Translanguaging in Action in English-Medium Classrooms

BLOOMSBURY GUIDEBOOKS FOR LANGUAGE TEACHERS

This series brings together books that enhance language educators' teaching practice. The books provide practical advice and applications, suitable for use in a range of contexts and for different learning styles, which are evidence-based and research-informed. The series appeals to practitioners looking to develop their skills and practice and is also suitable for use on a variety of language teacher education courses. The books feature a range of topics and themes, from critical pedagogy, to using drama, poetry or literature in the language classroom, to supporting language learners who have anxiety.

Also available in the series:

Teaching English to Young Learners, edited by Janice Bland
Critical Pedagogies for Modern Languages Education, edited by Derek Hird
A Poetry Pedagogy for Teachers, Maya Pindyck, Ruth Vinz, Diana Liu and Ashlynn Wittchow
Using Literature in English Language Education, edited by Janice Bland
Designing World Language Curriculum for Intercultural Communicative Competence, Jennifer Eddy
Performative Language Teaching in Early Education, Joe Winston
Using Theories for Second Language Teaching and Learning, Dale T. Griffee and Greta Gorsuch
Researching Language Learning Motivation, edited by Ali H. Al-Hoorie and Fruzsina Szabó
Language Learner Strategies, Michael James Grenfell and Vee Harris
Compelling Stories for English Language Learners, Janice Bland
Process Drama for Second Language Teaching and Learning, Patrice Baldwin and Alicja Galazka
Psychology-Based Activities for Supporting Anxious Language Learners, Neil Curry and Kate Maher
Pedagogical Translation for Language Teaching, Sarah Albrecht
Teachers as Curriculum Designers for Transcultural Communicative Competenece, Jennifer Eddy

Forthcoming in the series:

Teaching Beginner Level English Language Learners, Lesley Painter-Farrell and Gabriel Díaz-Maggioli

Translanguaging in Action in English-Medium Classrooms

A Resource Book for Teachers

Edited by

ZHONGFENG TIAN AND SUNNY MAN CHU LAU

BLOOMSBURY ACADEMIC
LONDON • NEW YORK • OXFORD • NEW DELHI • SYDNEY

BLOOMSBURY ACADEMIC
Bloomsbury Publishing Plc, 50 Bedford Square, London, WC1B 3DP, UK
Bloomsbury Publishing Inc, 1359 Broadway, New York, NY 10018, USA
Bloomsbury Publishing Ireland, 29 Earlsfort Terrace, Dublin 2, D02 AY28, Ireland

BLOOMSBURY, BLOOMSBURY ACADEMIC and the Diana logo are trademarks of Bloomsbury Publishing Plc

First published in Great Britain 2026

Copyright © Zhongfeng Tian, Sunny Man Chu Lau and contributors, 2026

Zhongfeng Tian, Sunny Man Chu Lau and contributors have asserted their right under the Copyright, Designs and Patents Act, 1988, to be identified as Authors of this work.

Series design: Grace Ridge
Cover image © J614 / Getty Images

All rights reserved. No part of this publication may be: i) reproduced or transmitted in any form, electronic or mechanical, including photocopying, recording or by means of any information storage or retrieval system without prior permission in writing from the publishers; or ii) used or reproduced in any way for the training, development or operation of artificial intelligence (AI) technologies, including generative AI technologies. The rights holders expressly reserve this publication from the text and data mining exception as per Article 4(3) of the Digital Single Market Directive (EU) 2019/790.

Bloomsbury Publishing Plc does not have any control over, or responsibility for, any third-party websites referred to or in this book. All internet addresses given in this book were correct at the time of going to press. The author and publisher regret any inconvenience caused if addresses have changed or sites have ceased to exist, but can accept no responsibility for any such changes.

A catalogue record for this book is available from the British Library.

A catalog record for this book is available from the Library of Congress.

ISBN: HB: 978-1-3504-5357-9
PB: 978-1-3504-5358-6
ePDF: 978-1-3504-5360-9
eBook: 978-1-3504-5359-3

Series: Bloomsbury Guidebooks for Language Teachers

Typeset by Deanta Global Publishing Services, Chennai, India
Printed and bound in Great Britain

For product safety related questions contact productsafety@bloomsbury.com.

To find out more about our authors and books visit www.bloomsbury.com and sign up for our newsletters.

Contents

Foreword: Translanguaging Futurism *Prem Phyak* vii

Introduction: Reimagining English-Medium Classrooms Through Translanguaging *Zhongfeng Tian and Sunny Man Chu Lau* 1

PART I Translanguaging Stance Development for Teachers

1. Metaphorical Affordances of Dominant Language Constellations (DLC) Artifacts in Pre-service Teacher Education: Developing a Translanguaging Stance *Nayr Correia Ibrahim* 17

2. Framing Teachers as Experts: Developing Translanguaging Spaces and Stances for Learning and Teaching *Gregory Child, Nicole King, and Kim Song* 39

PART II Translanguaging Practices in Elementary Classrooms

3. Promoting Translanguaging Pedagogical Practice Through Co-Teaching and Co-Learning: Insights from "Incipient" Bilingual Teachers *Haiyan Li, Woongsik Choi, Wayne E. Wright, and Trish Morita-Mullaney* 61

4   Translanguaging for Multilingual Proficiencies: From an English language into a Languages Classroom *Rachel Muchira* 83

5   Translanguaging Teaching Strategies in South Korea: Reframing EFL Elementary Classrooms as Multilingual Classrooms *Michael Rabbidge* 99

6   A Critical Approach to Reading Assessment of Multilingual Language Learners: A Case Study of Translanguaging Pedagogies, Teacher Knowledge, and Know-How *Laura Ascenzi-Moreno and Jennifer Conte* 119

PART III Translanguaging Practices in Secondary Classrooms

7   Translanguaging as a Decolonial Option: Exploring Curricular Cracks for Critical Literacy in EFL Classrooms *Phelippe Oliveira and Sunny Man Chu Lau* 139

8   Translanguaging in Action with Youth from Refugee Backgrounds *Saskia Van Viegen* 157

9   Aware-Explore-Apply Strengths Model: Translanguaging and Transknowledging for Critical Embodied Engagement *Joanna Rowe and Sunny Man Chu Lau* 179

How Can I Keep from Translanguaging?: An Afterword for Difficult Times *Ofelia García* 201

Index 209

Foreword

Translanguaging Futurism

Prem Phyak

Modern schooling has naturalized the coloniality of monolingualism as a pedagogical mantra to address the learning challenges of students from diverse linguistic, cultural, and racial backgrounds. This mantra is deeply rooted in the ideological coloniality of English as the language of civilized and educated people. Solidified through various mechanisms such as language policy, textbook/curriculum, assessment, and pedagogy in modern education, the hegemony of English monolingualism has created an "abyssal line" (Santos, 2014), invisibilizing and erasing the space of other languages in shooling. As English is historically framed as the language of economic and political power in global neoliberalism and cosmopolitanism, its use as the sole medium of instruction generally remains uncontested. However, this monolingual mantra reproduces colonial, capitalistic, and modernist imaginations, shaping what counts as legitimate language, ways of learning/teaching, and forms of knowledge. This edited volume resists and transforms this mantra from a bottom-up perspective. Taking an action-oriented approach to translanguaging, the co-editors and authors in the volume collectively break monolingual boundaries created by English-medium policies and practices and encourage us (teachers, teacher educators, and researchers) to become critical and reflective of pedagogies, epistemologies, and assessment practices that have been naturalized.

By taking interdisciplinary perspectives to show how translanguaging offers equitable, inclusive, and transformative spaces for multilingual learners, this volume shows how translanguaging (re)imagines classrooms as fluid, dynamic, and inclusive social spaces in which students from diverse linguistic, cultural, and racial/ethnic backgrounds feel safe, heard, and recognized as "epistemic subjects" (Phyak, 2023). Translanguaging as a pedagogy goes beyond teaching and learning named languages separately, and embraces the simultaneity of diverse language practices, including nonstandard and oral traditions (García & Li Wei, 2014). While challenging the normative power of monolingualism shaped by the history of colonialism, neoliberalism, and racism, translanguaging in this volume is discussed as an approach that disrupts boundaries between school and home/community by legitimizing students' diverse languaging embodying a wide range of semiotic and epistemic resources. This volume focuses on the following three broad areas of translanguaging in English-medium classes:

- Teacher agency for action-based translanguaging pedagogies.
- Critical multilingual awareness for translanguaging stance in designing and implementing translanguaging pedagogies.
- Translanguaging pedagogies as an approach to resist deficit views against multilingual speakers' language practices and affirm their identities, creating hope for transformative learning.

As each chapter in the volume focuses on practical activities, teachers across curricula will find them helpful in designing and implementing translanguaging pedagogies in English-medium classrooms. It is important to note that the practical activities and strategies discussed in the chapters are not technocratic but are informed by ideological stances that resist and transform monolingualism.

Teacher Agency and Translanguaging Stance

Teachers are key actors in making meaningful changes in education. Because of their familiarity with the linguistic, cultural, and social backgrounds of their students, teachers understand the centrality of language in pedagogical activities. However, teachers' agency, knowledge, and struggles are hardly recognized and included in education policies. This volume fills this gap by keeping teachers at the center of creating "translanguaging spaces" (Li Wei, 2011) for multilingual students. While focusing on actionable plans and activities, the authors collectively promote the agenda of equity and linguistic justice by offering teachers practical strategies and models for integrating translanguaging into pedagogy and assessment for multilingual learners.

Translanguaging stance (García et al., 2017) remains at the center of teacher agency in translanguaging pedagogies. It refers to ideological awareness involving the transformation of hegemonic assumptions about language and their roles in shaping pedagogical practices. As Ibrahim's chapter in this volume reminds us, translanguaging pedagogy engages teachers in analyzing their own "dominant language constellations" (DLC) to create spaces for students' total linguistic repertoires in the classroom. This implies that teachers' critical agency in relation to translanguaging pedagogy involves reflective engagement with diverse ideologies at the structural and personal levels. While reclaiming their identity as transformative agents, the teachers discussed in this volume have shown their power to break the hard linguistic boundaries that inflict linguistic, racial, and epistemic injustice. While challenging broader sociopolitical conditions, they demonstrate the importance of reflective practices in resisting and transforming unequal ideological and pedagogical assumptions and practices.

Translanguaging pedagogy in multilingual classrooms is not about the random use of languages; rather, it is a purposeful recognition and integration of multilingual students' linguistic, cultural, and semiotic abilities and skills. In their chapter, Child, King, and Song discuss the importance of staged, purposeful, and design-based pedagogical activities to show how teachers can put a translanguaging stance into action to create an equitable learning environment in multilingual classrooms. Similarly, Li, Choi, Wright, and Morita-Mullaney discuss "co-teaching" and "co-learning" as planned strategies to support "English monolingual" teachers in implementing translanguaging pedagogies in a Spanish-English bilingual education program. These and other chapters suggest that translanguaging pedagogies need spatial reconfiguration of the classroom as a "translanguaging space" (Li Wei, 2011). As Li Wei (2018) argues, a translanguaging space is created by and for translanguaging and involves collaborative teaching and learning with colleagues and students. In this space, both teachers and students transcend the given roles and boundaries to create multiple opportunities and ways of learning. In this sense, a translanguaging space is the space of "transpositioning" which involves the breaking of the predetermined roles and identities to explore and embrace new and greater ideas that challenge the status quo (Hawkins, 2021; Li Wei, 2024). By engaging teachers in risk-taking activities, transpositioning frees them from hegemonic ideologies about language pedagogies and allows them to recognize full linguistic repertoires, modalities, and epistemologies in the learning process.

Critical and Decolonial Awareness and Action

Translanguaging pedagogy is not a language-teaching method; rather, it is a transformative approach that focuses on resisting and transforming the mindset and practices that reproduce the monolingual status quo. The authors of this volume embrace this principle to counter the historical hegemony of monolingual mindset in language education. For example, in their chapters Muchira, Rabbidge, and Oliveira and Lau discuss how translanguaging engages teachers in resisting and transforming monolingual English and standard language ideologies in Kenya, South Korea, and Brazil, respectively. These chapters show how EFL teachers are brave and agentive in integrating translanguaging into the classroom. The field of TESOL/EFL is historically colonial and shaped by Western ideologies such as native speakerism and linguistic purism. EFL teachers are expected and forced to teach monolingually using standard and monoglossic English. This creates a vulnerable, exclusionary, and unsafe learning environment for multilingual students. As their home and community languages, epistemologies, and cultures are considered illegitimate in EFL pedagogy, assessment, and textbook, multilingual students feel excluded and deficient in the classroom. Translanguaging, as Oliveira and Lau have discussed in this volume, allows teachers to find "curricular cracks" to disrupt such monolingual orientations and create an inclusive learning environment where multilingual students feel belonged and recognized as legitimate members in the pedagogical process.

Decoloniality is one of the major approaches this volume highlights as an integral aspect of translanguaging pedagogy (Li Wei & García, 2022). By providing space for teachers to unpack the historical-structural conditions that shape the coloniality of monolingualism, native speakerism, and standard language ideology, translanguaging helps to build a decolonial awareness of teachers and take necessary actions to dismantle the coloniality of Western ideologies. Ubuntu translanguaging (see Muchira in this volume), critical literacy (see Oliveira and Lau in this volume), multilingual and cultural frames (see Ascenzi-Moreno and Conte in this volume) and Inuit Qaujimajatuqangit epistemology (Rowe and Lau in this volume) provide alternative approaches to transforming monolingual pedagogies. These approaches not only legitimize fluid, non-standard, and home languages (in EFL teaching) as resources for equitable and inclusive education but also, and more importantly, create space for diverse epistemologies that go beyond knowledge in official textbooks and curricula. Another important aspect of decoloniality in translanguaging pedagogy is its power to counter "deficit ideology" (Gorski, 2011) that dehumanizes and misrecognizes the linguistic, cultural, and epistemic identities of multilingual students. As Ascenzi-Moreno and Conte have discussed in this volume, translanguaging helps to correct biased assessment practices that position multilingual learners as deficient and less able. Similarly, Van Viegen's chapter shows that translanguaging creates creative spaces (e.g., poetry) that support refugee students' counter-narratives, challenging deficit views against their identities and language practices.

Translanguaging Praxis and Hope

Reading the chapters in the volume reminds me of Paulo Freire's "praxis" and "pedagogy of hope" (Freire, 1972, 1994) for transformative schooling. The plans and activities discussed and suggested in the volume are not universal and technocratic strategies aimed at fixing language problems; rather, they are the embodiment of critical awareness and transformative agency of teachers in multilingual contexts. Translanguaging pedagogies are grounded in teachers' critical and reflective awareness of how language intersects with broader sociopolitical issues. Freire (1972) argues that pedagogy should engage teachers and students in the critical analysis of social problems and take necessary action to address them. Defining this process as "praxis," Freire (1972) urges that pedagogical activities should be informed by the values and goals of transforming social inequalities and injustices. The plans, strategies, and pedagogies for translanguaging in this volume promote "transgressive praxis" (Lau et al., 2017) by countering hegemonic monolingual and monoglossic ideologies for socially just classroom spaces for multilingual students. More importantly, this volume signals the need for "decolonial praxis" (Odugu, 2022) in teacher education programs for multilingual education. This praxis engages teachers in epistemic pluralization, ideological resistance, and critical awareness-raising activities through translanguaging.

While offering practical activities for implementing translanguaging, this volume germinates hope for equitable classrooms in which minoritized language speakers' identities, epistemologies, and language practices are valued. Translanguaging actions in this volume promote a "pedagogy of hope" (Freire, 1972) that embodies the struggle, agency, and power of teachers to disrupt monolingual, monoglossic, and standard language ideologies. This volume shines the light of "a hope future" (Wright, 2023) by showing how translanguaging pedagogy "democratizes the learning space, allowing access and opportunity for linguistically diverse language learners to engage and participate in education" (Sembiante & Tian, 2023, p. 921). I conclude this foreword by reiterating the role of translanguaging pedagogy as a hope for reconciliation (Rowe and Lau, in this volume) between the colonial and Indigenous/local worlds. This hope is not only futuristic, but also, and more importantly, reparative. This implies that translanguaging pedagogies need to focus on truth-telling activities by creating a safe and inclusive classroom that allows students to use diverse language practices, epistemologies, and positionalities. This volume invites teachers and educators to join the path of a reparative future by embracing the power and praxis of translanguaging.

References

Freire, P. (1972). *Pedagogy of the oppressed*. Penguin.

Freire, P. (1994). *Pedagogy of hope*. Continuum.

García, O., Johnson, S. I., & Seltzer, K. (2017). *The translanguaging classroom: Leveraging student bilingualism for learning*. Caslon.

García, O., & Li Wei. (2014). *Translanguaging: Language, bilingualism, and education*. Palgrave MacMillan.

Gorski, P. C. (2011). Unlearning deficit ideology and the scornful gaze: Thoughts on authenticating the class discourse in education. *Counterpoints, 402*, 152–173.

Hawkins, M. R. (Ed.). (2021). *Transmodal communications: Transpositioning semiotics and relations*. Multilingual Matters.

Lau, S. M. C., Juby-Smith, B., & Desbiens, I. (2017). Translanguaging for transgressive praxis: Promoting critical literacy in a multiage bilingual classroom. *Critical Inquiry in Language Studies, 14*(1), 99–127.

Odugu, D. I. (2022). Translanguaging as decolonial praxis. *Journal of Multilingual Theories and Practices, 3*(1), 27–52.

Phyak, P. (2023). Translanguaging as a space of simultaneity: Theorizing translanguaging pedagogies in English medium schools from a spatial perspective. *The Modern Language Journal, 107*(1), 289–307.

Santos, B. d. S. (2014). *Epistemologies of the South. Justice against epistemicide*. Paradigm Publishers.

Sembiante, S. F., & Tian, Z. (2023). Translanguaging: A pedagogy of heteroglossic hope. *International Journal of Bilingual Education and Bilingualism, 26*(8), 919–923.

Li Wei. (2011). Moment analysis and translanguaging space: Discursive construction of identities by multilingual Chinese youth in Britain. *Journal of Pragmatics, 43*(5), 1222–1235.

Li Wei. (2018). Translanguaging as a practical theory of language. *Applied Linguistics, 39*(1), 9–30.

Li Wei. (2024). Transformative pedagogy for inclusion and social justice through translanguaging, co-learning, and transpositioning. *Language Teaching, 57*(2), 203–214.

Li Wei & García, O. (2022). Not a first language but one repertoire: Translanguaging as a decolonizing project. *RELC Journal, 53*(2), 313–324.

Wright, W. E. (2023). Translanguaging for a hopeful future. *International Journal of Bilingual Education and Bilingualism, 26*(8), 924–927.

Introduction

Reimagining English-Medium Classrooms Through Translanguaging

Zhongfeng Tian and Sunny Man Chu Lau

Setting the Stage: From Theory to Action in Multilingual Classrooms

In recent years, translanguaging has become a central topic in Applied Linguistics and TESOL, sparking significant interest among researchers and educators alike. Since its early conceptualizations (e.g., Canagarajah, 2011; Creese & Blackledge, 2010; García, 2009; García & Li, 2014; Hornberger & Link, 2012; Li, 2011), translanguaging theory has provided a transformative lens for rethinking language, communication, and learning. By emphasizing the fluid and dynamic use of multilingual learners' entire linguistic repertoires, translanguaging challenges traditional monolingual norms and offers a more inclusive, culturally sustaining, and justice-oriented approach to education. Despite the growing body of research, however, many teachers and practitioners remain unsure how to strategically and sustainably implement translanguaging pedagogies in their classrooms. This propelled us to create this book project as a platform for teachers and educators to share their translanguaging work in their unique contexts and to inspire others to try out their own.

This book, *Translanguaging in Action in English-Medium Classrooms: A Resource Book for Teachers*, seeks to bridge the gap between research and practice by offering evidence-based, research-informed, and practitioner-friendly applications of translanguaging pedagogies. Aimed at pre- and in-service K-12 teachers and teacher educators, the book provides a wealth of concrete, situated examples of translanguaging practices across diverse English-medium contexts, including underrepresented perspectives from the Global South. By showcasing how translanguaging can be used to foster linguistic and cultural equity, engage students in critical social inquiry, and affirm learners' identities and knowledge systems, this resource book equips educators with the tools to reimagine their classrooms as heteroglossic spaces for transformative learning.

Organized into three parts, the book begins by focusing on translanguaging stance development in teacher education, providing an entry point into the philosophy and ideological underpinnings of translanguaging pedagogy. It then transitions to translanguaging practices in elementary and secondary classrooms, illustrating how these practices played out in each unique context. Drawing on case studies from diverse geographical contexts—North and South America, Europe, Asia, and Africa—the chapters highlight key guiding principles, contextual challenges, and actionable strategies for implementing translanguaging in instruction and assessment. Each chapter follows a practitioner-oriented format, featuring research-informed insights, practical vignettes, and reflections to support teachers' independent development of translanguaging practices tailored to their unique teaching contexts. We invite teachers and educators to adopt and/or adapt these translanguaging practices as deemed relevant and pertinent to their own contexts.

The objectives of this book are fourfold: (1) to provide empirical evidence of situated translanguaging applications in various English-medium/TESOL contexts, where students are learning (in) English as an additional language which may or may not be the dominant language in society; (2) to guide pre-/in-service teacher efforts to develop a translanguaging stance and adapt translanguaging pedagogy to any teaching and learning contexts; (3) to offer key guiding principles of designing and implementing translanguaging across different contexts in instruction and assessment; and (4) to refine translanguaging theory, develop context-relevant practices, and strengthen the research-practice nexus. Ultimately, we aim to demystify translanguaging pedagogy—not as a prescriptive or one-size-fits-all method, but as a dynamic and adaptable framework that can complement other effective teaching practices to create equitable, meaningful learning experiences for multilingual students.

Translanguaging Theory and Pedagogy: Questions from the Field

While the transformative potential of translanguaging has been widely acknowledged in research (e.g., García & Kleyn, 2016; Tian et al., 2020;

Paulsrud et al., 2021), many educators continue to grapple with how to implement these practices effectively in their classrooms. Questions about its practical application, equity-focused implications, and alignment with curricular goals remain at the forefront of the discussion. This section addresses these burning questions, drawing on the case studies and research featured in this book to provide clarity and actionable guidance. Rooted in the lived experiences of practitioners, these inquiries highlight both the challenges and opportunities of translanguaging, serving as a roadmap for the volume. Each chapter builds on these questions, offering a blend of theoretical insights and practical strategies designed to help teachers navigate the complexities of translanguaging in action.

What Is Translanguaging?

At its core, what does translanguaging mean for educators and learners? Translanguaging is both a theoretical framework and a pedagogical approach. As a theory, it redefines language not as separate, labeled entities (e.g., "English" or "Spanish"), but as fluid, interconnected resources that multilingual individuals draw on to make meaning (Otheguy et al., 2015). Depending on the situation, learners may draw on a combination of linguistic and non-linguistic resources, including not only named languages but also language varieties and registers, gestures, and multimodal resources (Lau et al., 2021; Lin, 2019) to make sense of what they are learning, express their opinions, and respond to their interlocutors. Hence, communication through a trans/languaging process is an emergent process, leveraging a dynamic united semio-linguistic repertoire for meaning construction and expression.

As a pedagogy, translanguaging shifts the focus from rigid monolingual norms to an inclusive framework that embraces students' full linguistic and cultural identities (Li & García, 2022). Originating from bilingual education, it acknowledges that bilingual learners use all their language practices as integrated tools for thinking, learning, and identity-building. Further, rather than seeing languages as isolated and existing in their pure forms, translanguaging scholars view languages in individual minds and broader society as interwoven, complementing and completing each other (Muchira, Ch. 4). Language education in English-medium or bilingual education contexts has often prioritized the so-called "full," "complete," and "balanced" development of proficiency in the target language(s) so much so that its broader goals of inter- or cross-cultural communication, knowledge construction, respect, and understanding are often neglected (Child, King & Song, Ch. 2). This reflects a monolingual ideology which does not focus on how language is actually used but rather how it is idealized for its pure, standard form (Rabbidge, Ch. 5).

The dynamic, asset-based orientation of translanguaging practices can help transform classrooms into spaces where students' diverse languages, identities, and cultural worldviews are not only validated but leveraged as critical resources for more meaningful learning and use (Heugh, 2021; Li, 2018; Tian & Lau, 2022; see also Oliveira & Lau, Ch. 7).

Where Do We Start if We Want to Implement Translanguaging Pedagogy?

Developing a translanguaging pedagogy begins with a fundamental shift in mindset, in other words, a translanguaging stance—a move from viewing languages as isolated systems to embracing their dynamic, interconnected nature and an ideological commitment to valuing students' full linguistic repertoires as assets (García et al., 2017). This ideological shift, however, is not easy; it requires ongoing professional development and reflective practices that allow teachers to understand and enact translanguaging as a meaningful, context-sensitive approach to multilingual education.

Ibrahim in Chapter 1 introduces the concept of Dominant Language Constellations (DLCs) as a powerful reflective tool for pre-service teachers to examine their linguistic repertoires and ideological positionings. By creating personal DLC artifacts, teachers engaged in a process of mapping out the languages, dialects, and varieties they use across different contexts and relationships. This activity allowed them to uncover hidden biases and assumptions about language, such as favoring standardized varieties or prioritizing English. For example, one teacher reflected on how their own multilingual background, including a nonstandard dialect, had been a source of both pride and marginalization. Through this process, pre-service teachers began to develop a translanguaging stance that acknowledged linguistic diversity as a strength, laying the groundwork for transformative teaching practices.

Building on this foundation, Child, King, and Song in Chapter 2 examine how in-service teachers who might not speak their students' languages could still enact a translanguaging stance in their classrooms over time. The chapter follows three teachers participating in a grant project aimed at supporting multilingual learners in US Midwest classrooms. These educators critically reflected on their language beliefs and teaching practices, leveraging peer feedback and iterative adjustments to co-construct translanguaging spaces with their students. For instance, one physics teacher transformed her classroom by integrating multilingual word walls and encouraging collaborative problem-solving in students' home languages, and another fourth-grade teacher greeted her students each day using multiple languages and designed culturally responsive activities, such as storytelling that incorporated students' linguistic and cultural backgrounds. These practices created inclusive, multilingual learning spaces that validated students' identities and fostered a sense of belonging.

Together, these chapters illustrate that developing a translanguaging pedagogy is an iterative process that combines theoretical understanding with practical application (Tian, 2020; Tian & Zhang-Wu, 2022). Teachers must engage in reflective activities, such as creating DLCs or critically analyzing their language beliefs, to cultivate a translanguaging stance. They should also actively experiment with translanguaging design by planning classroom activities, learning from their students to embrace their linguistic and cultural resources in teaching and learning. Additionally, ongoing reflection during implementation allows for necessary shifts and flexible adaptations, such as rethinking monolingual policies and responding to students' diverse needs. This interplay of stance, design, and shifts (García et al., 2017) empowers educators to create equity-centered classrooms that harness the full potential of multilingual learners.

Is Translanguaging Just About Shuttling Between Languages?

One of the most common misconceptions about translanguaging is that it is merely about code-switching or alternating between languages. Translanguaging practices and pedagogy transcend language boundaries to encompass multimodal and interdisciplinary practices (Tai, 2024) that enrich both learning and identity development. Translanguaging, as highlighted in this volume, is a dynamic process that incorporates diverse semiotic, linguistic, and cultural resources to foster meaningful learning experiences.

Li, Choi, Wright, and Morita-Mullaney in Chapter 3 showcase how the Spanish and English teachers in a dual-language bilingual education program incorporated bilingual songs, visuals, movements, and performance to support vocabulary and concept learning on the topic of habitats, which reinforced children's understanding in both languages. Van Viegen's Chapter 8 discusses how translanguaging could transform classrooms into inclusive and empowering spaces. The teacher participants from a Canadian secondary school worked with refugee-background students and had them write bilingual "Where I Am From" poems, which allowed them to express their personal histories, cultural connections, and aspirations through both their home languages and English. This purposeful use of a mix of languages affirmed students' linguistic and cultural identities, sending a strong message about the relevance and legitimacy of these learners' identities and heritage in an

English classroom. Furthermore, translanguaging pedagogies through using bilingual vocabulary charts, graphic organizers, and collaborative discussions in multiple languages in math lessons also helped build language awareness and conceptual understanding that support authentic learning.

This expanded definition of translanguaging that includes the "multimodal forms" of language and communication situated in sociocultural contexts is also well discussed in Chapter 6 by Ascenzi-Moreno and Conte. The authors explain how this expanded notion of translanguaging reconfigured their way of assessing multilingual students' reading abilities (to be elaborated further in "What about Assessment?"). To sum up, far from being limited to switching between languages, translanguaging approaches move beyond the confines of traditional monoglossic paradigms, creating dynamic, multimodal, and interdisciplinary learning environments that reflect the realities of multilingual students. Importantly, most chapters in this volume articulate the collaborative and communal nature of language learning and teaching. By drawing on multilingual exchanges in the classroom, translanguaging pedagogy can potentially promote co-learning, crafting "a shared responsibility of knowledge, language and culture exchange" (Child, King, and Song, Ch. 2) not only among students but also between students and teachers, and even among teachers (see, e.g., Ch. 3, 8, and 9). The co-learning spaces make language classrooms more inclusive and equitable (Tai & Li, 2021).

Why Does Translanguaging Matter in English-Medium Classrooms?

Why is translanguaging essential in English-medium classrooms, especially those serving multilingual learners? Traditional monolingual approaches do not align with how multilingual learners function, restricting them from using their full range of conceptual knowledge, multiliteracies, and strategies for making meaning and communicating their learning (Lin, 2019). For example, Muchira in Chapter 4 describes how the strict English-only policy in Kenyan education has reduced lessons to simple repetition, memorization, and imitation of teachers' input, hindering students' more in-depth learning. In contrast, translanguaging allows students to draw on their entire linguistic and cultural repertoires, fostering equity in language learning, promoting critical thinking, and validating students' lived experiences, identities, and knowledge systems (Li, 2024).

Achieving Equity: Affirming Minoritized Languages, Identities, and Knowledge Systems: Most chapters in this volume illustrate how translanguaging offers language-minoritized students an effective pathway to acquire the language of instruction while valuing their existing linguistic resources. Rather than erasing home languages in favor of the dominant language, translanguaging integrates students' entire linguistic repertoires, enabling deeper engagement with content and building confidence as learners while reinforcing and affirming diverse students' identities, cultural worldviews, and funds of knowledge. By incorporating students' lived experiences, translanguaging creates spaces where students feel seen, heard, and valued. For example, Rowe and Lau highlight in Chapter 9 an interdisciplinary project with Indigenous students from the Inuit communities in Northern Quebec, Canada, that aims to strengthen students' English development while honoring their cultural and linguistic heritage. Grounded in Seligman's (2011) PERMA model of well-being and using the Aware-Explore-Apply (AEA) coaching model (Niemiec, 2014), the project encourages students to reflect on character strengths, using translanguaging to discuss and compare concepts in English and Inuktitut. Weaving Indigenous language and beliefs into the lesson fosters students' intercultural and metalinguistic awareness in understanding how languages convey knowledge of the world in different and complementary ways, that is, transknowledging (Heugh, 2021). Moving beyond conventional instruction, it reframes language learning as an evolving, intercultural process of "becoming" (Maturana & Varela, 1992) that empowers students to navigate multiple linguistic and cultural worlds.

Promoting Critical Engagement with Social Issues: Translanguaging is more than a linguistic tool; it fosters critical literacy and social awareness. In Chapter 7, Oliveira and Lau illustrate how Oliveira, as an EFL teacher in a Brazilian secondary school, used translanguaging approaches to create "curricular cracks" (or openings) in standardized textbooks for critical literacies education. Exploring the topic of globalization through a translanguaging lens, the teacher invited critical discussions in multiple languages that disrupted the dominant neoliberal discourses on globalization and English language education. This approach also allowed the teacher to gain insight into students' full linguistic and semiotic repertoires, existing critical perspectives, as well as their transdisciplinary and out-of-school knowledge, which helped signal further curricular cracks for more in-depth critical engagements.

These chapters demonstrate why translanguaging matters in English-medium classrooms: it bridges equity, critical engagement, and identity affirmation. By leveraging students' full communicative repertoires, translanguaging fosters in-depth learning while honoring cultural pride, challenges monolingual norms to critique inequities, and positions students' identities and lived experiences as central to learning. These transformative practices create inclusive, socially conscious, and justice-oriented educational spaces.

How Can We Balance Access to English with Translanguaging Practices?

One of the most common challenges teachers face is striking a balance between students' access to English as an additional language and the use of translanguaging in instruction. High-stakes exams often pressure educators to prioritize English at the expense of students' home languages, limiting opportunities for multilingual learning (see, e.g., Ch. 4). Neoliberal discourse on English as a global language for academic, professional, and socioeconomic advancement also deters teachers from adopting translanguaging for fear of "distracting" students from "real" learning (see, e.g., Ch. 5 and 7). The use of students' home or Indigenous languages in the classroom is often considered irrelevant. Teachers also often feel worried, and even guilty, that drawing on students' home languages and knowledges will compromise their English attainments, even though they often intuitively recognize how it can effectively support and scaffold their students' learning in/of English (Sah & Li, 2022). This tension, often referred to as the "access paradox" (Janks, 2004), is particularly evident in contexts where high-stakes exams prioritize English proficiency. The question then becomes—How can educators leverage translanguaging to support language learning while ensuring students achieve the English proficiency needed for academic success?

In Chapter 4, Muchira challenges this dynamic by demonstrating how an ESL lesson can serve as a launchpad for metalinguistic awareness, enhancing students' vocabulary knowledge, grammatical and phonemic awareness, and fostering collaborative learning across diverse linguistic backgrounds. Drawing on Makalela's (2016) concept of Ubuntu translanguaging, Muchira illustrates how languages and collective community knowledge can be integrated to support children's learning. Specifically, she explores the implementation of this approach in Kenyan schools, where teachers incorporated community languages alongside English to teach linguistic concepts such as adjectives. This multilingual pedagogy not only expanded students' linguistic repertoires but also deepened their understanding of English grammar and vocabulary, reinforcing the value of leveraging all linguistic resources for academic success.

Many chapters in this volume (see, e.g., Ch. 5, 7, 8, and 9) highlight how translanguaging bridges the gap between the demands of English language development and the need for culturally and linguistically sustaining pedagogy. These case studies demonstrate that translanguaging is not an "either-or" proposition but a "both-and" approach. By strategically integrating translanguaging into classroom practices, educators can help students navigate high-stakes academic contexts while fostering a deeper engagement with both the target language and their linguistic resources. This balanced approach ensures that students meet curricular expectations and testing requirements without losing their connection to their cultural and linguistic identities, ultimately creating more inclusive and equitable language learning environments.

How Do We Employ Translanguaging Strategically in Classrooms?

What does it mean to use translanguaging strategically, and how can educators ensure its effectiveness? While translanguaging is fluid and dynamic, its implementation in classrooms must be intentional and purposeful. All the chapters in this volume emphasize that effective translanguaging pedagogy begins with knowing one's students—their linguistic backgrounds, learning needs, and identities. Strategic translanguaging practices involve aligning instruction with clear learning objectives, intentionally planning activities that support meaning-driven language development, and fostering an equitable classroom environment where students' full linguistic repertoires are valued and leveraged for deeper learning.

In particular, Rabbidge in Chapter 5 provides compelling examples from South Korean EFL classrooms, where teachers deliberately integrated translanguaging into their lessons to scaffold students' understanding of complex concepts. These educators combined planned pedagogical translanguaging with spontaneous language use, while also signaling clear linguistic intentions to guide students in navigating academic tasks. Similarly, Li and colleagues in Chapter 3 highlight another approach to strategic translanguaging through co-teaching in a US dual-language program. In this setting, English- and Spanish-medium teachers collaboratively designed and implemented "bridging lessons" to integrate translanguaging practices effectively. A vivid example comes from a first-grade English Language Arts class. During a lesson on animal habitats, both teachers used a bilingual song and a read-aloud of *The Magic School Bus Hops Home* in English and Spanish to engage students. They encouraged students to discuss habitat essentials in their language of choice—English, Spanish, or a mix of both—fostering linguistic flexibility and cultural inclusivity. By alternating instructional roles and reiterating key concepts in both languages, the co-teaching model not only enhanced biliteracy development but also positioned students as active co-constructors of knowledge. The strategic use of translanguaging in this lesson enabled students to bridge linguistic gaps while exploring academic content collaboratively.

Furthermore, Van Viegen in Chapter 8 highlights an asset-based approach to translanguaging, particularly for refugee students navigating resettlement and educational integration. Instead of focusing on what students lacked or how they struggled to meet curricular demands, teachers supported and expanded upon students' self-initiated multilingual strategies. Based on an empirical study with refugee youth and their teachers in a Canadian secondary school, the chapter illustrates how students used digital tools, peer collaboration, and personal translation apps to mediate meaning, reinforcing their learning in self-directed ways. For instance, Ahmed, a Grade ten student attending school for the first time, combined a graphic organizer, picture dictionary, iPad, and translation software to complete a literacy task. Teachers observed these strategies and reflected on how to build upon them, acknowledging that allowing students agency over their linguistic resources enhanced engagement and learning. This chapter underscores how strategically embracing students' translanguaging moves fosters inclusion, affirms students' identities, and transforms classrooms into more empowering spaces.

These examples illustrate that when translanguaging is purposefully aligned with instructional goals, embedded in reflective teaching practices, and reinforced through collaborative approaches, it fosters an inclusive learning environment that supports linguistic diversity, academic attainments, and cultural affirmation. By strategically embracing translanguaging, educators can help ensure that minoritized students thrive in multilingual classrooms.

What about Assessment? Can We also Apply Translanguaging in Assessment?

How can assessment practices better reflect the diverse linguistic repertoires of multilingual learners? Traditional assessment frameworks often fail to capture the full range of multilingual learners' abilities, as they are primarily designed with monolingual native speakers in mind. This creates inherent biases against multilingual students from drawing on multiple languages to make meaning (Heugh et al., 2017; Shohamy, 2011). Translanguaging, when incorporated into assessment practices, can address these biases and better align evaluations with students' multilingual linguistic and academic capabilities.

First and foremost, educators are encouraged to gather holistic background information for instruction and assessments, which include students' linguistic histories and repertoires, prior schooling experiences, home and community literacy practices (see, e.g., Ch. 2, 4, 7, and 8). This approach allows teachers to view students as individuals with rich linguistic and cultural resources, beyond their current English proficiency.

Ascenzi-Moreno and Conte in Chapter 6 provide a compelling framework for how translanguaging can transform reading assessments for multilingual learners. For example, taking note of students' language approximations (i.e., producing similar but not exact sounds of the word) and posing follow-up questions about these approximations could help teachers differentiate between students' decoding abilities, word knowledge, and comprehension. Allowing students a choice to retell the stories monolingually or bilingually, and taking into account their multimodal expressions, also helped teachers to more accurately assess students' performance and identify areas of need and improvements. In Chapter 7, Oliveira and Lau encourage teachers to see assessment as a "critical literacy resource" that creates learning-oriented spaces for students to reflect on what they learn and what they think of the new perspectives emerging in class discussions. Assessments that promote self-reflection, such as portfolios and self-assessments, in translingual ways, not only help students examine their own assumptions and beliefs but also enable teachers to identify students' values, critical knowledge, and repertoires. These insights can then be further engaged in the learning process.

Translanguaging in assessment goes beyond merely accommodating multilingual learners; it actively disrupts monolingual biases by valuing the interplay between students' languages. These practices send a powerful message: linguistic diversity is an asset, not a barrier. By adapting assessments to reflect multilingual and cultural frames, educators can create more equitable evaluation systems that truly capture students' abilities, fostering an inclusive environment where multilingualism is celebrated.

Conclusion and Future Directions

This book offers real classroom examples on how translanguaging, when implemented with intentionality and context-sensitivity, can create justice-oriented educational environments where students' linguistic and cultural resources are not merely accommodated but celebrated and leveraged for deeper learning. By drawing on theoretical insights, practical applications, and authentic examples from diverse educational contexts, we aim to inspire educators to embrace a translanguaging stance and pedagogies to emulate linguistically and culturally sustaining practices in their own contexts.

Our work, however, does not stop here. While the guiding principles and case studies outlined in this volume offer a roadmap for integrating translanguaging into classrooms, they also underscore the need for ongoing inquiry and systemic support. Sustained research on translanguaging theory and practice is needed to explore its affordances and challenges in diverse settings. Future studies should examine how translanguaging operates in underrepresented regions, across various disciplines, and within evolving educational paradigms. Such research can further refine translanguaging theory and illuminate innovative practices that respond to the complexities of multilingual education.

To prepare educators for this paradigm shift, translanguaging must be integrated into teacher education and professional development programs (Tian & Zhang-Wu, 2022). Pre- and in-service teachers need opportunities to critically examine their language ideologies, develop a translanguaging stance, and experiment with context-specific strategies for implementation. These programs should include reflective activities, collaborative projects, and access to research-informed resources that equip teachers to navigate the dynamic realities of linguistically and culturally diverse classrooms.

At the systemic level, meaningful support for translanguaging requires structural changes in curricula, assessment frameworks, and educational policies. Current systems, often rooted in monolingual ideologies, must evolve to accommodate the fluid linguistic practices of multilingual learners. This includes revising curricula to include multilingual and multicultural content, designing assessments that value students' full linguistic repertoires, and implementing policies that legitimize and encourage translanguaging practices. Advocacy efforts must target policymakers, administrators, and other stakeholders to create the institutional conditions necessary for translanguaging to thrive.

In conclusion, translanguaging offers a bold vision for the future of education—one that celebrates linguistic diversity, advances equity, and empowers students to thrive academically, socially, and culturally. This book offers a foundation for educators to begin or deepen their journey with translanguaging, and it also calls for collective action to sustain equitable practices. We sincerely invite teachers and educators to join us in our collaborative and collective efforts to honor the multilingual realities of our world and equip our students to navigate it with confidence and pride.

References

Canagarajah, S. (2011). Translanguaging in the classroom: Emerging issues for research and pedagogy. *Applied Linguistics Review*, *2*(2011), 1–28. https://doi.org/10.1515/9783110239331.1

Creese, A., & Blackledge, A. (2010). Translanguaging in the bilingual classroom: A pedagogy for learning and teaching. *Modern Language Journal*, *94*(1), 103–115. https://doi.org/10.1111/j.1540-4781.2009.00986.x

García, O. (2009). *Bilingual education in the 21st century: A global perspective*. Wiley/Blackwell.

García, O., & Kleyn, T. (Eds.). (2016). *Translanguaging with multilingual students: Learning from classroom moments*. Routledge.

García, O., & Li, W. (2014). *Translanguaging: language, bilingualism and education*. Palgrave Macmillan.

García, O., Johnson, S. I., & Seltzer, K. (2017). *The translanguaging classroom: Leveraging student bilingualism for learning*. Caslon.

Heugh, K. (2021). Southern multilingualisms, translanguaging and transknowledging in inclusive and sustainable education. In P. Harding-Esch & H. Coleman (Eds.), *Language and the sustainable development goals: Selected proceedings of the 12th Language and Development Conference* (pp. 37–47). British Council.

Heugh, K., Prinsloo, C., Makgamatha, M., Diedericks, G., & Winnaar, L. (2017). Multilingualism(s) and system-wide assessment: A southern perspective. *Language and Education, 31*(3), 197–216. https://doi.org/10.1080/09500782.2016.1261894

Hornberger, N. H., & Link, H. (2012). Translanguaging and transnational literacies in multilingual classrooms: A bilingual lens. *International Journal of Bilingual Education and Bilingualism, 15*(3), 261–278. https://doi.org/10.1080/13670050.2012.658016

Janks, H. (2004). The access paradox. *English in Australia, 139*, 33–42. https://search.informit.org/doi/10.3316/informit.849538151512751

Lau, S. M. C., Tian, Z., & Lin, A. M. Y. (2021). Critical literacy and additional language learning: An expansive view of translanguaging for change-enhancing possibilities. In J. Z. Pandya, R. A. Mora, J. H. Alford, N. A. Golden, & R. S. de Roock (Eds.), *The handbook of critical literacies* (pp. 381–390). Routledge.

Li, W. (2011). Moment analysis and translanguaging space: Discursive construction of identities by multilingual Chinese youth in Britain. *Journal of Pragmatics, 43*(5), 1222–1235. https://doi.org/10.1016/j.pragma.2010.07.035

Li, W. (2018). Translanguaging as a practical theory of language. *Applied Linguistics, 39*(1), 9–30. https://doi.org/10.1093/applin/amx039

Li, W. (2024). Transformative pedagogy for inclusion and social justice through translanguaging, co-learning, and transpositioning. *Language Teaching, 57*(2), 203–214. https://doi.org/10.1017/S0261444823000186

Li, W., & García, O. (2022). Not a first language but one repertoire: Translanguaging as a decolonizing project. *RELC Journal, 53*(2), 313–324. https://doi.org/10.1177/00336882221092841

Lin, A. M. Y. (2019). Theories of trans/languaging and trans-semiotizing: Implications for content-based education classrooms. *International Journal of Bilingual Education and Bilingualism, 22*(1), 5–16. https://doi.org/10.1080/13670050.2018.1515175

Makalela, L. (2016). Ubuntu translanguaging: An alternative framework for complex multilingual encounters. *Southern African Linguistics and Applied Language Studies, 34*(3), 187–196. https://doi.org/10.2989/16073614.2016.1250350

Maturana, H. R., & Varela, F. J. (1992). *The tree of knowledge: The biological roots of human understanding*. Shambhala Publications.

Niemiec, R. M. (2014). *Mindfulness and character strengths: A practical guide to flourishing, mindfulness and character strengths: A practical guide to flourishing*. Hogrefe Publishing.

Otheguy, R., García, O., & Reid, W. (2015). Clarifying translanguaging and deconstructing named languages: A perspective from linguistics. *Applied Linguistics Review, 6*(3), 281–307. https://doi.org/10.1515/applirev-2015-0014

Paulsrud, B., Tian, Z., & Toth, J. (Eds.). (2021). *English-medium instruction and translanguaging*. Multilingual Matters.

Sah, P. K., & Li, G. (2022). Translanguaging or unequal languaging? Unfolding the plurilingual discourse of English medium instruction policy in Nepal's public schools. *International Journal of Bilingual Education and Bilingualism, 25*(6), 2075–2094. https://doi.org/10.1080/13670050.2020.1849011

Seligman, M. E. P. (2011). *Flourish: A visionary new understanding of happiness and well-being*. Free Press.

Shohamy, E. (2011). Assessing multilingual competencies: Adopting construct valid assessment policies. *The Modern Language Journal, 95*(3), 418–429. http://www.jstor.org/stable/41262376

Tai, K. W. H. (2024). Cross-curricular connection in an English Medium Instruction Western History classroom: A translanguaging view. *Language and Education, 38*(3), 435–464. https://doi.org/10.1080/09500782.2023.2174379

Tai, K. W. H., & Li, W. (2021). Co-Learning in Hong Kong English medium instruction mathematics secondary classrooms: A translanguaging perspective. *Language and Education, 35*(3), 241–267. https://doi.org/10.1080/09500782.2020.1837860

Tian, Z. (2020). Faculty first: Promoting translanguaging in TESOL teacher education. In S. M. C. Lau & S. Van Viegen (Eds.), *Plurilingual pedagogies: Critical and creative endeavors for equitable language in education* (pp. 215–236). Springer International Publishing.

Tian, Z., Aghai, L., Sayer, P., & Schissel, J. L. (Eds.). (2020). *Envisioning TESOL through a translanguaging lens: Global perspectives*. Springer International Publishing.

Tian, Z., & Lau, S. M. C. (2022). Translanguaging flows in Chinese word instruction: Potential critical sociolinguistic engagement with children's artistic representations of Chinese characters. *Pedagogies: An International Journal, 17*(4), 282–302. https://doi.org/10.1080/1554480X.2022.2139261

Tian, Z., & Zhang-Wu, Q. (2022). Preparing pre-service content area teachers through translanguaging. *Journal of Language, Identity & Education, 21*(3), 144–159. https://doi.org/10.1080/15348458.2022.2058512

PART I

Translanguaging Stance Development for Teachers

1

Metaphorical Affordances of Dominant Language Constellations (DLC) Artifacts in Pre-service Teacher Education

Developing a Translanguaging Stance

Nayr Correia Ibrahim

Introduction

We have witnessed in recent years an exponential growth in translanguaging research and a generalized acknowledgment of, and interest in its pedagogical affordances (Cenoz, 2017; Lau & Van Viegen, 2020; Shi, 2023; Song et al., 2022). The "translanguaging turn" (García & Li Wei, 2014) has contributed to decentering the monolingual bias in language education, shifting the core theoretical underpinnings of language learning and teaching from static to fluid processes (Donley, 2022) and normalizing the dynamic use of named language(s) by multilingual individuals. Spotlighting the prefix "trans," a translanguaging stance (García et al., 2017; Seltzer, 2022) can decenter monoglossic language ideologies, demonolinguize discourse (Ibrahim, 2022a), so it becomes more inclusive of linguistic diversity, and disrupt the language borders of classroom communication and teaching approaches. Despite this paradigm shift, there is still considerable uncertainty among teachers about how to operationalize flexible language practices in the classroom. Research into teachers' beliefs about multilingualism may highlight a general positive attitude toward the phenomenon (Haukås, 2016), without a real understanding of translanguaging as a sense-making, contextualized practice, where languages coexist and entangle in fluid communication. In order to bridge the chasm between ideologies and practice, researchers are calling for approaches that give pre-service teachers more opportunities to explore their own perceptions and ideological positionings in relation to translingual practices so as to better support multilingual learners in the classroom.

This chapter is based on a study that used the concept of Dominant Language Constellations (DLCs) (Aronin, 2021) as a tool for exploring pre-service teachers' subjective, experiential engagement with their languages. The student teachers (#28) (henceforth STs) were in a Master's Program in Primary and Secondary Education, with English as an elective, at a university in Northern Norway. They created DLC artifacts (Ibrahim, 2022b), a visual, artifactual activity, which required STs to engage with their full linguistic repertoires and identify their most expedient languages. The four DLC artifacts selected for this chapter, together with the STs' oral and written reflections, exemplify the metaphorical affordances of this creative activity, as it helps STs to unpack their relationships with their languages. After addressing the recent interest in translanguaging, as a concept and a practice, the DLC artifacts are analyzed as a material tool for uncovering STs' language ideologies, multilingual identities, and translanguaging stance (Seltzer, 2022). This is followed by a step-by-step description of the DLC activity, highlighting the pedagogical opportunities for engaging with linguistic diversity at an individual and class level. Finally, the chapter concludes with suggested concrete steps for teacher educators to further explore DLC artifacts as creative and critical tools for enhancing understanding of translanguaging and for demonolingualizing the English classroom (Ibrahim, 2022a).

Literature Review

A Translanguaging Stance in Teacher Education

From its inception, as an explicit pedagogical practice in the Welsh context (Williams, 1996), translanguaging has been described as a "potent concept" (Prilutskaya, 2021, p. 1) that "captured people's imagination" (Li Wei, 2018, p. 9). There are many definitions of translanguaging, but ultimately they all presuppose the breakdown of language barriers, for example: "a systematic, strategic, affiliative and sense-making process" (Gutiérrez et al., 2001, p. 128); "the deployment of a speaker's full linguistic repertoire without regard to watchful adherence to the socially and politically defined boundaries of named languages" (Otheguy et al., 2015, p. 281); "an eco-system of mutual interdependence" (García & Li Wei, 2014, p. 21); "primarily an interactional, practice-based theory of language and multilingualism" (Donley, 2022, p. 3). Cenoz (2017) differentiates between spontaneous translanguaging, as the naturally occurring language mixing in multilingual communication, and pedagogical translanguaging as a planned classroom strategy that uses "different languages for input and output or other planned strategies based on the use of students" resources from the whole linguistic repertoire' (194). A holistic approach to translanguaging legitimizes learners' natural translanguaging practices, evident in personal and family contexts. These practices should be replicated in educational contexts, both inside and outside the classroom walls. In the English classroom, this reconceptualization of language use provides a "translanguaging lens to speak back to traditional TESOL theory" (Tian et al., 2020, p. 1). It positions translanguaging as socially just pedagogy, which contributes to decolonizing and demonolingualizing teaching and learning practices (Ibrahim, 2025).

Moving in this direction requires a comprehensive approach to teacher education supported by an ideological shift in policy and personal beliefs. For example, Wong et al. (2023), report on a study that aimed to develop students' pedagogical knowledge of translanguaging through explicit course design. They observed a significant shift in student teachers' practices and beliefs but insisted "that purposeful, gradual, and consistent instruction is needed while introducing translanguaging to TCs due to the complexity of translanguaging and its application" (p. 831). In Luxembourg, an official multilingual policy covering all levels of education is accompanied by compulsory teacher education in multilingualism. Yet, as revealed by Aleksić and García's (2022) observation of a pre-school in Luxembourg, the "teachers' actions and discourse reveal raciolinguistic ideologies and misappropriation of the term translanguaging" (p. 3836). Ibrahim (2024b) concludes that this may simply reflect an overemphasis on the *multi* perspective in teacher education, where multilingualism is associated with a celebration of an accumulation of separate languages, and consequently teachers are unable to truly enact a translanguaging stance.

A translanguaging stance describes a "teacher's belief that a bilingual student has one holistic language repertoire that he or she draws on at school" (García et al., 2017, pp. 49–50). A comprehensive strategy for integrating a translanguaging stance in teacher education compels student teachers to question and reevaluate their own language identities. This process can help them perceive children as having a variety of sense-making resources that they can draw on to engage in and communicate their learning. Seltzer (2022) urges training programs to attend to the personal, political, and pedagogical elements of teachers' stances that can spark critical reflection on, and discussion around personal ideologies. Going beyond a focus on *multi*lingualism as a prerequisite for engaging with linguistic diversity, we need to educate teachers as advocates of and activists for *trans*languaging practices. These practices contribute to constructing a knowledge base and practice of translanguaging that escapes the binding concepts of monolingualizing discourse and the dichotomization of concepts and terminology (Ibrahim, 2022a; Ortega, 2014). One such approach is the visual material affordances of dominant language constellations, described in the section below.

Dominant Language Constellations: A Visual and Artifactual Window to a Translanguaging Stance

The concept of the Dominant Language Constellations (DLC) (Aronin, 2006; Lo Bianco & Aronin, 2020) was developed to capture the complexity, multidimensionality, and unpredictability of contemporary multilingual communication. It defines "the group of a person's most expedient languages, functioning as an entire unit and enabling an individual to meet all his/her needs in a multilingual environment" (Aronin, 2019, p. 21). Recently, DLC has been employed as a material pedagogical tool in teacher education (Ibrahim, 2022b; Pinho, 2023), with increasing applications in school contexts (Gkaintartzi & Triantou, 2023). The objective being to acknowledge and raise awareness of the hidden linguistic diversity in classrooms today. Aronin (2018) developed different ways to visualize an individuals' DLCs, including 2D DLC maps, 3D DLC modeling with plasticine and sticks, and computer-assisted modeling (Aronin & Moccozet, 2021). Ibrahim (2022a) employed DLC artifacts as concrete representations of an individual's languages. A DLC artifact can be defined as a concrete subjective external representation of an individual's full linguistic repertoire and naturally occurring DLCs, encapsulating creative, aesthetic, and kinaesthetic processes. The activity described in this chapter is based on an ongoing study, which collects DLC artifacts from STs in order to increase engagement with their multilingual identity.

Translanguaging-in-action: Developing a Translanguaging Stance through Artifactual and Narrative Exploration

Context and Participants

In the Norwegian context, the DLC artifact activity described in this chapter is a creative response to the revised curriculum, which explicitly mentions multilingualism in the Curriculum for English (Norwegian Directorate of Education and Training, 2020): "Pupils should be given a basis for seeing their own and the identity of others in a multilingual and multicultural context" (3), and where English is positioned as a key subject in developing multilingualism: "English is an important subject when it comes to cultural understanding, communication, all-round education and identity development"; "Language learning involves seeing connections between English and other languages the students know"; "English shall help the pupils to develop an intercultural understanding of different ways of living, ways of thinking and communication patterns" (2). Despite an apparent positive attitude to linguistic diversity in Norway, qualified by Lanza (2020) as a "linguistic paradise" (131), there is no mention of translanguaging, and there is a scarcity of concrete guidelines and appropriate materials for integrating translanguaging practices. Kalaja and Pitkänen-Huchta (2020, p. 7) denounce the fact that national curricula remain "at the level of buzzwords and lack any concrete applications." Myklevold and Speitz (2021) conclude that there is a disconnect between ideological intentions and operational realities.

The DLC artifact activity was conducted at the beginning of two English courses in a Masters in Primary and Secondary Teacher Education in Norway: a first year Grades 1–7 course, where STs require thirty credits of English, and a fourth year Grades 5–10 course with sixty credits of English. The aim of the activity is to encourage critical reflection on STs' subjective, experiential, and lived multilingualism (Ibrahim, 2023). Overall, twenty-eight DLC artifacts, together with the STs' written reflections, were collected between 2019 and 2023: twenty-one from Grades 1–7 and seven from Grades 5–10. The majority of STs have Norwegian, English, and a third language in their DLC, with six STs identifying a different heritage language. The Grades 1–7 STs were exposed to plurilingual practices integrated into the English course, for example, exploring dual-language picturebooks (Ibrahim, 2022c). Grades 5–10 STs took a module on Multilingualism and Plurilingual Practices as part of the 15-credit course, Literacy, Diversity, and Intercultural Citizenship in the English Language Classroom.

Analyzing the DLC Artifacts: From Multiple Monolingualism to a Translanguaging Stance

Content and semiotic analysis of the artifacts explored STs' relationships with their languages (Ibrahim, 2022b) from a visual and metaphorical perspective. They identified cross-linguistic and cross-modal opportunities to move the narrative from merely identifying *multi*lingualism as an accumulation of languages to perceiving or even representing *trans*lingual perspectives (Ibrahim, 2024b). The visual and design elements, that is, the layout of the DLC artifact, the choice of materials, color, size and shapes, and their positionings in the artifact are analyzed in the vignettes that follow. The interplay between these elements in each artifact revealed the inception of a *trans*languaging stance and the potential willingness to engage in cross-linguistic practices. The selected artifacts for this chapter (ST18, ST2, ST15, ST28) provided a concrete resource to exemplify this shift in perception, on a continuum of: describing multilingualism as multiple monolingualisms (Vignette 1 ST18) with a discourse that started recognizing language interdependence (Vignette 2 ST2) to a recognition of interconnected communicative practices (Vignette 3 ST28) and ultimately explicit engagement with translingual communicative practices (Vignette 4 ST15) and a translanguaging stance. On a pedagogical level, these vignettes can serve as guidelines for teachers to identify the elements to highlight when guiding their students' creation and explanation of their artifacts.

Moving from Distinct Languages to Acknowledging Language Interdependence

The majority of DLC artifacts identified teachers' perception of multilingualism as a collection of languages. This is clearly represented by the use of flags or objects that associated the respective language with a unique geographical, political, or cultural space, as in Vignette 1. Yet, both Vignettes 1 and 2 acknowledge language connection and interdependence.

Vignette 1: ST18—*T-shape*

ST18's DLC artifact (Figure 1.1) represented languages through the flag analogy, which delineates political spaces. According to the ST, the T-shape refers to the first letter of his name, thus imbuing the artifact with a personal identity. The DLC is depicted on the horizontal part of the T-shape, with Norwegian in the middle, "my mother tongue. It is the language I speak, and it is the language I have learnt the most." On either side, the ST added Swedish and Danish:

> because I know them based on them being similar to Norwegian. I also have Danish relatives so I am a little bit used to listen to it. I have also been a lot in Sweden, so I can understand mostly of what they are saying. And because these are languages I just know and have not tried to learn.

FIGURE 1.1 *ST18's DLC artifact—T-shape.*

The ST's static representations of his DLC are reinforced by the visual association of language as a separate geographical and political space. However, the ST simultaneously acknowledged intercomprehension and language interdependence, as a rationale for including Swedish and Danish.

Vignette 2: ST2— *Apple tree*

As identified in Ibrahim (2024a), trees were a common metaphor in STs' DLC artifacts, as they encapsulated solidity, timelessness, and rootedness in a heritage language. ST2's DLC (Figure 1.2) consists of a tree with a thick brown trunk, four green leaves, and a red apple in the middle, straddling all four leaves. The different shades of green and the positioning of the leaves are significant as this design decision was made to explain ST2's relationship with multilingualism:

> The highest leaf represents the Norwegian language, as it is the language, and part of the culture, that I most strongly identify with. [. . .] The second leaf is English, as English is the language I would answer immediately if someone were to ask me if I speak any other language. I speak English fluently, and there are topics I find easier to discuss in English than in Norwegian although my nationality is Norwegian. The bottom leaves, which represent Danish and Swedish, are in a paler shade of green as I do not have a strong relationship with these languages. I cannot speak either and I do not have a Danish or a Swedish language identity, but I understand Danish when I read it, and I understand Swedish when I hear it.

FIGURE 1.2 *ST2's DLC artifact—apple tree.*

The apple, representing Spanish, takes center stage in the DLC artifact, both in color (red) and position, even though it was the ST's foreign language, but this position is significant, as described below:

> The apple hangs lower than the Norwegian and the English leaves, but it is placed so that it touches both leaves. I chose this placement deliberately because I wanted to show that I feel a stronger connection to English than Spanish, and because this apple is nourished by the Norwegian and the English leaves as I learned Spanish using Norwegian and English. I doubt that select leaves nourishes select fruits on a tree, but I find this to be a fitting portrayal of my linguistic journey. If I were to learn other languages they would also be apples that I must take care of in order for them to flourish.

This metaphor of the leaves nourishing the apple is a fitting analogy of how language learning can and should depend on our knowledge of other languages. Hence, this is a clear and artistic reference to linguistic interconnection, which defies the separate language ideology, that supports a monolingual bias. Despite its inherent immobile stance, the DLC sows the seeds for developing a translanguaging stance.

Moving from Language Interdependence to an Emerging Translanguaging Stance

Vignettes 3 and 4 describe DLC artifacts that go further than simply identifying and connecting languages. They already reflect a conscious understanding of multilingualism as translingual practice and use unique metaphors to create complex representations of language identities and practices.

Vignette 3: ST28— *wheel mechanism*

ST28's DLC consists of six wheels in a gear or clockwork mechanism that turns all the wheels simultaneously. In the words of the ST, the rationale for this metaphor was to demonstrate function and dynamism: "I also wanted to illustrate that my DLC is not something static, but rather it is in a constant state of movement". The varying sizes of the wheels reflect the function of these languages in the ST's life: the big wheels are the ST's DLC, and provided the energy and the driving force to make the mechanism of her multilingualism function:

> The biggest wheel, Norwegian, is causing a motion. Drives the understanding of Swedish and Danish wheels as well, but those two I have nothing more than understanding of, I can't use them myself, so those two wheels are not contributing to my dominant language constellations, they are just there as part of my repertoire. Then English comes in, and has become an equally large wheel, then came French, which also has a considerable size.

This metaphor of intricate interdependence and linkage becomes an analogy for the interconnectedness of languages with the potential for normalizing a translanguaging stance in the classroom. This mechanism is flexible and open to additional wheels or languages that join the mechanism, not as separate parts, but as an indispensable contribution to the functioning of the whole:

> I for example am currently adding sign language [. . .] Wheels can be added to better the performance of the mechanism as well.

Besides the shift in the ST's perception of her language identity, as she admitted to not considering herself multilingual, there is a clear reassessment of the ST's perception of translanguaging in the English classroom:

> I have asked students in the past to "speak English", but have encouraged their peers to help them with words they get stuck on. This is not something I will be doing in the future. No matter the utterances of the students, if they are able to say the sentence, they are trying to say by using two Norwegian words—I will allow them to do so.

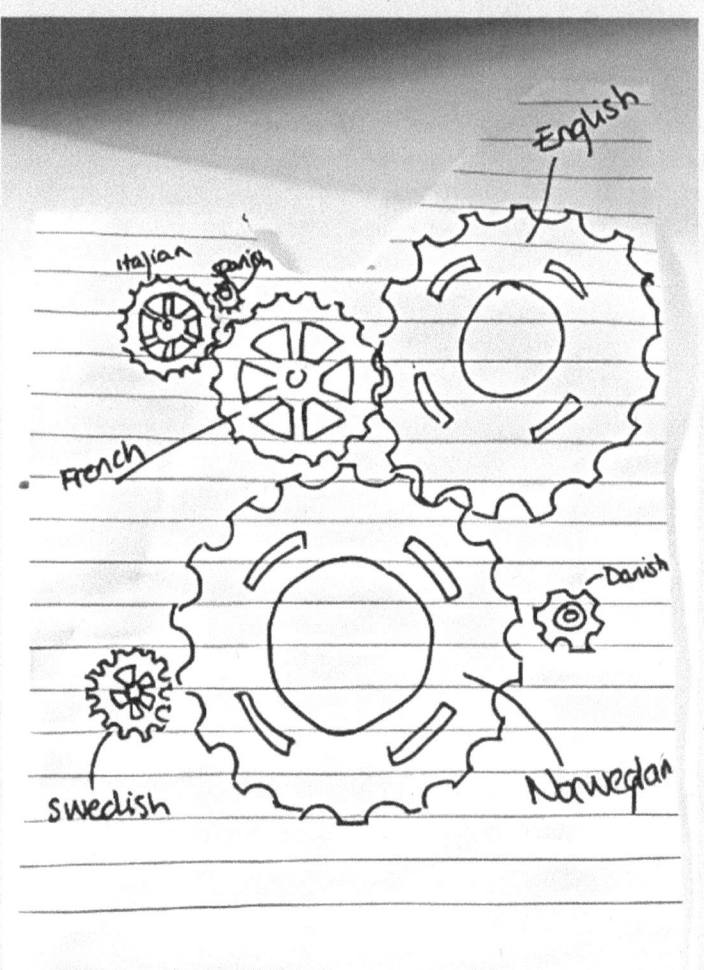

FIGURE 1.3 *ST28's DLC artifact—wheel mechanism.*

Vignette 4: ST15— *a dream catcher*

ST15 called her DLC artifact a dream catcher or a cobweb. It is made of a hoop with an elaborate star-like design, and pink and blue thread attached by three white beads. The two-colored design in the hoop represents Icelandic and Norwegian, ST15's two heritage languages, and the hanging threads, her other languages, that is, English, Castellano (Spanish),

Catalán, Danish, and Swedish. For ST15, the hoop or cobweb, "aligned with my explanation of how and why I translanguage daily." She goes on to say:

> I have described previously to my bilingual partner why I mix up words and sentence structures. I have described it as each language being a thread and they are woven into themselves and each other, creating a cobweb. My cobweb consists of many different threads woven into each other, making me mix up words and such.

The complex interweaving of thread in the dream catcher, which is soft and fluid and malleable, represents the delicate crisscross, interweaving reality of ST15's translanguaging practices, which she referred to on three different occasions, emphasizing the active nature of her language mixing: "I listen to English and use it when translanguaging; my explanation of how and why I translanguage daily; This is because I use English to think and translanguage."

The dream catcher represents a personal translanguaging stance (Seltzer, 2022), which is borne out of ST15's complex language experiences that have shaped her identity and the descriptions of her language mixing practices. Naming languages, which is absent from the DLC, only occurred during written reflection, where she needed to engage with her languages as separate social constructs (Ibrahim, 2024a). This is the only DLC where the ST uses the term translanguaging.

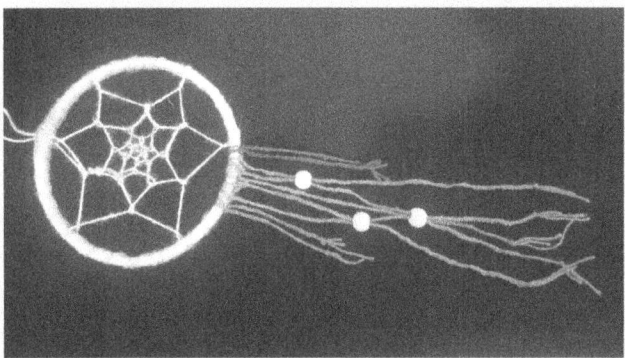

FIGURE 1.4 *ST15's DLC artifact—dream catcher.*

Pedagogical Opportunities for Embracing a Translingual Stance

Based on the analyses of the selected DLC artifacts in the four vignettes above, this creative, concrete activity presents multiple pedagogical opportunities.

First and foremost, it constitutes an innovative approach to engaging future teachers of English in describing their complex repertoires of languages, linguistic competencies, and identities. Second, it constitutes a space for initiating reflections around language mixing and the potential acceptance of translanguaging as both a practice and a communicative strategy in the classroom.

Consequently, designing a sequence of work around the DLC artifact from a translanguaging perspective needs to include a clear framework guiding teachers through the creative and reflective processes. Based on classroom experience, this framework includes an explicit sequential structure, as depicted in Figure 1.5:

Stage One: Activating Prior Knowledge and Awareness Raising—Whole-class Activity

In Stage One, the teacher educator first engages STs in a whole-class discussion around their languages. The main discussion points revolve around which languages they "know" vs "speak," why and where they learnt these languages, if they enjoyed the experience of learning those languages, how well they think they know the languages. Below are some examples of questions that can be used at this stage:

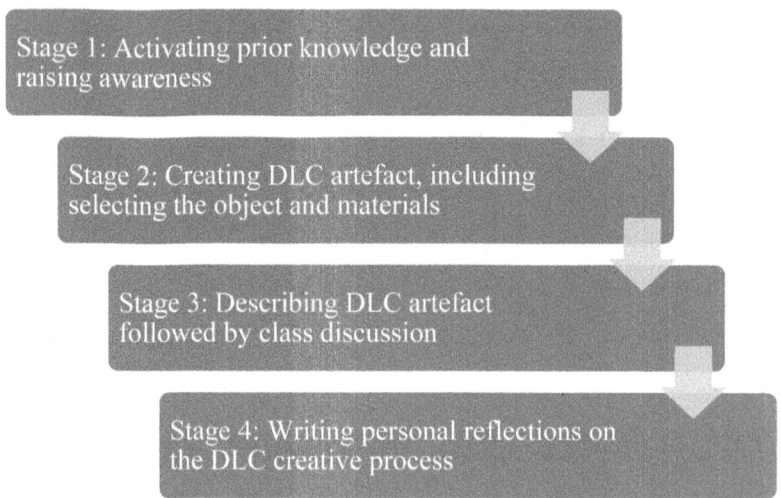

FIGURE 1.5 *DLC artifact teaching framework.*

- Which languages do you know?
- Where did you learn these languages: at school, at home, in a new country?
- How old were you when you started learning these languages?
- How well do you feel you speak and/or understand these languages?
- How well do you feel you read and/or write these languages?
- Do you still speak any of these languages? Why/Why not?
- Did you enjoy learning these languages?
- Which languages are you learning now or would you like to learn in the future?

During this initial discussion, STs are encouraged to mention all their language learning experiences as this sets the stage for engaging with their full language repertoire. Furthermore, it encourages reflecting on their attitudes toward and knowledge about multilingualism in their communities, schools, as well as national and international contexts. This whole-class discussion also sets the scene for introducing the concept of DLCs versus linguistic repertoires in a PowerPoint presentation.

The idea of a tangible DLC artifact is then introduced, and STs are asked to consider what their linguistic repertoire/DLC would look like as an object. They are presented with some sample DLCs created by past students, such as the atom (Ibrahim, 2022b) or the dream catcher (Figure 1.4) or the teacher educator's own DLC artifact. A careful selection of the sample DLC artifacts (see Ibrahim, 2022a, 2024a; Ibrahim & Lourenço, forthcoming), which are not necessarily representative of a particular culture, encourages metaphorical reflections through their uniqueness and subjectivity. STs have artistic freedom to create their DLC artifact, with no restrictions, the emphasis being on their creativity and originality to avoid the overuse of flags or other stereotypical symbols as representations of personal linguistic identities. Some teachers may need reassurance that they do not need to be "artistic" or "creative," but that the artifact they create, simple or complex, will be perfect to tell their linguistic story.

Stage Two: Creating DLC Artifacts Including Selecting the Object and Materials—Individual Free Choice Activity

The creation of the DLC artifacts can be executed in class or at home. At this stage, the time and space for individual reflection about materials to be used, choice of object to represent the multiple languages, and layout and positioning

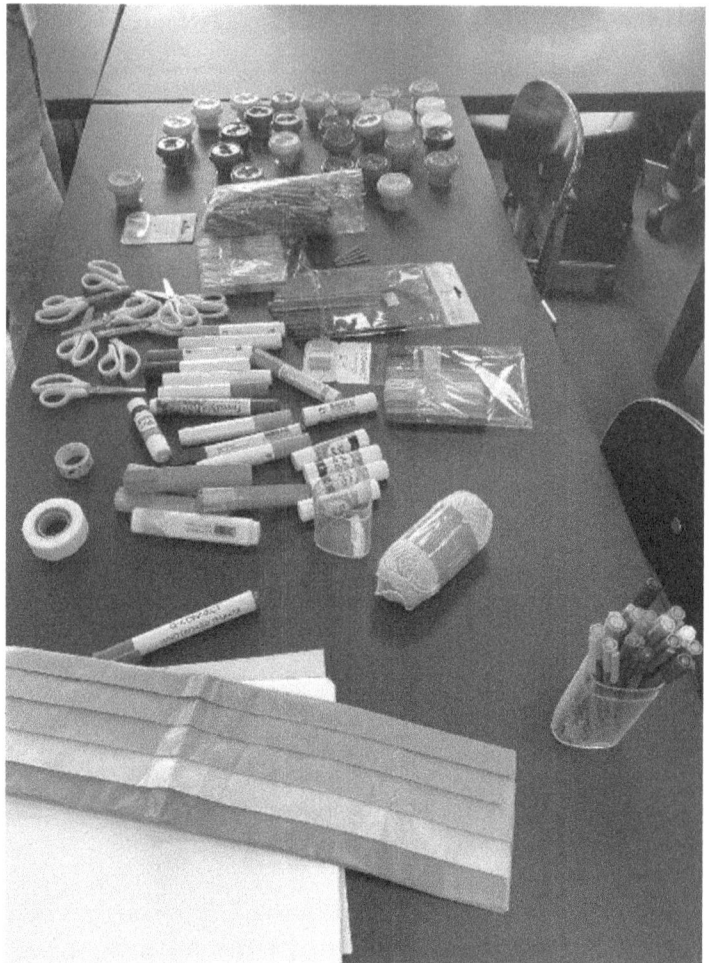

FIGURE 1.6 *Examples of materials provided for participants in the workshop at EDiLiC conference in Copenhagen, June 2023.*

decisions are key considerations. The freedom of choice of materials allows for subjectively created personal representations of languages. STs can use any type of material at their disposal, including card, ribbon, plastic, string, beads, twigs, playdough, matches to create objects with very personal meanings. In the original study, the STs were given a week to work on their DLC artifacts. When the artifacts are to be done in class or in a time-bound session, as in a workshop, a range of materials needs to be provided with around an hour for the actual creation. See Figure 1.6 for an example of materials provided at the *tenth International Conference of the Association EDiLiC* in Copenhagen, for the workshop *From early childhood to adulthood: DLC materialities for continuity and transition in plurilingual education*, conducted by Aronin and Ibrahim (2023).

Stage Three: Oral Description of DLC Artifact Followed by Whole-Class Discussion

Once the artifact has been created, the STs present their DLC to the class: they start by describing their DLC artifacts, which includes naming the object, describing the layering, and the chosen colors, shapes, and materials; then they explain the rationale for their creative choices and the respective metaphorical affordances of these choices to encapsulate the special relationship with their languages. In the end, the other STs in the class are invited to comment or ask questions for clarification.

This stage highlights the importance of the narrative for exploring objects and contributes to creating a collective multilingual class identity. It reveals the scope of multilingualism, debunks the myth that multilingualism is only associated with the "other," that is, immigrants, foreigners, or minority/heritage/Indigenous groups. This perception risks "otherising multilingualism as something uniquely foreign that teachers and schools must learn to cope with" (Calafato, 2020, p. 605), reinforces the unequal status of minority languages, and excludes majority language students with knowledge of multiple languages from identifying as multilingual. The subsequent questions, comments, and discussions around the DLC artifacts allowed for a discovery by the STs of the ubiquitousness of multilingualism. STs' comments below illustrate the impact on their perceptions of having listened to the other STs' language stories:

> With this DLC activity, and the conversation afterward, hearing the students explain how they came to their choices ensures deep learning, as they are thinking critically about their language journey as they communicate with others. (ST28)
>
> I also observed that other students have not seen themselves as multilingual individuals what was surprising and tells a lot about the teaching system and self-assessment and reflections about learning in schools in Norway (or lack of it). (ST1)

Stage Four: Writing Personal Reflections on the DLC Creative Process—Individual Reflective Activity

The DLC artifact creation was complemented by a reflective written narrative, in which the STs were required to address the following questions:

1. How did you organize your DLC and why did you choose this specific shape, materials, colors, and so on, to represent your named languages?

2. How did creating a visual and manual (craft) representation of all your languages, in this specific shape, help you visualize your multilingualism and see yourself as a multilingual individual and multilingual teacher?

3. How do you think this will change the way you approach your students' other languages in your English lessons?

4. How does this manual, visual, multimodal activity support and enhance creative teaching and ensure deep learning in the language classroom?

This last stage is key for unpacking the metaphorical affordances of the object and an opportunity to explore the personal meanings of objects that at first may seem rather mundane or idiosyncratic. Reflective narratives provide a window into "the inner mental worlds" of language users as they are more closely tied to "the lived reality of phenomena" than other modes (Chik et al. 2014: 2). In the words of the STs, these reflections highlight:

1. the discovery of a multilingual self:

    > By creating my own DLC I felt inspired by the linguistic story that this language map illustrates [. . .] The DLC helped me think of myself as a multilingual individual as it made me focus on my relationships with language. (ST2)

    > Creating a visual and manual representation of the connections and relationships between the languages in which I am proficient, made me aware that I too am multilingual. This is not something I have considered before, despite speaking three languages, learning a fourth, and understanding several others. (ST28)

2. the satisfaction of discovering the interrelatedness of languages or translanguaging stance:

    > I experienced that putting the separate languages in a DLC was like putting pieces of a puzzle together. This puzzle illustrated my language journey as a whole and I am able to explain each piece and how they fit together with the next piece. I found this whole-ness very satisfying. (ST2)

3. the critical pedagogical implications for their future teaching:

    > I believe I would be able to get great insight into the students' thoughts about language, language learning, and how they view themselves as multilingual through their DLCs. (ST28)

> It is interesting to think of other individuals' linguistic stories and it makes me curious to know more about an aspect of my students' identity that I previously did not take much into consideration. (ST2)
>
> I am very aware of the difficulties of being multilingual in a classroom that expects monolingualism, so I am always aware of how it impacts students. (ST15)

According to Li Wei (2020), teacher education needs approaches that "raise the critical awareness amongst teachers and teacher trainers of their own multilingual background, their own learning trajectories and their own attitudes toward plurilingualism and plurilingual practices" (274). The four-stage framework provides several opportunities to raise critical awareness and engage STs in the journey toward a translanguaging stance. The recognition and appreciation of all their languages as part of their identity is the first step. Yet, a thread of discussion, reflection, and creativity around personal language diversity is present throughout the framework. The four DLC artifacts analyzed in the vignettes reflect the journey from an awareness raising of language interdependence to a self-proclaimed translanguaging stance. However, as observed in Vignettes 1–3, even though there was an acknowledgment of linguistic diversity and language connections, not all DLCs reflect the translanguaging stance explicitly. It is therefore recommended that discussions address translanguaging by specifically exploring the implications of language interdependence and language mixing on the STs' language repertoire. Students can also recreate their DLC artifacts at the end of the academic year or the course to evaluate the extent to which there is a shift in perspectives. Ultimately, these personal objects constitute fertile ground for teacher educators to sow the seeds of linguistic diversity.

Concluding Thoughts

This chapter explores DLC artifacts as an innovative creative approach to engaging teachers in a translanguaging stance through the development of identity texts. The DLC artifacts provided concrete and narrative spaces for visibilizing linguistic diversity. Furthermore, they contributed to developing a translanguaging stance, with reported pedagogical implications for the STs' future practice. At the stage of creating their DLCs, the STs were unaware of, or had not reflected on, the extent of their multilingualism and the reality of translanguaging in their lives as well as its potential uses in the classroom. The artifact, as a tangible arts-based platform, provided a metaphorical space for exploring language mixing and translanguaging that would have been denied through an exclusively lingual approach. The visual and creative object allowed for a much wider and deeper exploration of real language use and initiated a more relaxed relationship with their languages.

The DLC teaching framework (Figure 1.5) provides teacher educators with a staged approach to engage STs in acknowledging the complex ways in which they use their linguistic repertoires and in reassessing their attitudes to translanguaging. From raising awareness, where STs embrace their linguistic diversity as a source of strength, to the creative process, enhanced through the narrative lens, the sequence of activities provided STs with tangible and age-appropriate examples of more socially just pedagogy. They also laid the groundwork for further critical reflection on the actual practice of multilingualism as language interdependence, language mixing, and, as explicitly mentioned in ST15's reflections, translanguaging. The careful choice of the object and the materials that constituted the artifact became an intentional act of identifying the different roles languages played in STs' life trajectory. Subsequently, the strong subjective narratives that emerged from the activity indicated a deeper understanding of translanguaging as a personal identity marker and a flexible pedagogical approach, thus contributing to expanding the multilingual mindset in teacher education. STs were able to envision a future imagined English classroom community, where other languages were welcome and could be used as teaching and learning resources in a reciprocal approach that contributed to creating safe multilingual learning environments.

Not all DLC artifacts presented a clear shift toward a translanguaging stance, hence the targeted selection of DLC artifacts in this chapter. However, the STs' awakening to the potential of translanguaging, evident in these artifacts, is an opportunity that educators need to seize in order to further the discussion of translanguaging pedagogical design. The DLC teaching framework offers teacher educators a structured teachable moment that supports future teachers in making informed decisions when considering the potential of the translanguaging stance as a communicative strategy in the classroom. The artifacts encapsulated fluid translingual spaces and contribute to reconceptualizing language practices and identities in education, providing "an ideological and pedagogical shift for linguistic rights and social justice in education in an increasingly diverse world" (Paulsrud et al., 2017, p. 17). These are acts of activism for a more linguistically just educational future.

References

Aleksić, G., & García, O. (2022). Language beyond flags: Teachers misunderstanding of translanguaging in preschools. *International Journal of Bilingual Education and Bilingualism, 25*(10), 3835–3848. https://doi.org/10.1080/13670050.2022.2085029

Aronin, L. (2006). Dominant language constellations: An approach to multilingualism studies. In M. Ó Laoire (Ed.), *Multilingualism in educational settings* (pp. 140–159). Schneider Publications.

Aronin, L. (2018). DLC: Relationships, patterns and contexts. Paper presented at the XIth International Conference on Third Language Acquisition and Multilingualism, Lisbon, Portugal, September 13–15.

Aronin, L. (2019). Dominant language constellation as a method of research. In E. Vetter & N. Jessner (Eds.), *International research on multilingualism: Breaking with the monolingual perspective* (pp. 13–26). Springer.

Aronin, L. (2021). Dominant language constellations in education: Patterns and visualisations. In L. Aronin & E. Vetter (Eds.), *Dominant language constellations approach in education and language acquisition* (pp. 19–42). Springer.

Aronin, L., & Moccozet, L. (2021). Dominant language constellations: Towards online computer-assisted modelling. *International Journal of Multilingualism*, 20, 1–21.

Aronin, L., & Ibrahim, N. (2023). *From early childhood to adulthood: DLC materialities for continuity and transition in plurilingual education*. Workshop presented at *10th International Conference of the Association EDiLiC / 10ème congrès international de l'association EDiLiC conference*, Copenhagen, 28–30 June 2023.

Calafato, R. (2020). Language teacher multilingualism in Norway and Russia: Identity and beliefs. *European Journal of Education*, 55(4), 602–617.

Cenoz, J. (2017). Translanguaging in school contexts: International perspectives. *Journal of Language, Identity and Education*, 16, 193–198.

Chik, A., Barkhuizen, G., & Benson, P. (2014). *Narrative inquiry in language teaching and learning research*. Routledge.

Donley, K. (2022). Translanguaging as a theory, pedagogy, and qualitative research methodology. *NABE Journal of Research and Practice*, 12(3–4), 105–120. https://doi.org/10.1080/26390043.2022.2079391

García, O., & Li, W. (2014). *Translanguaging: Language, bilingualism and education*. Palgrave Macmillan.

García, O., Ibarra Johnson, S., & Seltzer, K. (2017). *The translanguaging classroom: Leveraging student bilingualism for learning*. Caslon.

Gkaintartzi, A., & Triantou, G. (2023). Activating diversity: The use of dual language books for critical plurilingual education. *Journal of Applied Linguistics*, 36, 30–56. https://doi.org/10.26262/jal.v0i36.9917

Gutiérrez, K., Banquedano-López, P., & Alvarez, H. (2001). Literacy as hybridity. In M. D. L. L. Reyes & J. J. Halcón (Eds.), *The best for our children: Critical Perspectives on Literacy for Latino Students* (pp. 122–141). Teachers College Press.

Haukås, Å. (2016). Teachers' beliefs about multilingualism and a multilingual pedagogical approach. *International Journal of Multilingualism*, 13, 1–18.

Ibrahim, N. (2022a). Mainstreaming multilingualism in education: An Eight-D's framework. In A. Krulatz, G. Neokleous, & A. Dahl (Eds.), *Theoretical and applied perspectives on teaching foreign languages in multilingual settings* (pp. 33–46). Multilingual Matters.

Ibrahim, N. C. (2022b). Visual and artefactual approaches in engaging teachers with multilingualism: Creating DLCs in pre-service teacher education. *Languages*, 7, 152. https://doi.org/10.3390/languages7020152

Ibrahim, N. C. (2022c). Examining a Northern Sámi-Norwegian dual language picturebook in English language education through a critical translingual-transcultural lens. *Intercultural Communication Education, 5*(3), 105–124. https://doi.org/10.29140/ice.v5n3.847

Ibrahim, N. C. (2023). Educating early years and primary English language teachers multilingually. In D. Valente & D. Xerri (Eds.), *Innovative practices in early English language education* (pp. 233–257). Palgrave Macmillan.

Ibrahim, N. C. (2024a). Exploring student teachers' multilingual identity through dominant language constellations: DLC artefacts in teacher education. In D. Gabryś-Barker & E. Vetter (Eds.), *Modern approaches to researching multilingualism: Studies in Honour of Larissa Aronin* (pp. 323–344). Multilingual Matters.

Ibrahim, N. C. (2024b). Multilingualism vs translingualism in teacher education: Changing perspectives. In S. Mourão & C. Leslie (Eds.), *Research into teacher education and professional development for multilingualism in childhood* (pp. 99–114). Bloomsbury.

Ibrahim, N. C. (2025). Translanguaging as inclusive pedagogy and multilingual oracy. In D. Karoulla-Vrikki & L. Lopriore (Eds.), *Oracy acquisition and development in early second language learning: Voices from diverse international contexts* (pp. 218–232). Multilingual Matters.

Kalaja, P., & Pitkänen-Huhta, A. (2020). Raising awareness of multilingualism as lived – in the context of teaching English as a foreign language. *Language and Intercultural Communication, 20*(4), 340–355.

Lanza, E. (2020). Urban multilingualism and family language policy. In G. Caliendo, R. Janssens, S. Slembrouck & P. Van Avermaet. *Urban Multilingualism in Europe: Bridging the Gap between Language Policies and Language Practices* (pp. 121–40). De Gruyter Mouton.

Lau, S. M. C., & Van Viegen, S. (Eds.). (2020). *Plurilingual pedagogies: Critical and creative endeavors for equitable language in education* (pp. 3–22). Springer.

Li, W. (2018). Translanguaging as a practical theory of language. *Applied Linguistics, 39*(1), 9–30.

Li, W. (2020). Dialogue/response: Engaging translanguaging pedagogies in higher education. In S. M. C. Lau & S. Van Viegen (Eds.), *Plurilingual pedagogies: Critical and creative endeavors for equitable language in education* (pp. 3–22). Springer.

Lo Bianco, J., & Aronin, L. (Eds.). (2020). *Dominant language constellations: A new perspective on multilingualism*. Springer.

Myklevold, G.-A., & Speitz, H. (2021). Multilingualism in curriculum reform (LK20) and teachers' perceptions: Mind the gap? *Norwegian Journal of Language Teaching and Learning, 9*(2), 25–50.

Norwegian Directorate of Education and Training. (2020). *Læreplan i engelsk*. https://www.udir.no/lk20/eng01-04?lang=eng

Ortega, L. (2014). Ways forward for a bi/multilingual turn in SLA. In S. May (Ed.), *The multilingual turn: Implications for SLA, TESOL and bilingual education* (pp. 32–53). Routledge.

Otheguy, R., García, O., & Reid, W. (2015). Clarifying translanguaging and deconstructing named languages: A perspective from linguistics. *Applied Linguistics Review, 6*, 281–307.

Paulsrud, B., Rosén, J. K., Straszer, B., & Wedin, Å. (2017). Perspectives on translanguaging in education. In B. Paulsrud, J. Rosén, B. Straszer, & Å. Wedin (Eds.), New perspectives on translanguaging and education (pp. 15–34). Multilingual Matters. https://doi.org/10.21832/9781783097821-003

Pinho, A. S. (2023). Pre-service teachers' professional identity and representations of English as a foreign language: Toward a dominant language (teaching) constellation? In L. Aronin & S. Melo-Pfeifer (Eds.), *Dominant language constellations: Language awareness and identity*. Springer. (pp 219–245)

Prilutskaya, M. (2021). Examining pedagogical translanguaging: A systematic review of the literature. *Languages*, *6*(180), 1–18. https://doi.org/10.3390/languages6040180

Seltzer, K. (2022). Enacting a critical translingual approach in teacher preparation: Disrupting oppressive language ideologies and fostering the personal, political, and pedagogical stances of preservice teachers of English. *TESOL Journal*, *13*(2), 1–11. https://doi.org/10.1002/tesj.649

Shi, L. (2023). Enriching early years English language education with translanguaging. In D. Valente & D. Xerri (Eds.), *Innovative practices in early english language education* (pp. 233–257). Palgrave Macmillan.

Song, J., Howard, D., & Olazabal-Arias, W. (2022). Translanguaging as a strategy for supporting multilingual learners' social emotional learning. *Education Sciences*, *12*(7), 475. https://doi.org/10.3390/educsci12070475

Tian, Z., Aghai, L., Sayer, P., & Schissel, J. L. (Eds.). (2020). *Envisioning TESOL through a translanguaging lens: Global perspectives*. Springer.

Williams, C. (1996). Secondary education: Teaching in the bilingual situation. In C. Williams, G. Lewis, & C. Baker (Eds.), *The language policy: Taking stock*. CAI.

Wong, C.-Y. (C.), Du, X., & Estudillo, A. G. (2023). 'I've grown so much more confidence in my actual instruction': Examining teacher candidates' pedagogical knowledge growth in translanguaging. *Language and Education*, *37*(6), 820–835.

2

Framing Teachers as Experts

Developing Translanguaging Spaces and Stances for Learning and Teaching

Gregory Child, Nicole King, and Kim Song

Introduction

Multilingual Learners (MLs) are the fastest-growing population within US schools (NCES, 2023); however, teachers remain predominantly white, middle-class, native English speakers (Boser, 2014). To address this misalignment, schools and teacher preparation programs are working to acknowledge the lack of diversity in teachers, recruit more diverse applicants (e.g., Yip & Xu, 2024), and incorporate more culturally and linguistically sustaining educational practices, such as translanguaging (García, 2023), into their curricula. However, given restrictive language and assessment policies, the enactment of translanguaging pedagogy remains controversial (Sembiante & Tian, 2020). Researchers call for collaborations with teachers to explore mindsets and pedagogical practices fostering equitable education for MLs (García, 2023; García et al., 2021).

In this chapter, we share how three in-service teachers from the US Midwest enacted translanguaging repertoires and reinvented their classrooms as translanguaging spaces (Li, 2011; Seltzer, 2022). The three teachers were participants in a grant project that sought to develop and enhance the capacity of in-service teachers to work with MLs. By design, we encouraged in-service teachers to develop a critical understanding of language and to leverage translanguaging pedagogy. As they enacted this new understanding of language and knowledge with their MLs, they helped to create more equitable and accessible environments for their MLs.

Ultimately, teachers transformed their practices, converting classrooms into translanguaging spaces where their beliefs were locally manifested by creating inviting, multilingual spaces of belonging, supporting home languages, and fostering collaboration between students. Translanguaging spaces do not develop in all classrooms because teachers and students are in the same space (Sanger, 2020); their development requires collaboration and planning. We contend that any space can become a translanguaging space. We further assert that when translanguaging spaces are co-constructed, this collaboration leads to socially just spaces that positively contribute to MLs' educational outcomes (Nieto, 2017).

Literature Review

The student population in US schools is becoming increasingly diverse; between 2010 and 2019, MLs became the fastest-growing proportion of the student body population (NCES, 2023). The teaching force, however, remains predominantly white, monolingual individuals largely underprepared to teach MLs, with a curriculum designed for linguistically and culturally white, middle-class students (Baker-Bell, 2020; Flores & Rosa, 2015; Song et al., 2021). Even with the unchanged teacher demographics, there has been substantial scholarship on culturally and linguistically sustaining practices, including translanguaging and multilingual, multicultural books and stories (Song & King, 2023), and the affordances that they provide to MLs (García et al., 2021; Sayer, 2013; Sembiante & Tian, 2020). Translanguaging pedagogy refers to a stance or mindset and instructional design (García et al., 2017; Seltzer, 2022); it creates opportunities for teachers in collaboration with their MLs to push against traditional monoglossic and monocultural practices to celebrate diversity (García & Kleyn, 2016; García & Li, 2014). Incorporating translanguaging into classrooms creates spaces of increased learning, equity, and engagement for the growing ML population.

Translanguaging as Theory and Pedagogy

Coined by Cen Williams, the term translanguaging originally described an approach to bilingual education where students would learn content in one language but demonstrate their comprehension in another (García & Li, 2014).

Since its inception, translanguaging has grown to represent both theory and pedagogy (García et al., 2017; García & Li, 2014). As a theory, translanguaging asserts that MLs flexibly leverage their communicative repertoires in self-expression without compartmentalizing by named languages (e.g., English, French) (García & Li, 2014). Translanguaging theory positions MLs as linguistic experts drawing from their resources as they interpret and engage with the world around them. This view of languaging contradicts traditional monolingual perspectives rooted within the language policies of US schools (Menken & García, 2010). Traditionally, named languages are conceptualized as separate, unconnected entities existing apart from and even to the detriment of each other; a position in direct contradiction with translanguaging as a theory of language (García et al., 2021; Li, 2018).

Translanguaging as pedagogy entails teachers' active, intentional, and purposeful design incorporating learners' home languages in classroom activities (Li, 2011) while acknowledging the use of multiple languages is the students' choice that should be respected (Abraham et al., 2021; Li, 2011). Regardless of their linguistic repertoire, teachers can either support translanguaging by encouraging and positively responding to student languaging or repress it through narrowly created educational activities or language policies (e.g., "English only" policies) (García et al., 2017). When teachers actively support and incorporate learners' entire linguistic repertoire, classrooms can become translanguaging spaces where students freely make meaning and express identities (García et al., 2017).

Teachers are uniquely positioned to resist dominant language ideologies that prioritize English-only spaces. Seltzer (2022) disentangled the concept of a translanguaging stance to shed light on the personal, political, and pedagogical beliefs that teachers hold and manifest with their students. Viewing a translanguaging stance through this lens encourages teachers to question how their language beliefs and policies either align with or separate them from their students, examine the power that English and white English speakers have (e.g., Baker-Bell, 2020; Flores & Rosa, 2015), and consider how students creatively leverage their linguistic and cultural assets in classrooms (Flores, 2020).

Defining Translanguaging Spaces

Translanguaging spaces are co-constructed. In the words of Li Wei (2011),

> The act of translanguaging then is transformative in nature; it creates a social space for the multilingual language user by bringing together different dimensions of their personal history, experience and environment, their

attitude, belief and ideology, their cognitive and physical capacity into one coordinated and meaningful performance, and making it into a lived experience. (p. 1223)

As translanguaging spaces are shared spaces, the linguistic and cultural norms, and personal histories are shared among MLs, peers, and teachers; English, middle-class white cultural practices are not the de facto standard. This directly opposes many classrooms that position mainstream linguistic and cultural practices in power. In translanguaging spaces, linguistic and cultural practices other than English are not only accepted but actively invited and recognized as assets to improve educational achievements and promote equity in these spaces (Abraham et al., 2021; García et al., 2017).

Translanguaging spaces are also built upon the fundamental concepts of MLs' everyday language practices. MLs' linguistic practices naturally incorporate multiple languages. García and Kleyn (2016) explain that everyone develops linguistic systems based on social interactions. Most individuals acquire a named language; however, as individuals engage with people who speak different named languages, or different varieties of the same language, they acquire features of those languages/varieties without distinguishing between them. An outsider with different experiences might readily identify the varieties of the same or different named languages, which the speaker may not as easily identify, yet represent the speaker's unique language repertoire. Consistent with a social stance toward education and the belief that teaching is a political act (Freire, 2000), translanguaging spaces are transformative spaces (Li & García, 2022) that encourage learners to recognize and utilize their linguistic and cultural resources as learning assets (García et al., 2021).

Finally, translanguaging spaces emancipate students' expression beyond simply safe spaces, to spaces of shared trust and responsibility (Zhang, 2021). In these spaces, teachers support students' translanguaging and assist in reframing flexible languaging as legitimate across all contexts. This reframing helps teachers and students who may have previously viewed language practices through a siloed, monolingual lens (Williams, 2023). Teachers and MLs build trust in classrooms as spaces where MLs can access their linguistic, cultural, and personal assets in flexible, meaningful ways. To do this, teachers must be willing to relinquish control of the space and share it with their MLs. Teachers are not expected to be linguistic experts in MLs' home languages, they must, however, be willing to ask for help from their MLs and their families (García et al., 2017). This creates opportunities to engage ML families in classroom activities and to ask students to help when developing materials; these opportunities craft a shared responsibility of knowledge, language, and cultural exchange. Teachers cannot establish translanguaging spaces alone, it requires collaboration from students, families, and communities (Sanger, 2020).

In this chapter, we will share how three in-service teachers—a fourth-grade teacher, a physics teacher, and a US history teacher—enacted translanguaging spaces in their classrooms. Each classroom's enactment and emergence as a translanguaging space will look unique, as the MLs in each classroom are unique. They will highlight the shared and co-constructed nature of these spaces (Blommaert et al., 2005; Li, 2011).

Translanguaging in Action

In this section, we would like to take you with us to three classrooms. Within these classrooms, you will be introduced to teachers who learned to enact translanguaging spaces. Key to these observations was that teachers had been taught about translanguaging and then positioned as experts within their spaces to interpret and implement translanguaging. The classroom teachers were content teachers seeking an ESL endorsement and taking courses at a university in the Midwest. While each teacher collaborated with their MLs to create and enact a translanguaging space differently, there are a few common threads: teachers supporting their MLs sense of belonging, encouraging and acknowledging flexible use of home languages, and collaboration among the students (and with the teachers).

Michelle

In Michelle's sheltered physics classroom, there were ten MLs who spoke Turkish, Swahili, and Vietnamese. During our visit, the class was in the middle of a unit on magnetism. Upon entering her classroom, our eyes were immediately called to the back wall where colorful papers hung above a whiteboard. Upon further inspection, we noticed that the papers contained translations of question words (who, what, where) color-coded by language. The whiteboard below the papers served as a multilingual word wall where key terms relating to magnetism were translated and similarly color-coded by language (Figure 2.1).

When we arrived, the classes were transitioning, and Michelle was at the door talking to students. She greeted her students in their home languages and flexibly languaged with them. When MLs entered the classroom speaking English, Michelle engaged with them in English; if they entered the classroom speaking Spanish, she would engage with them in Spanish. In our interactions with Michelle, we had learned that she has a great interest in language learning and connecting with her students. She frequently sought opportunities to

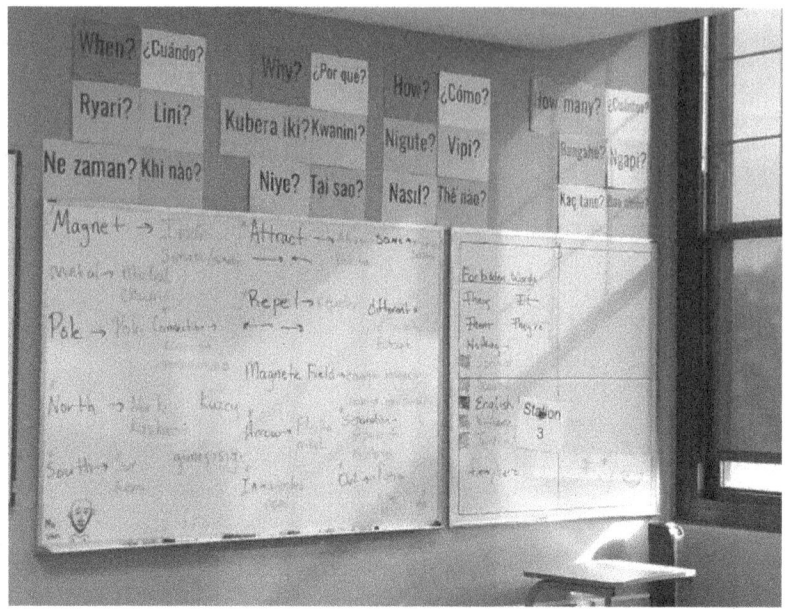

FIGURE 2.1 *Multilingual word wall.*

learn the home languages of her MLs, resulting in her ability to converse in Spanish, Vietnamese, and her growing proficiency in Arabic. Her desire to interact with MLs in their home language was observed throughout our visit as she frequently languaged flexibly in her communications.

What stood out to us most about Michelle's linguistic flexibility was the way she brought her MLs' out-of-class linguistic practices into the classroom. As previously mentioned, translanguaging is the fluid linguistic practice of MLs and positions their linguistic fluidity as the norm. Michelle met students where they were outside of the classroom and brought those practices into her interactions and instruction. She did not impose linguistic rules demanding that English or home languages be used at specific times for specific purposes; she shifted with them.

When the bell rang to start class, Michelle immediately welcomed everyone and referred to them as her "team." This seemingly simple greeting was representative of more than a label used to refer to her students; it was illustrative of the importance she placed on collaboration and co-construction. She continually emphasized peer interaction by instructing her MLs to first work with classmates and to ask them questions because they knew the content before bringing the question to her. Throughout the lesson, Michelle and her students discussed magnetism using Spanish, English, and Vietnamese together. She built on their knowledge of concepts, such as separation, in their home languages using visuals before introducing the word in English.

As Michelle walked around to check in on each group, she could hear her "team" using the key vocabulary in a variety of languages.

Michelle and her "team" established the classroom as a translanguaging space beginning with the greetings at the door and the interactions at the beginning of class. Critically, the normalized practice of home language use in the classroom created an opportunity for Michelle to deliver an academically challenging curriculum that fully affirmed and leveraged her students' sense-making across languages. Creating a translanguaging space that allowed and encouraged her MLs to use their entire linguistic repertoire as an asset and resource for learning facilitated deeper conversations about content. Through their conversations about magnetic fields, MLs progressed from the simplistic notion that magnets are separated from each other to statements like the following, "Because magnetic fields are going in different directions; magnetic fields are separating," and "The magnets are repelling. I know this because the magnetic fields are separated."

The observed translanguaging is a result of several small but meaningful actions. Firstly, Michelle greeted her students in their home language and/or English depending on the language they were using in the classroom. She demonstrated through her actions that languages other than English were welcome and accepted in her classroom space. Second, a multilingual word wall with key vocabulary terms available in all her MLs' home languages ensured that MLs had the vocabulary needed to carry out deeper conversations about magnetism. This word wall was used in coordination with multilingual slides and the anchor chart of question words in different languages. Third, in positioning MLs as a team, learning became a collaborative endeavor where Michelle was a facilitator and her MLs were responsible for learning. This practice is particularly important because it allowed Michelle to ask difficult questions and provide high-quality instruction without compromise; when MLs have access to their entire linguistic repertoire, they can use their language skills as an asset for learning. Finally, what was not explicitly seen but learned through conversation with Michelle, was her open seating chart. MLs were allowed to select who they would like to work with, which created opportunities for students to converse in their home languages.

Madison

The next classroom we visited belongs to Madison. Madison was a fourth-grade elementary teacher who taught in a large urban area. The community surrounding her school was a tight-knit, diverse community, including a large population of refugees from Bosnia, that eagerly engaged with the school when opportunities were available. During the observations, there were only fifteen students present. Of those fifteen, six were MLs speaking seven languages (Bosnian, Croatian, Vietnamese, Arabic, French, Swahili, and Nepali). When we arrived at the classroom, students had not yet returned from another class, allowing us to explore the classroom a little.

During our exploration, the first thing we noticed were hand-drawn flags representing the home countries of each student. All her students, ML and mainstream alike, created a flag recognizing their home country. The effort to ensure all students were represented avoids the practice of trivializing or even tokenizing individuals who are linguistically, racially, or culturally diverse. Madison was creating a space where all students were seen and heard. What stood out about this practice was we could see and get a sense of who was in the class before students were even there. As we continued to explore, we found *All About Me* projects where students listed their favorite colors, pets, and future careers with hand-drawn pictures of themselves (Figure 2.2).

The students soon returned to the classroom, and Madison gave a quick introduction to Greg and Nicole. She informed the students that we were her teachers and that we wanted to come and see what was happening in the classroom. Admittedly, when the students returned, they caught us looking at their flags and posters. Throughout our visit, we joined the students in their activities. In our interactions, they frequently asked if we saw their flag or

FIGURE 2.2 *Madison's ML-welcoming practices.*

poster. We would ask which was theirs, and we would go and look at it. Upon our return, they would excitedly tell us more about themselves and their flags and about the things they could not put on the poster. The students were excited to see themselves in the space, and they wanted us to see them as well. These flags and posters not only told us about the students in the class, but they served as a starting point for students to engage with us and to welcome us into their classroom, for them a co-constructed space.

This co-constructed space continued in the way Madison opened the lesson. Madison's slides began with the welcome slide from Figure 2.3. As shown in the figure, the word "hello" had been translated into eight languages including English, representing the languages spoken in her classroom. She put the slide up and invited students to teach each other greetings in their home languages. At first, there was some hesitancy, but slowly students started to teach each other. Over five minutes, each greeting was taught, and all the students were invited to repeat them in their respective languages.

Several items stood out to us from this practice. First, Madison did not require any student to teach their greeting if they were not ready or did not desire to do so; she made the offer and then respected MLs' choice, whatever it was. However, we noticed that those who were initially reticent to teach/share their home language greetings became more engaged as peers taught their greetings and ultimately chose to teach theirs. The translanguaging space was an inviting one. Second, Madison positioned her students as language experts and shared the control and responsibility of teaching and

FIGURE 2.3 *Multilingual greetings.*

learning with them. When she invited students to teach their greetings, she listened and participated, even asking questions about her pronunciation and potential different greetings she had heard in the past, all the while respecting her students as teachers. Finally, this multilingual opening to the class demonstrated that languages other than English were invited and encouraged in their translanguaging space. One of Madison's initial concerns as she learned about translanguaging was that she did not speak the home languages of her MLs. She was worried that this would prevent her from supporting translanguaging. However, her classroom was a model of how a teacher who does not speak the languages of her students can thoughtfully and strategically design a lesson that leverages translanguaging.

Madison's lesson continued with a review of inferences and how one makes an inference. Throughout her instruction, she maintained a student-centered approach using images that reflected the cultures of the MLs in her class. For example, after reviewing inferencing, they began a guided practice where Madison projected pictures and students had to infer what was happening in each. Included with those pictures was an image of a family celebrating Ramadan. Students worked with partners to describe what they saw and infer what was happening. There were many responses about families sharing a large meal. One group of students used their cultural and linguistic resources to identify a Muslim family breaking their fast in the evening during Ramadan (Figure 2.4), and then the group worked together to complete the inferencing form (Figure 2.5). Similar occurrences were observed throughout the lesson; Madison purposefully connected the content to students' backgrounds.

FIGURE 2.4 *Multilingual and multicultural inferencing.*

FRAMING TEACHERS AS EXPERTS

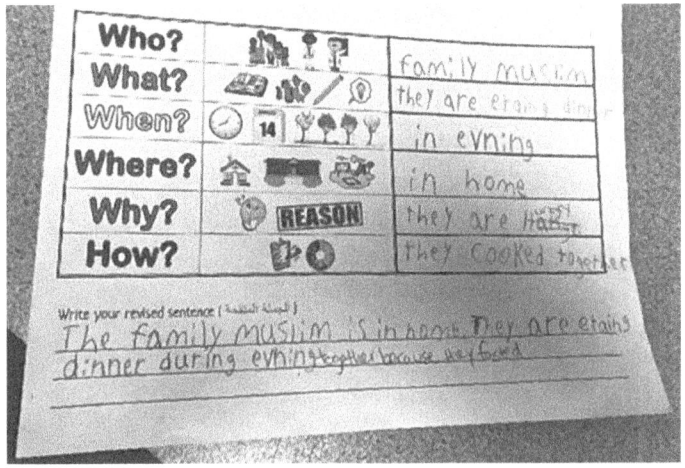

FIGURE 2.5 *Multilingual and multicultural inferencing.*

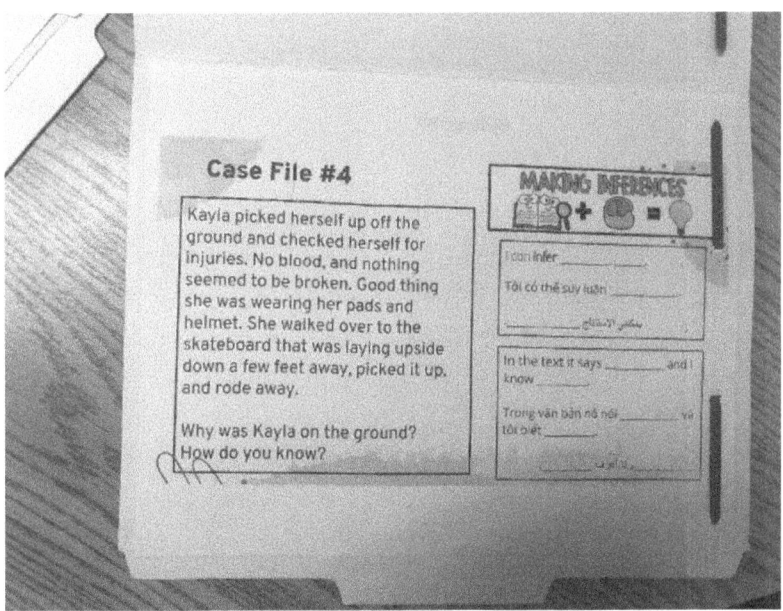

FIGURE 2.6 *Inferencing detective case file.*

The final activity required students to become inference detectives. Working through case files (Figure 2.6), Madison's students had to infer what happened with text evidence. Her prework included purposeful grouping. MLs were placed in groups with students who shared a home language or with groups that did not share a home language, depending on the specific needs of each ML. Akilah, an ML working on a case file, emerged as the group leader. The scenario her group was assigned described skateboarding. Akilah was unfamiliar with this topic and found herself in a group where she was the only ML. She asked questions about helmets, pads, and potential injuries. Through her questions, her peers engaged in and created inferences supported by text evidence. Akilah's peers were initially not on task and were busy distracting each other until she began to ask questions and refocus their work; Akilah was the glue that bound this group together.

Madison created a translanguaging space through several purposeful, yet simple steps. First, students found themselves in the classroom through the decorations and posters that acknowledged who they were and who they wished to become. Her MLs and mainstream students alike were excited that we would look at their work and they wanted to share more about themselves with us. We later learned that Binti, one of the MLs, was so excited to be in their space that she brought a Swahili dictionary (Figure 2.7) into the class her cousin had helped create; she wanted to share her language with her classmates. Second, Madison allowed students to choose the language they

FIGURE 2.7 *Swahili dictionary.*

used in classroom activities and then respected their choices; no student was required to use/teach their home language with peers. Finally, Madison utilized her resources to create multilingual materials and meaningful groups where students could complete their work. Madison was concerned that her ability to support translanguaging would be limited based on her linguistic skills; however, with careful planning and knowledge of her MLs cultural and linguistic backgrounds, she was able to design activities where students worked together to meet the educational objectives of the day.

Andrea

The last classroom we visited belonged to Andrea. Andrea was a secondary social studies teacher of US history who taught in the same urban school as Michelle. During this visit, we heard students using English, Spanish, and Somali. (There were two Somali speakers, and one had only been in the United States for less than a month.) The room was large, and in the back, Andrea had a copy of the translated question words that Michelle had created, as well as a word wall that contained a map labeled with key vocabulary (Figure 2.8). To the right of the map was a prominent flag with an image depicting Frida Kahlo. Her classroom was in the middle of a unit on colonization prior to the formation of the United States.

During the passing time between classes, Andrea was in the hallway conversing with students in Spanish, similar to Michelle. However, unlike Michelle, Andrea did not take up the identity of being multilingual even though she used English and Spanish as resources for instruction. For example, when the class started, the warm-up activity asked MLs to look at different images and describe how the people in the pictures felt before, during, and after the event depicted in the image. Their content focus was the causes of colonization; therefore, the images depicted colonizers from different eras. She showed a picture of a colonizer carrying a flag to a presumably "undiscovered" land. She asked students to identify objects in the picture and to consider how the colonizers felt. At first, there was no response, so after a short silence, Andrea modeled how students could respond. She said they looked proud and started to sound out the word proud, "*orgulloso*," in Spanish. It took her a moment to recall the word; she stumbled a few times trying to recall and pronounce it, but as soon as she did, her Spanish-speaking students repeated the word and told her she had gotten it correct. The students then continued to help her with the word *orgulloso* and further taught her more terms for the objects they identified in the image. With each image, Andrea returned to the question about feelings, and added another question, how do you know they

FIGURE 2.8 *Word wall map.*

feel that way? Positioning herself as a language learner created a space where the students were excited to teach her new terms while they focused on the deeper questions of feelings associated with colonization.

Andrea's culminating assignment required students to create posters describing three causes of colonization (Figure 2.9). One requirement of the poster was that students include home languages. This was explicitly added to the activity because Andrea wanted to create an opportunity for everyone to be active participants in creating the final product. While students worked on this project, Andrea walked from group to group providing support. She reached a group composed of Spanish speakers, one of whom primarily communicated their ideas in Spanish—Miguel. In this group, the students worked together to construct their posters, with one student serving as a language broker between Andrea and Miguel. However, Andrea wanted to connect more directly with Miguel, and she shifted to primarily using Spanish, with some English for vocabulary terms. After the conversation, Andrea was overheard saying, "Somos el equipo de Spanglish here." [*We're the Spanglish team here*]. Even though Andrea did not self-identify as multilingual, she utilized the linguistic skills available in her classroom to make meaning and to position herself in the group with her MLs.

FRAMING TEACHERS AS EXPERTS 53

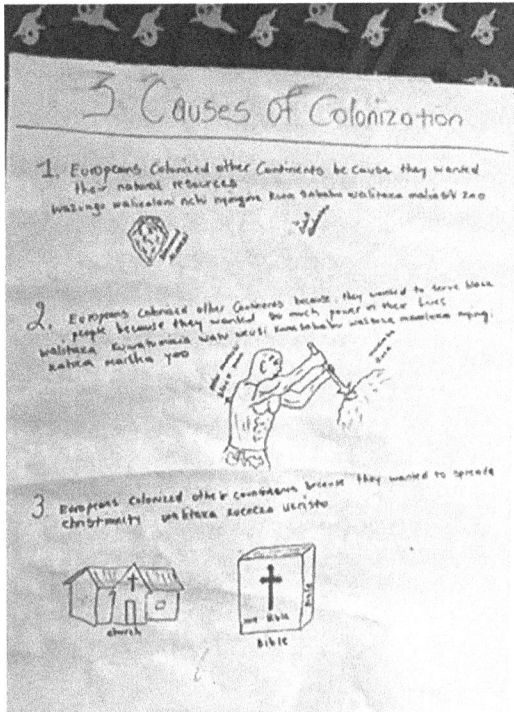

FIGURE 2.9 *Multilingual colonization poster.*

Another critical feature of this activity was Andrea's purposeful grouping of MLs. Andrea crafted student groups to complete the colonization posters mentioned above. However, she had an instance where an ML pushed against the grouping structure. Most groups shared a home language, however, there was one group that did not. To ensure everyone could participate in this group, Andrea included students who could serve as language brokers, instructing them to use Google Translate when needed. Esteban, a group member in the mixed language group, realized he was with a peer who did not speak English, he looked directly at the teacher and asked, "Are you serious?" He continued to question what his peer could contribute to their work if they could not communicate. Andrea responded that she was, in fact, serious and reminded Esteban to respect everyone's language. She encouraged him to focus on what everyone could add, not what they couldn't. At the end of the conversation, Esteban offered suggestions for ways his group could work together.

While the actions Andrea took were similar to Michelle and Madison's, there are a few things we would like to highlight as key to creating translanguaging spaces. First, Andrea demonstrated a willingness to engage with a language in which she lacked both comfort and confidence in her proficiency. However, her willingness to try modeled for her students that it is okay to make mistakes, as everyone in the classroom was both a language learner and a language teacher. A willingness to place herself in the same position MLs are placed in every day at school created a space where her MLs were willing to share and engage in activities. Second, including a language component in her assignment created opportunities, and even a necessity, for all students to contribute to the final project regardless of their English proficiency. Finally, grouping structures and explicit conversations about working across languages served as a vital catalyst in resolving the pushback expressed by Esteban. Once they were able to voice concerns and solutions for those concerns, Andrea's MLs found ways to creatively work with each other and recognize the assets everyone brings to the table.

Conclusion

In this chapter, we shared three examples of translanguaging and translanguaging spaces in action in very different classrooms. In visiting each classroom, we saw how teachers operationalized and created translanguaging spaces in their unique classrooms and communities. We observed each teacher's creativity and use of their resources to craft spaces where multilingual learners not only felt seen and heard but were simultaneously provided with a rigorous and equitable education. Translanguaging spaces were established by inviting student participation, supporting home languages, and fostering collaboration. These deliberate actions created opportunities for MLs to experience success in the classroom and express their desired identities. In conclusion, we would like to provide a list of suggestions that can help teachers, teacher educators, and students develop and, more importantly, implement their translanguaging stance:

- Seek to learn about the languages, cultures, and personal histories of the MLs.
- Create instructional activities that model translanguaging and provide opportunities for teachers and students to implement and reflect upon what they are learning.
- Provide opportunities for teachers to observe and learn from one another on their planning, teaching, and reflection practices.

- Create opportunities for collaborative learning.
- Be purposeful in designing activities that incorporate MLs' home languages.
- Don't be afraid to try, we frequently ask MLs to try with content and language practices that are new to them; we, as teachers, must be willing to do the same.

References

Abraham, S., Kedley, K., Fall, M., Krishnamurthy, S., & Tulino, D. (2021). Creating a translanguaging space in a bilingual community-based writing program. *International Multilingual Research Journal, 15*(3), 211–234. https://doi.org/10.1080/19313152.2021.1883791

Baker-Bell, A. (2020). *Linguistic justice: Black language, literacy, identity, and pedagogy.* Routledge.

Blommaert, J., Collins, J., & Slembrouck, S. (2005). Spaces of multilingualism. *Language & Communication, 25*(3), 197–216. https://doi.org/10.1016/j.langcom.2005.05.002

Boser, U. (2014). *Teacher diversity revisited: A new state-by-state analysis.* Center for American Progress.

Flores, N. (2020). From academic language to language architecture: Challenging raciolinguistic ideologies in research and practice. *Theory Into Practice, 59*(1), 22–31. https://doi.org/10.1080/00405841.2019.1665411

Flores, N., & Rosa, J. (2015). Undoing appropriateness: Raciolinguistic ideologies and language diversity in education. *Harvard Educational Review, 85*(2), 149–171. https://doi.org/10.17763/0017-8055.85.2.149

Freire, P. (2000). *Pedagogy of the oppressed* (30th anniversary edition). Continuum.

García, O. (2023). Re-seeing translanguaging in teacher education and research. In Z. Tian & N. King (Eds.), *Developing translanguaging repertoires in critical teacher education* (pp. IX–XIII). de Gruyter Mouton.

García, O., Flores, N., Seltzer, K., Wei, L., Otheguy, R., & Rosa, J. (2021). Rejecting abyssal thinking in the language and education of racialized bilinguals: A manifesto. *Critical Inquiry in Language Studies, 18*(3), 203–228. https://doi.org/10.1080/15427587.2021.1935957

García, O., Johnson, S. I., & Seltzer, K. (2017). *The translanguaging classroom: Leveraging student bilingualism for learning.* Caslon.

García, O., & Kleyn, T. (2016). Translanguaging theory in education. In Ofelia García, Tatyana Kleyn (Eds.), *Translanguaging with multilingual students: Learning from classroom moments.* (pp. 9–33). Routledge.

García, O., & Li, W. (2014). *Translanguaging: Language, bilingualism and education.* Palgrave Macmillan.

Li, W. (2011). Moment analysis and translanguaging space: Discursive construction of identities by multilingual Chinese youth in Britain. *Journal of Pragmatics, 43*(5), 1222–1235. https://doi.org/10.1016/j.pragma.2010.07.035

Li, W. (2018). Translanguaging as a practical theory of language. *Applied Linguistics, 39*(1), 9–30. https://doi.org/10.1093/applin/amx039

Li, W., & García, O. (2022). Not a first language but one repertoire: Translanguaging as a decolonizing project. *RELC Journal, 53*(2), 313–324. https://doi.org/10.1177/00336882221092841

Menken, K., & García, O. (Eds.). (2010). *Negotiating language policies in schools: Educators as policymakers*. Routledge.

National Center for Education Statistics. (2023). *English learners in public schools*. Condition of education. U.S. Department of Education, Institute of Education Sciences. Retrieved January 26, from https://nces.ed.gov/programs/coe/indicator/cgf

Nieto, S. (2017). Becoming sociocultural mediators: What all educators can learn from bilingual and ESL teachers. *Issues in Teacher Education, 26*(2), 129–141.

Sanger, C. S. (2020). Inclusive pedagogy and universal design approaches for diverse learning environments. In C. S. Sanger & N. W. Gleason (Eds.), *Diversity and inclusion in global higher education* (pp. 31–71). Springer Singapore. https://doi.org/10.1007/978-981-15-1628-3_2

Sayer, P. (2013). Translanguaging, TexMex, and bilingual pedagogy: Emergent bilinguals learning through the vernacular. *TESOL Quarterly, 47*(1), 63–88. https://doi.org/10.1002/tesq.53

Seltzer, K. (2022). Enacting a critical translingual approach in teacher preparation: Disrupting oppressive language ideologies and fostering the personal, political, and pedagogical stances of preservice teachers of English. *TESOL Journal, 13*(2), e649. https://doi.org/10.1002/tesj.649

Sembiante, S., & Tian, Z. (2020). The need for translanguaging in TESOL. In Z. Tian, L. Aghai, P. Sayer, & J. Schissel (Eds.), *Envisioning TESOL through a translanguaging lens: Global perspectives* (pp. 43–66). Springer.

Song, K., & King, N. (2023). Collaborative multilingual families' story making that transcends school policies and practices of inequity at community translanguaging spaces. In V. Lee & L. Grant (Eds.), *Advancing culturally responsive and socially just approaches to multilingual family-school partnerships* (pp. 3–27). Rowman & Littlefield.

Song, K., Kim, S., & Preston, L. R. (2021). "No difference between African American, immigrant, or white children! They are all the same": Working toward developing teachers' raciolinguistic attitudes towards ELs. *International Journal of Multicultural Education, 23*(1), 47–66. https://doi.org/10.18251/ijme.v23i1.1995

Tian, Z., & King, N. (Eds.). (2023). *Developing translanguaging repertoires in critical teacher education* (Vol. 1). de Gruyter Mouton.

Williams, D. G. (2023). Trust and translanguaging in English-medium instruction. *ELT Journal, 77*(1), 23–32. https://doi.org/10.1093/elt/ccac016

Yip, S. Y., & Xu, Y. (2024). Increasing the diversity of teaching workforce: A review of minority teacher candidates' recruitment, retention, and experiences in initial teacher education. *Pedagogy, Culture & Society*, 1–18. https://doi.org/10.1080/14681366.2024.2384492

Zhang, H. (2021). Translanguaging space and classroom climate created by teacher's emotional scaffolding and students' emotional curve about EFL learning. *International Journal of Multilingualism*, *21*(1), 298–324. https://doi.org/10.1080/14790718.2021.2011893

PART II

Translanguaging Practices in Elementary Classrooms

3

Promoting Translanguaging Pedagogical Practice Through Co-Teaching and Co-Learning

Insights from "Incipient" Bilingual Teachers

Haiyan Li, Woongsik Choi, Wayne E. Wright, and Trish Morita-Mullaney

Introduction

Translanguaging as a teaching project requires a robust understanding of its purpose before it can be transformed into a meaningful practice that recognizes the collective assets of a multilingual classroom. Yet, within translanguaging's conceptualization and application, the language proficiencies of teachers may mediate their willingness to explore and implement translanguaging pedagogies. While English monolingual teachers may be reluctant to investigate the merits of translanguaging, it is possible to draw them into its praxis (Flores & Schissel, 2014; Shi & Rolstad, 2023; Wong & Tai, 2023). Scholars in language ideologies argue that moving teachers from monoglossic to heteroglossic thinking is not exclusively an exercise in gaining additional named languages. Flores and Schissel (2014) argue that a monoglossic orientation toward teaching and learning dismisses the linguistic and cultural bodies of knowledge that children bring to the classroom. With a monolingual stance, multilingual students are marginalized, not empowered to draw from their varied resources. Alternatively, a heteroglossic stance considers all the rich resources children bring to the classroom, including their named and expressed languages and varieties of those languages. Teachers with this stance see students' rich linguistic resources as part of students' self-determination. They can express themselves more fully without concern or risk of poor treatment in whatever setting (Morita-Mullaney, 2024).

The myth that bilingual teachers automatically draw from a heteroglossic stance and monolingual English teachers draw from a monoglossic stance suggests an overly simple binary view (García et al., 2018; Kloss, 1998). Teachers have the possibility to think heteroglossically, regardless of their claimed proficiencies in such languages. Yet an enduring conceptualization within bilingual education is that full proficiency in English and the partner language is the only definition of bilingualism (Howard et al., 2018; Morita-Mullaney et al., 2022). Proficiency in the standard variety of both named languages has become more of an emphasis in dual-language bilingual education (DLBE) programs, thus dismissing the more emancipatory efforts of bilingual education surrounding developing students' linguistic tolerance and cross-cultural understandings (Morita-Mullaney, 2024; Valdez et al., 2016). This focus on standardized language varieties maps onto how teachers may feel about their own and their students' proficiency in English and the partner language. For example, a Spanish-speaking bilingual teacher from Spain may have concerns about teaching mostly Mexican American students in their classroom, because the students' varieties of Spanish differ and may be viewed by the teacher as "inferior" to Standard Castilian Spanish. The same teacher may also feel concerned that their own English proficiency is notably lower relative to their Spanish proficiency—and different from the Standard American English variety spoken by their monolingual English teacher peers—and thus regard themselves as an incomplete or developing bilingual. For English dominant speakers who have no proficiency in any other language, they may have constructed themselves as incapable of becoming bilingual. For those teachers who identify as full or balanced bilinguals, they may also ascribe to a native speaker perfection ideal and believe that such native-like performances are required by their students (Faltis, 2024). Such ideologies often mediate resistance to adopting a translanguaging pedagogy. Biliteracy in two languages in the context of our study demonstrates that mastery of both languages is seemingly needed to most effectively integrate the logics and practices of translanguaging.

One method of addressing a translanguaging praxis is by way of co-learning and co-teaching. Co-learning suggests teachers can be learners of bilingual students' languages in the classroom and come together with students to discuss their language ideologies within the context of translanguaging classrooms. Co-teaching is when teachers work together to incrementally adopt translanguaging strategies as they transform their beliefs around language teaching and learning. Co-learning and co-teaching can emerge from interaction among professionals and instructional coaching (Renn et al., 2023; Teemant et al., 2014). In this chapter, we investigate how co-learning and co-teaching manifest over an eighteen-month period through an intensive project of graduate studies and instructional coaching with dual-language bilingual education teachers. We first lay out the setting and context of our inquiry and situate it within the literature related to translanguaging, co-teaching, and co-learning. In so doing, we augment how translanguaging as praxis can be the role of all teachers within the DLBE program, even those who are English monolinguals. We conclude with suggestions for teachers to engage in co-teaching and bridging lessons to facilitate effective translanguaging practices.

Setting and Context

This study takes place in the state of Indiana where the phenomenon of DLBE has scaled up substantively since 2015, given the state's adoption and funding of a DLBE pilot program for schools across the state (Chesnut & Morita, 2023; Indiana Dual language Pilot Program, 2015; Morita-Mullaney & Chesnut, 2022). Adopted by a very conservative legislature, its original intent was to create economic opportunities for English dominant speakers (Chesnut & Morita-Mullaney, 2023). DLBE programs differ from other models of bilingual education that focus specifically on addressing the needs of linguistic minority students classified as English Language Learners (ELLs) (e.g., transitional and developmental bilingual education models) (Wright & Choi, 2024). While Indiana's legislation may have envisioned more one-way dual-language programs focused exclusively on dominant English-speaking children, the Indiana Department of Education articulated the benefits of a two-way model serving equal proportions of English-majority speakers and ELL-classified speakers of the partner language in the same classroom. Two-way programs represent a "strong form" of bilingual education, meaning they are designed to develop high levels of bilingualism and biliteracy for both student populations (Wright & Baker, 2025). However, there are nonetheless legitimate concerns about the role DLBE programs may play in the "gentrification" of bilingual education, meaning such programs may be more tailored to the needs and interests of white majority parents and their children (Valdez et al., 2016).

Through a federally funded DLBE professional development grant, we worked with eighteen in-service teachers over five school years. DLBE teachers within the project took five graduate courses in English language development and teaching, plus a course on the foundations of bilingual education and a course on bilingual teaching methodologies. The coursework focused primarily on addressing the strengths and needs of ELL-classified students, thus countering prior practice in the state that centered on English-dominant students in DLBE programs. During this eighteen-month period, teachers were also committed to our classroom observations, which happened three times in a given school year and one time in the fall semester of the following school year. In addition to the coursework, teachers also received instructional coaching from a bilingual coach who worked for our project and not the school district. As such, the coach was able to have bold conversations about their instruction and their transformation toward a translanguaging classroom.

For this chapter, we focus on two "monolingual English" teachers—Connie and Beth—who taught Kindergarten and Grade 1 respectively in a Spanish-English DLBE program at Mapleton Elementary School (pseudonym), serving as the English partner teachers. Mapleton Elementary, located in a Northern Indiana town of 35,000, has seen a demographic shift, with Latinx ELLs now making up 22 percent of its students. The school's DLBE program, established in 2017, uses a state-supported 50/50 model for kindergarten and first-grade students. This involves a paired classroom approach, with one class taught in English and another in Spanish. As monolingual teachers from the English-partner of the DLBE program participated in our project's coursework and coaching, they ultimately came to recognize themselves as "incipient bilinguals," given their efforts to learn and use a little Spanish in their classrooms. According to Wright and Baker (2025), incipient bilinguals have one well-developed language while the other is in the early stages of development. We adopted this term to highlight the evolving nature of the teachers' language proficiency and views of themselves as they engaged in teaching in the DLBE program, as they appropriated a translanguaging stance over time, and as they engaged in co-learning and co-teaching.

Literature Review

Translanguaging allows students to use their entire linguistic repertoire without being restricted by traditional language boundaries (García & Wei, 2014). In a multilingual classroom, the approach helps students make connections across languages, fostering target language skills in listening, speaking, reading, and writing (García & Kleyn, 2016). It values the unique strengths that culturally and linguistically diverse students bring to language learning. However, implementing translanguaging in a classroom can be challenging. Some scholars, such as Hamman (2018), argue that it is essential to protect pedagogical spaces for low-status languages in bilingual programs. Without careful consideration and planning, translanguaging could reduce students' exposure to and opportunities to develop proficiency in these languages.

In response to these challenges, research supports co-teaching and co-learning as effective ways to implement translanguaging. Co-teaching, involving both Spanish-speaking and English-speaking teachers, presents valuable opportunities for translanguaging pedagogy (Lachance & Honigsfeld, 2023). Beeman and Urow (2013) introduced the "Bridge," a co-teaching strategy that merges two languages to help students transfer knowledge. While emerging from a traditional bilingual perspective, certain aspects of this method can be productively reframed through a translanguaging lens. This method encompasses "bridging lessons" where teachers deliberately use two languages to help students develop proficiency, build metalinguistic awareness, and understand academic content. For example, teachers might highlight English-Spanish cognates to show the connection between similar words, reinforcing students' language skills and further developing their vocabulary.

Ríos and Castillón (2018) explore contemporary trends in bilingual literacy development and education, shedding light on the literacy strengths that immigrant children bring to the classroom. Lachance and Honigsfeld (2023) emphasize the importance of co-teaching in enhancing language development, academic achievement, and multilingual identity for bilingual learners. Dove and Honigsfeld (2017) provide practical models and tools for dual-language classrooms, helping teachers align their instruction and integrate translanguaging into everyday practice. Wright et al. (2023) highlighted challenges in implementing co-teaching as a standard practice. Teachers in a 50/50 English-Spanish model faced coordination issues, with some noting inconsistent translanguaging and limitations in Spanish proficiency. Concerns included inadequate bridging, disjointed language transitions, and a curriculum that did not fully support bilingual objectives. These challenges emphasize the need for alignment between teaching practices, professional development, and curriculum design to effectively incorporate translanguaging in DLBE programs.

Collaborative co-learning, where teachers and students learn together, also plays a significant role in translanguaging (García & Wei, 2014). In this approach, teachers act as facilitators rather than instructors, engaging in a shared learning process. Hansen-Thomas et al. (2021) found that when high school teachers used translanguaging as a scaffolding tool for instruction, students were positioned as experts, and both students and teachers benefited from the mutual exchange of knowledge. This method respects students' linguistic diversity and uses their languages as valuable resources for learning. Studies like Tai and Wong (2023) emphasize that co-learning helps create a space where students can use their first language alongside English, improving their understanding and engagement. Teachers take on the role of learners, gaining insight into their students' linguistic backgrounds and integrating these into lessons. This approach supports students' social-emotional well-being and multilingual identities. Monolingual teachers can also become effective co-learners by acknowledging their students' linguistic knowledge (Stewart & Hansen-Thomas, 2020). This approach aligns with the idea of transformative pedagogy, which aims to foster inclusion and social justice through translanguaging (Li Wei, 2024). Co-learning and "transpositioning," where teachers and students switch perspectives to co-construct knowledge, emphasize the need for a holistic approach to both teaching and learning.

Current literature emphasizes the vital role of co-teaching and co-learning in implementing translanguaging pedagogy. This chapter explores practical methodologies, focusing on instructional strategies, collaborative approaches, and assessment techniques tailored to foster language development and content mastery. These methods leverage the benefits of translanguaging to create a more dynamic and effective learning environment, with the goal of enhancing both linguistic and academic outcomes. Through two classroom vignettes, we aim to provide practical insights that help educators seamlessly incorporate translanguaging into their teaching. These real-world examples enrich the bilingual education landscape, fostering an inclusive and productive learning environment for all students.

Translanguaging and Co-teaching

Bridging lessons (Beeman & Urow, 2013) co-taught by Spanish and English teachers are conducive to implementing translanguaging as pedagogical practice and facilitating emergent biliteracy. In co-planned bridging lessons in a 50/50 paired-classroom DLBE model, the partner teachers purposely integrate two languages (e.g., Spanish and English) to facilitate bilingual learners' academic content knowledge, language, and literacy transfer and metalinguistic awareness. Such bridging can be done by comparing languages in bilingual vocabulary charts generated by the teachers or students or reading and producing side-by-side bilingual texts. The teachers can draw students' attention to the similarities and differences in written and spoken languages. Then, the students engage in discussions about the key content concepts through translanguaging.

Vignette #1

To demonstrate how co-teaching can activate and facilitate translanguaging practices for both teachers and students, we present a vignette of a bridging lesson from a first-grade English Language Arts class within the DLBE program (50/50 English-Spanish model) at Mapleton Elementary School. In this bridging lesson, English and Spanish classes were combined for a lesson on animal habitats. The students were taught a song about habitats in both languages. Next, the teachers took turns reading from the picture book *The Magic School Bus Hops Home: A Book About Animal Habitats*, with one reading the English version and the other reading the Spanish version. The students then collaborated in groups to talk about the essentials for an animal habitat. They were encouraged to translanguage during their discussions.

Context and Setting

At the beginning of the dual-language habitat unit, Luz (the Spanish partner teacher) and Beth (the English partner teacher) combined their classes. This collaboration launched a strategic co-teaching approach that embraced translanguaging practices. Beth, the lead teacher for the lesson, encouraged students to communicate in their preferred language—Spanish, English, or a blend of both—fostering a classroom environment where linguistic flexibility supported learning.

Pedagogical Approach

Beth catalyzed the discussion by posing the question, "What is a habitat?" and encouraged pair discussions. The responses from students varied (e.g., one student asked, "Is habitat the same as habit?"), indicating differing levels of comprehension. This led Beth to articulate the session's objectives clearly:

> *Today we're going to do it in English and in Spanish. Both. You might notice some things about the English words and the Spanish words. You might notice how they are alike, how they're different. You might notice that in a book that we read, you might hear some words that are alike and different. But our goal overall is to be able to know what a habitat is and what a habitat has to have.*

The instructional material included bilingual habitat slides (Figure 3.1), enhancing the visual and linguistic association vital for academic language

Home or natural environment of an animal or plant.
Hogar o ambiente natural de un animal o una planta.

FIGURE 3.1 *Bilingual Habitat visual furnished by DLBE teachers.*

development. This approach facilitated a deeper understanding of habitat components—food, water, shelter, and space—with terms introduced in both languages.

A notable feature of this session was the inclusion of a bilingual song about habitats (Figure 3.2). Beth told the students, "So we're going to teach you a song that helps us remember the four things that a habitat has. You might recognize the tune. But we switch the words." The song, performed with accompanying motions, was presented in both English and Spanish, utilizing the melody of the familiar children's song "Head, Shoulders, Knees, and Toes." A visual bilingual slide (Figure 3.3) was used to teach the students the key vocabulary in English and Spanish, and to support their learning and performing of the song. The activity then transitioned to a quicker pace, adding an enjoyable dynamic to the bilingual singing (Figure 3.4). This interactive approach, which lasted about six minutes, exemplified effective scaffolding, combining language learning with the fun of music and movement.

The session transitioned to a bilingual read-aloud of *The Magic School Bus* book (Figure 3.5). Beth asked the students which language to start with, and they chose to begin with English. The teachers took turns modeling expressive reading aloud, holding the books up to display images and using gestures to enhance student engagement and comprehension. As they read, they frequently paused to check for understanding, asking questions like, "Did she have everything she needed in her habitat?," and inviting predictions. The teachers also commented during the reading. For example, Beth pointed to a vocabulary slide on the screen (Figure 3.3) and suggesting, "Maybe we should add *friends, amigos*, to the habitat." Students responded in both

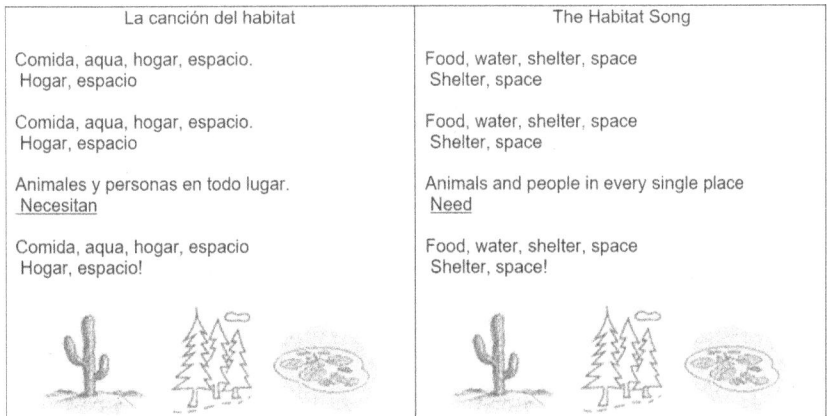

FIGURE 3.2 *The Habitat Song in Spanish and English.*

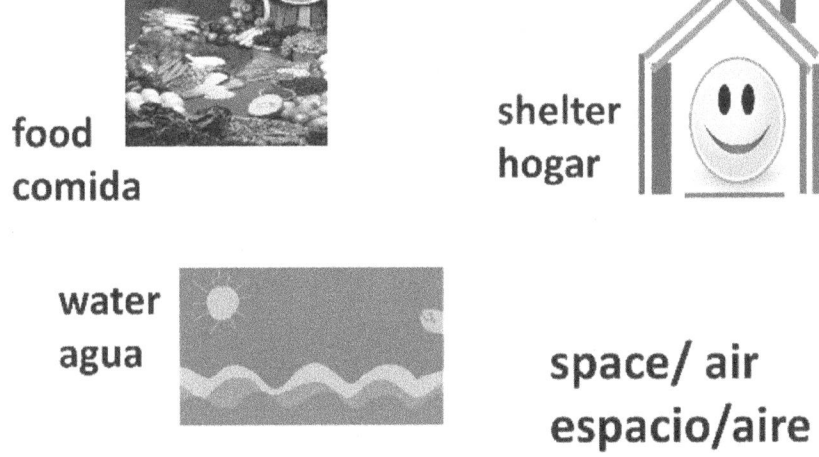

FIGURE 3.3 *Bilingual slide to support singing of The Habitat Song in English and Spanish.*

English and Spanish. One student commented on the image in the book, "*El autobús es una rana. Sí, sus ojos también dan vueltas.*" (The school bus is a frog. Yes, its eyes are also going round and round). Another student asked in Spanish, "*¿Qué dijo lo tuviste al pájaro que ver con esta, la rana?*" (What did it say about what the bird had to do with the frog?). Luz asked, "*¿Qué cosa escucharon?*" (What did you all hear?). A student responded in English, "or somebody said . . . and be like 'ahh'." Though 70 percent of the exchanges happened in English, the teachers' modeling of switching between both

FIGURE 3.4 *Learning and performing The Habitat Song in English and Spanish.*

FIGURE 3.5 *Bilingual read-aloud of The Magic School Bus Hops Home: A Book About Animal Habitats.*

languages helped bridge the students' linguistic resources, making space for them to use their preferred language. This approach fostered an inclusive atmosphere, promoting both linguistic and cultural diversity.

Assessment and Feedback

In the concluding phase of the lesson, Beth instructed the students, "Turn right now to your thinking partner and tell them the four things a habitat has . . . you can choose to say it in English, Spanish, or both." As the students discussed habitat essentials in their language of choice, Beth and Luz walked around the classroom, listening to the students and providing them with feedback in English and Spanish. After the think-pair-share, Beth announced, "We are going to sing our song one more time. This time, you get to choose whether you want to sing in English, Spanish, or both." Some students enthusiastically responded, "Spanish!" Luz then repeated the instruction in Spanish, ensuring all students understood. The repetition of the bilingual song served as a dual tool for reinforcing the concept and exploring language preferences. During review sessions, flexibility in language use was encouraged, promoting translanguaging expressions.

Throughout the lesson, Beth and Luz actively engaged in co-teaching by alternating their instructional roles and blending their language practices. For instance, when Beth posed the initial question in English, Luz followed up by reiterating the question in Spanish, ensuring that all students comprehended the discussion topic. During the pair discussions, they provided support and clarified questions in students' preferred language, fostering a bilingual learning environment. Their co-led bilingual song activity demonstrated seamless interaction and coordination between the teachers, reinforcing the habitat concepts in both languages. In summary, co-teaching served as a bridge that activated and supported translanguaging practices led by both teachers and students. It allowed the teachers to effectively draw on each other's language resources to coordinate instructional targets and practices. It also created the ecology for students to demonstrate their linguistic flexibility and utilize their own language repertoires.

Discussion and Suggestions for Co-teaching

This section provides discussion and suggestions for the observed co-teaching lesson, with strategies for educators adopting similar practices. We highlight effective co-teaching methods with translanguaging, addressing implementation, challenges, and benefits to foster a more inclusive and dynamic learning experience across teaching contexts. We utilize the collaborative instructional cycle of Lachance and Honigsfeld (2023) (Figure 3.6) to discuss how to augment co-teaching lessons, thereby facilitating a more effective integration of languages.

The collaborative instructional cycle is a framework for co-teachers to plan, deliver, assess, and reflect on instruction for English learners in integrated settings, as introduced by Dove and Honigsfeld (2017). They discuss co-teaching between general education teachers and ELL specialists. Lachance and Honigsfeld (2023) extend the cycle (co-planning, co-teaching, co-assessment, and co-reflection) to dual-language programs. This cycle is helpful for bridging lessons co-taught by English and Spanish (or other languages) teachers in DLBE programs. Co-planning involves establishing a shared vision, goals, and expectations for co-teaching, as well as designing differentiated and scaffolded lessons that address both language and content objectives. For the bridging lessons taught by both Spanish and English teachers, teachers need to collaboratively develop language objectives that support the linguistic needs of students while reinforcing key content concepts. This entails identifying essential vocabulary, language structures, and language functions that align with the academic content. Furthermore, teachers should strategically integrate language supports, such as visual aids,

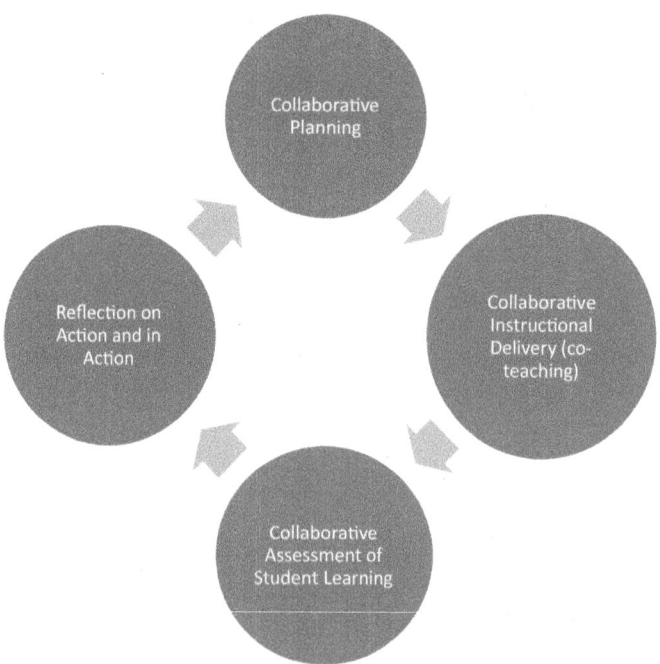

FIGURE 3.6 *The collaborative instructional cycle. (Lachance & Honigsfeld, 2023).*

graphic organizers, and language frames, to facilitate comprehension and language development for all students.

Co-teaching involves selecting and implementing one of the seven co-teaching models (Lachance & Honigsfeld, 2023), based on the needs of the students, the content, and the context (see Table 3.1).

For Spanish and English co-teaching lessons, it is particularly beneficial to choose co-teaching models that capitalize on the linguistic expertise of both teachers. For example, the *one group–one leads, one teaches on purpose* model allows each teacher to lead in their language of expertise, fostering shared learning goals. The *habitat* lesson adopts two models: the *one group-one leads* (when Beth facilitated the whole lesson as a lead teacher), and the *one group-two teach the same content* (when the bilingual read-aloud and bilingual song-learning were led by both teachers). Additionally, the *two groups-one pre-teaches, one teaches alternative information* model can be instrumental in addressing diverse language proficiency levels among English learners, as it enables targeted language support before introducing new content. In addition, the selection of co-teaching models should align with the linguistic and academic goals set during the co-planning phase. Integrating language objectives seamlessly into the chosen co-teaching model ensures

Table 3.1 Co-teaching Models

Model	Description
One Group—One Leads, one Assists	One teacher leads the lesson while the other provides targeted support.
One Group—Two Teach the Same Content	Both teachers jointly deliver the same content to the entire class.
One Group—One Teaches, One Assesses	One teacher instructs while the other assesses student understanding.
Two Groups—Two Teach the Same Content	The class is divided, with each teacher instructing their group on the same material.
Two Groups—One Pre-Teaches, One Teaches Alternative Content	One teacher introduces foundational content, while the other presents different, complementary information.
Two Groups—One Reteaches, One Teaches Alternative Content	One teacher reviews content for students needing reinforcement, while the other teaches new or supplemental content.
Multiple Groups—Two Monitor/Teach	Both teachers circulate among multiple small groups, providing instruction and support as needed.

Source: *Lachance & Honigsfeld, 2023.*

all learners receive comprehensive language support while engaging with content. Moreover, the collaborative nature of co-teaching in both languages not only enriches students' language development, but also fosters a culturally responsive and inclusive learning environment for them to translanguage to cross the traditional strict line between two languages.

In bilingual co-teaching, effective co-assessment involves analyzing students' language skills, strengths, and challenges using both formative and summative assessments. For instance, in the *habitat* lesson, formative assessment was conducted through group discussions and bilingual song repetition, allowing teachers to gauge both content and language learning outcomes. Reflection in bilingual co-teaching includes collaboratively evaluating teaching strategies, identifying strengths and areas for improvement, and setting actionable goals to enhance language integration, support diverse language proficiency levels, and increase student engagement.

Translanguaging and Co-Learning

When incipient bilingual teachers are not co-teaching with their partner proficient bilingual teachers, they can be co-learners with their emergent bilingual students and learn from the students as resources for translanguaging. The first step of co-learning is, whenever possible, to try to learn new words and phrases in students' languages other than English, paying attention to how they are spoken and written. Next, the teachers should go out of their comfort zone and try to write and say out loud the words and phrases in front of the whole class. Then, the teachers can ask their bilingual students for affirmation.

In the following vignette, Connie, an incipient bilingual teacher, positions herself as a co-learner, invites her students' translanguaging, and tries to pronounce a phrase in Spanish.

Vignette #2

Connie is an "English partner" teacher in a DLBE program at Mapleton Elementary School. She taught a kindergarten class in English and her partner teacher taught the same students in Spanish. As a two-way DLBE program, approximately half of her students were Spanish-speaking ELL-classified students, and the other half were English-majority students, all of whom were learning to be proficient bilinguals in Spanish and English.

It was the exciting first day of the Spring semester. Connie got to reunite with her kindergarten students after the Winter break. In the middle of a language arts lesson, Isaiah, a curious English-majority child, asked Connie a question out of the blue. He asked, "What were all those decorations in the cafeteria for?" Connie smiled and responded, "Oh yes, you guys were asking me about that during breakfast." She continued, "Um, that was from the Hispanic celebration. The fifth graders actually made those. Do you remember what it is called in Spanish?" Some students quietly raised their hands. Connie, making a theatrical hand gesture to indicate an imaginary hanging decoration (Figure 3.7), prompted the class again, "I mean they use them for a lot of holidays, but we really started that word with the Day of the Dead. Does anybody remember?" More students raised their eager hands. Connie asked again, "What are those called in the cafeteria, those banners that are hanging?" More students raised their hands. Brandon, an English-majority student sitting right in front of Connie, whispered in Spanish "*Papel picado.*" (Papel picado is a colorful paper art used to decorate Día de Muertos ofrendas/altars.) Connie heard Brandon and encouraged him, "Say a little bit louder so everyone can hear it." Brandon repeated with a louder voice, "*Papel picado!*" Connie attempted to repeat the phrase, "*Papel . . . ,*" but ended up bursting into laughter. Connie chuckled and jokingly said, "When I try to speak Spanish, you guys just laugh at me, so I don't want to say it." The children laughed, too. Undeterred, with a shy smile and blushing, Connie gave it another try. She slowly pronounced the phrase, "*Papel picado.* Did I say it?" "Yes!" shouted the students with big nods.

FIGURE 3.7 *Connie asking a question with a hand gesture.*

Discussion and Suggestions for Co-Learning

In Vignette 2, Connie acknowledged the students' bilingualism and tried to learn from the students. When a student asked a question about the hanging banner, she knew the phrase "papel picado" and tried to elicit the Spanish words from students. She did not end there, and she tried to pronounce the phrase, repeating it after her students. When incipient bilingual teachers come across words or phrases in other languages than English, including even emergent bilingual learners' names, it can be challenging for them to pronounce or remember them. Due to the fear of making mistakes, the teachers may shy away from saying the words out loud. However, in this vignette, instead of avoiding pronouncing the phrase or simply using the English translation like "paper banners," Connie encouraged the students' translanguaging. She then attempted to pronounce the Spanish phrase in the way that her students pronounced it, and asked students if she did it right. This process was not just about learning and pronouncing unfamiliar words; it was about embracing the teacher's vulnerability. Transpositioning the teacher's traditional role as a knowledge holder into being a co-learner entails teachers becoming vulnerable (Brantmeier 2013, as cited in Li Wei, 2024). Connie accepted and demonstrated that she was also a learner of a language in which students were more proficient than her. Such a shared moment of vulnerability may create shared camaraderie between the incipient bilingual teacher and emergent bilingual learners. In other words, this was a moment of connection, or "bridging," between the teacher and her students, who were on the same journey of learning language and culture. By trying to learn and pronounce unknown words and taking the risk of making a mistake, the teacher can convey the message to students that language learning provides opportunities for connection and growth. Most importantly, co-learning is an empowering act. By asking for affirmation from students, as Connie did, the teacher can empower students to take an expert role, which is traditionally assumed by the teacher in the classroom.

Students are the most beneficial resources for enacting a translanguaging classroom, and "incipient bilingual" teachers should position themselves as co-learners to facilitate students to take an active role in co-constructing knowledge leveraging their bilingualism (Hansen-Thomas et al., 2021; Li Wei, 2024). As Connie demonstrated, teachers can learn new words or phrases in students' languages directly from bilingual students. Then, the teachers can try to use the new language and ask students to confirm if they did it right. More importantly, in a similar fashion, we suggest that the teachers should try to learn more in-depth about the students' funds of knowledge (Moll et al., 1992) beyond commonly used words and phrases. In other words, co-learning can and should be more meaningful than just reciting the

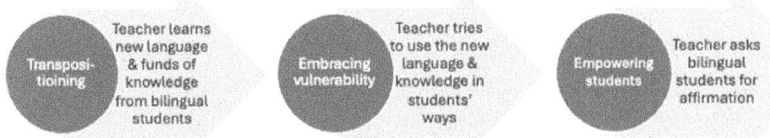

FIGURE 3.8 *The process of co-learning.*

names of cultural objects. Teachers can tap into "historically accumulated and culturally developed bodies of knowledge and skills" that are meaningful to bilingual students and their household (Moll et al., 1992, p. 133). For instance, in the case of Connie's class, the teacher can learn more about how bilingual students might celebrate the Day of the Dead (*Día de Muertos*) in their homes and communities or how they might use *papel picado* in other occasions. Figure 3.8 summarizes the essential points and process of co-learning.

There is one critical thing to consider particularly in two-way dual-language bilingual education programs. Knowing that co-learning is an empowering act, the teacher should make sure to invite the minoritized language learners (Spanish-minoritized students in Connie's case) to teach the teacher through translanguaging, rather than asking for help from the dominant language learners (English-majority students in Connie's case). Research shows that English-majority students tend to be more vocal, and they tend to benefit more from translanguaging in Spanish-English dual-language classrooms than their Spanish-minoritized peers (Hamman, 2018; Wright et al., 2023). To empower marginalized students and their bilingualism, teachers should be more intentional about whom to invite as bilingual experts in the classroom. Teachers should create translanguaging and co-learning opportunities for emergent bilingual students from a linguistically marginalized background to teach about their languages and culture to the class and the teacher, voluntarily assist their emergent bilingual peers in groups, and become a leader of the class.

Concluding Thoughts

This chapter has brought attention to the potential for teachers on the "English partner" of paired-classrooms in a 50/50 DLBE model to engage in translanguaging pedagogical practices. The very nature of the 50/50 model and typical use of "monolingual English" teachers for English instruction reinforces a monoglossic view of bilingualism and the strict unnatural separation of the two languages. However, as Beth and Connie completed the coursework in our project (including courses on foundations of bilingual education and bilingual teaching methods), worked closely with a bilingual coach, and made efforts to start learning Spanish, they came to recognize themselves as "incipient bilinguals" and began to develop a translanguaging stance. The first vignette demonstrates the potential for co-teaching between English and Spanish partner teachers to engage in translanguaging pedagogical practices through bridging lessons. As Beth and Luz co-taught their lesson on habitats, they broke down the monolingual walls that separated their two classrooms and provided their students with a safe space to be emergent bilinguals and draw on their entire linguistic repertoires to actively engage in learning. The second vignette demonstrates ways English partner teachers can be co-learners with their emergent bilingual students through translanguaging to further develop their own Spanish-language development while facilitating student learning through meaningful interaction. As Connie relied on her emergent bilingual students to help her learn and properly pronounce *papel picado* as they discussed the cafeteria decorations, she also demonstrated that she highly valued her students' bilingualism and served as a role model of a language learner who is not afraid to make mistakes. Thus, co-teaching and co-learning hold strong potential for incipient bilingual teachers to develop a translanguaging stance and implement effective translanguaging pedagogical practices, even on the "English partner" of dual-language bilingual education programs.

Some Suggestions for Bridging and Co-Teaching:

- Co-Planning and Bridging Lessons:

1. Schedule regular planning sessions where both English partner and Spanish partner teachers collaborate to design lessons that incorporate both languages.
2. Identify key concepts that can be taught in both languages and create activities that allow students to use their entire linguistic repertoire.
3. Co-teach lessons where both teachers are actively involved, alternating between languages to reinforce concepts and vocabulary.

- *Fostering a Supportive Bilingual Environment*

1. Create a classroom environment that celebrates bilingualism by displaying multilingual signs, labels, and student work.
2. Encourage students to assist each other and teachers in language learning journeys, fostering a sense of community and mutual support.

By considering these strategies, incipient bilingual teachers may develop a translanguaging stance and begin to integrate translanguaging pedagogical practices, even within the "English partner" of dual-language bilingual education programs.

References

Beeman, K., & Urow, C. (2013). *Teaching for biliteracy: Strengthening bridges between languages*. Caslon Publishing.

Brantmeier, E. J. (2013). Pedagogy of vulnerability: Definitions, assumptions, and applications. In J. Lin, R. L. Oxford, & E. J. Brantmeier (Eds.), *Re-envisioning higher education: Embodied pathways to wisdom and social transformation* (pp. 95–106). Information Age Publishing.

Chesnut, C., & Morita-Mullaney, T. (2023). Dueling roles in dual language education: Exploring leader identity development in dual language strands. *Educational Administration Quarterly*. https://doi.org/10.1177/0013161X2312118

Dove, M. G., & Honigsfeld, A. (2017). *Co-teaching for English learners: A guide to collaborative planning, instruction, assessment, and reflection*. Corwin Press.

Faltis, C. (2024). The hegemonic power of English (and Spanish of elsewhere) and its impact in dual language education. In J. A. Freire, C. Alfaro, & E. de Jong (Eds.), *The handbook of dual language bilingual education* (pp. 495–513). Routledge.

Flores, N., & Schissel, J. L. (2014). Dynamic bilingualism as the norm: Envisioning a heteroglossic approach to standards-based reform. *TESOL Quarterly*, *48*(3), 454–479.

García, O., & Kleyn, T. (2016). Translanguaging theory in education. In O. García & T. Kleyn (Eds.), *Translanguaging with Multilingual Students: Learning from Classroom Moments* (pp. 9–33). New York, NY: Routledge.

García, O., Ibarra-Johnson, S., & Seltzer, K. (2018). *The translanguaging classroom: Leveraging student bilingualism for learning*. Caslon.

García, O., & Wei, L. (2014). Language, bilingualism and education. In *Translanguaging: Language, bilingualism and education*. Palgrave Pivot. https://doi.org/10.1057/9781137385765_4

Hamman, L. (2018). Translanguaging and positioning in two-way dual language classrooms: A case for criticality. *Language and Education*, *32*(1), 21–42. https://doi.org/10.1080/09500782.2017.1384006

Hansen-Thomas, H., Stewart, M. A., Flint, P., & Dollar, T. (2021). Co-learning in the high school English class through translanguaging: Emergent bilingual newcomers and monolingual teachers. *Journal of Language, Identity & Education*, *20*(3), 151–166.

Howard, E., Lindholm-Leary, K. Rogers, D. Olague, N., Medina, J., Kennedy, F., Sugarman, J. Christian, D. (2018), *Guiding Principles for Dual Language Education* (3rd ed.). Washington, DC: Center for Applied Linguistics.

Indiana Dual Language Pilot Program, Indiana Code § 20-20-41. (2015). http://iga.in.gov/legislative/2015/bills/senate/267#document-d98be4d3

Kloss, H. (1998). *The American bilingual tradition*. ERIC Clearinghouse on Languages and Linguistics.

Lachance, J., & Honigsfeld, A. (2023). *Collaboration and co-teaching for dual language learners: Transforming programs for multilingualism and equity*. Corwin.

Li, W. (2024). Transformative pedagogy for inclusion and social justice through translanguaging, co-learning, and transpositioning. *Language Teaching, 57*, 203–214. https://doi.org/10.1017/S0261444823000186

Moll, L. C., Amanti, C., Neff, D., & Gonzalez, N. (1992). Funds of knowledge for teaching: Using a qualitative approach to connect homes and classrooms. *Theory Into Practice, 31*(2), 132–141. https://doi.org/10.1080/00405849209543534

Morita-Mullaney, T. (2024). *Lau v. Nichols and Chinese American language rights: The sunrise and sunset of bilingual education*. Multilingual Matters.

Morita-Mullaney, T., & Chesnut, C. (2022). Equity traps in the deselection of English learners in dual language education: A collective case study of school principals. *NABE Journal of Research and Practice*, 1–20. https://doi.org/10.1080/26390043.2022.2079390

Morita-Mullaney, T., Renn, J., & Chiu, M. M. (2022). Spanish language proficiency in dual language and English as a second language models: The impact of model, time, teacher, and student on Spanish language development. *International Journal for Bilingual Education and Bilingualism, 25*, 1–19.

Renn, J., Li, H., Choi, W., Wright, W., & Morita-Mullaney, T. (2023). Making "small waves of change": Dual language and general education teacher transformation through instructional coaching. *TESOL Quarterly, 57*(1), 1–241.

Ríos, C., & Castillón, C. (2018). Bilingual literacy development: Trends and critical issues. *International Research and Review, 7*(2), 85–96. ERIC. https://eric.ed.gov/?id=EJ1188732

Shi, L., & Rolstad, K. (2023). "I don't let what I don't know stop what i can do"— How monolingual English teachers constructed a translanguaging Pre-K Classroom in China. *TESOL Quarterly, 57*(4), 1490–1517.

Stewart, M. A., & Hansen-Thomas, H. (2020). Co-learning, translanguaging and English language acquisition. *Research Outreach*, (116).

Tai, K. W., & Wong, C. Y. (2023). Empowering students through the construction of a translanguaging space in an English as a first language classroom. *Applied Linguistics, 44*(6), 1100–1151.

Teemant, A., Leland, C., & Berghoff, B. (2014). Development and validation of a measure of critical stance for instructional coaching. *Teaching and Teacher Education, 39*, 136–147.

Valdez, V. E., Freire, J. A., & Delavan, M. G. (2016). The gentrification of dual language education. *The Urban Review, 48*(4), 601–627. https://doi.org/10.1007/s11256-016-0370-0

Wong, C.-Y., & Tai, K. W. H. (2023). "I made many discoveries for myself": The development of a teacher candidate's pedagogical knowledge of translanguaging. *System, 116*, Article 10305. https://doi.org/10.1016/j.system.2023.10305

Wright, W. E., & Baker, C. (2025). *Foundations of bilingual education and bilingualism* (8th ed.). Multilingual Matters.

Wright, W. E., & Choi, W. (2024). DLBE program types for different target populations. In J. A. Freire, C. Alfaro, & E. de Jong (Eds.), *The handbook of dual language bilingual education* (pp. 94–114). Routledge. https://doi.org/10.4324/9781003269076-9

Wright, W. E., Morita-Mullaney, T., Choi, W., & Li, H. (2023). Building bilingual teachers' translanguaging repertoires in a new immigrant destination state. In Z. Tian & N. King (Eds.), *Developing translanguaging repertoires in critical teacher education*. De Gruyter Mouton. https://doi.org/10.1515/9783110735604-007

4

Translanguaging for Multilingual Proficiencies

From an English language into a Languages Classroom

Rachel Muchira

Introduction: The Kenyan School and Language

Linguistic fluidity is the norm in Kenya, like in many multi-ethnolingual settings, and especially in urban spaces where communities from diverse linguistic backgrounds congregate. Using translanguaging practices to integrate the learners' linguistic fluidity in the classroom has been shown to be of immense benefit to the learning process for the learners on the African continent, especially where the mastery of the other languages in the learners' repertoires is more advanced than the medium of instruction, since these are taught and used as the languages of instruction in the first years of school and are embraced and encouraged in home and/or community languaging practices (Carstens, 2016; Kiramba & Harris, 2019; Krause, 2022; Norro, 2022; Omidire & Ayob, 2022; Setyaningrum et al., 2022).

The Kenyan educational situation varies in that despite policy stipulation for teaching and use of the repertoires of the catchment area[1] as the medium

---

[1] Referring to the geographical area surrounding a school from which its learners are drawn, the optimal walking distance being 2 KM from the learners' homes (GoK, MoE, 2018; Macharia et al., 2023).

of instruction in the first three years of schooling, only Kiswahili is taught, while an English-only medium is enforced from the onset—even in the pre-primary levels—in a bid to promote its fluency. The other languages are largely prohibited in the schools, with their use often punishable, as they are seen as an obstruction to English fluency (Oduor, 2010, 2015).

The schools' enforcement of a purist-separatist approach to language is a reflection of the society's hierarchical view of language, which pedestalizes (standard) English as the epitome of social-economic actualization.[2] This view persists in spite of (or perhaps because of) the linguistic fluidity that characterizes everyday expression and interactions of and by Kenyans. From this stance, the ability to sort through the fluidity of everyday linguistic practices and perform "fluently" in a standard code (in this case English) sets one apart as belonging to the educated, upwardly mobile elite (Kioko & Muthwii, 2003).

The reality, however, is that the English-only medium of instruction in primary schools is counterproductive because the imposition of monolingual practice(s) does in fact hamper proficiency (Cummins, 2019). It is therefore not surprising that the Kenyan approach ends up adversely affecting the learners' proficiency in the English language—and medium, and consequently their ability to engage fully in classroom discourses (Athiemoolam & Kibui, 2013; Kembo-Sure & Ogechi, 2016). The lessons, therefore, are reduced to repetition, memorization, and imitation of the teachers' input by the learners. To mitigate this, there have been calls to implement a mother tongue medium in primary school (Kembo-Sure & Ogechi, 2016).

It is unclear how the mother tongue medium would be defined and implemented in settings where children's linguistic practices are characterized by super- and hyper-diversity from the very onset. Additionally, even in regions that have traditionally been said to be linguistically homogeneous—hence could be assigned a "language of the catchment area" as the medium of instruction in the lower grades—family language policies are increasingly enforcing what they regard as more prestigious English (and in some cases Kiswahili) varieties as the family language. As a result, fewer children are acquiring Indigenous codes as L1, which poses a challenge to the application of the "mother tongue medium." There is need, therefore, to consider techniques that consider the fluid nature of learners' linguistic repertoires and leverage them to improve fluency in the multiple codes enmeshed therein, hence the suggestion to take an (Ubuntu) translanguaging approach and use

---

[2]Muchira (2020, p. 26) highlighted the role of the Kenyan media and film industry in the entrenchment of English linguistic hegemony in their portrayal of the linguistic practices of the various socioeconomic classes.

the English language classroom to explore and enhance the other linguistic resources of the pupils.

Bridging the Gap: Ubuntu Translanguaging

Despite the schools' and (some) parents' impositions, the Kenyan everyday linguistic practices defy the puritanical-separatist expectations and are characterized by the pliability with which the various linguistic strands are woven into versatile and functional languaging, akin to what is also being referred to as Kenyanese (Githiora, 2018). The complex diversity of the Kenyan linguistic practices calls for a theoretical outlook that takes into account their continually adaptive and accommodative nature, hence the Ubuntu Translanguaging framework (Makalela, 2016). As a starting point, the framework explains Kenyans' simultaneous acquisition of multiple linguistic codes resulting in complex repertoires, contrary to the sequential development of L1/Mother tongue → L2 → L3. As a result, in the Kenyan setting—unlike the South African one, terminology has shifted from "mother tongue" to "indigenous languages" associated with the different ethnolinguistic communities, (Kenya Institute of Curriculum Development, 2017) and these markers are not necessarily tied to linguistic proficiency, as illustrated by the children we worked with.

While some aspects of varieties of Kenyan English have previously been regarded as deviating and ungrammatical (Buregeya, 2006, 2013; Kanyoro, 1991; Okombo, 2015), the Ubuntu Translanguaging framework recognizes these "peculiarities" as the result of the interconnectedness of not only the speakers' various linguistic codes, but also all their knowledge in the sense-making process.

The permeation of non-Englishes[3] in the English-only spaces (e.g., schools), despite the rules and restrictions forbidding it, is a natural consequence of the incompletion of the learners' linguistic repertoire, which necessitates that the different linguistic codes interwoven in the learners' repertoires complement and complete each other. It is therefore inconceivable that these codes exist in a "pure" form; if anything, there cannot be one without the others (Makalela, 2016, p. 192).

A holistic development of a speaker's repertoire is a culmination of all the components it comprises. Locking out the other linguistic codes making up

---

[3] I am using this here to refer to all the other linguistic codes apart from what is regarded as "standard English," including Kenyan varieties that exhibit deviations—phonetic-phonologically, morpho-syntactically, and even semantically—from the said standard.

the learners' repertoires out of the school system is therefore self-inhibiting. We should instead be exploring techniques that allow and encourage the learners to explore, embrace, and capitalize on the rich diversity of their repertoire to enhance overall proficiency, which is what our experiment based on the Ubuntu Translanguaging pedagogy aims for.

Our Experiment: Why the Cart before the Horse?

Some Kenyan teachers, in a bid to improve the situation, challenge the monolingual school policy and find ways to integrate the learners' repertoires into their lessons so as to engage learners more and include them in the co-construction of knowledge, although the practice is largely considered illegitimate, as in the case presented by Kiramba and Harris (2019). In their study, Kiramba and Harris observe the integration of varieties of Kiswahili and Kimeru in Science and Hygiene lessons to optimize interaction and ensure comprehension. In the English lesson, however, the teacher switches to Kiswahili—only to scold the pupils when he gets frustrated with their failure to grasp the concepts in the English language, and not to support learning (2019, p. 23).

Why is he not using the same facilitative translanguaging techniques that seem to work in other subjects? How do the fluid linguistic backgrounds of learners, characterized by simultaneity, interconnectedness, and incompletion of linguistic codes, relate with the abstract, intangible grammatical concepts? We explore this by adapting the Ubuntu Translanguaging pedagogical propositions of word/sentence walls in different languages and multilingual literacy corners fronted by Makalela (2016, p. 193).

We worked through the English explanations and exercises of foods and adjectives in class, while encouraging pupils to apply whatever linguistic variation that enables their most unencumbered expression. As homework, we asked the pupils to work with their guardians, friends, relatives, and so on, to fill in a worksheet (Table 4.1) with the equivalences of comparatives and superlatives in what they identify as their Indigenous Languages. Pupils who share an ethnolinguistic background then worked in groups to compare and discuss findings in the next session. In doing this, we integrated and leveraged the Ubuntu philosophy of community and collective knowledge—within and beyond the school setting—and foster the learners' awareness of, and the role of their various communities in language(s) learning (Back, 2020; Kim et al., 2021).

We worked with pupils of Grade five in a community school based in the Kawangware area of Nairobi, an area of superdiverse (ethno)linguistic

Table 4.1 Worksheet

Name:	Age:
1. Languages you speak "Mother tongue" With parents With siblings With cousins With aunties and uncles With grandparents With home friends With school friends In class	
2. How would you say this in your "mother tongue"? a. An unripe mango is sour b. Peppers are hot c. Goat meat is delicious d. Ripe bananas are sweet e. Black tea is bitter	
3. How would you say this in your "mother tongue"? a. Mangoes are sweeter than bananas b. Honey is the sweetest c. Goat meat is more delicious than beef d. Chicken is the most delicious e. Black/African nightshade is more bitter than tea	

heterogeneity, where one hears varieties of codes, depending on the interlocutors. For this reason, it is difficult (if not impossible) to assign the children brought up in the area a fixed L1, as linguistic fluidity is the norm from the onset, similar to other (urban) settings with linguistic superdiversity (Banda, 2018; Krause, 2022; Makalela, 2016).

This notwithstanding, identities tied to the ethnolinguistic backgrounds are very much alive, and as observed, children are aware of their being Luhya, Kukuyu, Luo, and so on, and even (jokingly) refer to each other using the tags *Mluhya, Mkamba, Mkikuyu, and so on.* The children, however, while eagerly proclaiming their ethnolinguistic identities, quickly gave the caveat that they were not really versed in the codes associated with these classifications, stating "I speak a little" and *nasikia, lakini sijui kuongea* (I hear but I do not know how to speak)[4] and similar phrases.

The phrase *nasikia, lakini sijui kuongea* gave insight into the nature of proficiencies evident among the pupils. In this case, the phrase is in nonstandard Kiswahili; *nasikia* is derived from the verb *kusikia*, which translates to "to hear," but is used to refer to "comprehend" (whose standard form is *kuelewa*). *Sijui* (from *kujua*) is equivalent to "to know," but is used here instead of *kuweza*, which would be the standard expression for the (lack of) ability the learners are referring to. The Ubuntu Translanguaging tenets of incompletion and interconnectedness explain the pupils' self-assessment of their proficiency in linguistic codes making up their repertoire, and their ability to appropriate their language skills in the different codes to ensure communication. Our lesson aims at enhancing proficiency in their Indigenous codes, which are excluded from formal education, with the reasoning that it will boost their overall multilingual proficiency, as there will be a richer pool of resources to draw from.

Our (Session) Plan

The topic of comparative and superlative adjectives is embedded in the context of healthier "traditional foods" juxtaposed against the non-healthy "junk food." Our choice for this topic was informed by the use of "traditional foods" as heritage artifacts for ethnolinguistic communities making up the Kenyan state on one hand—such that *githeri*[5] is a Kikuyu delicacy, while *muthokoi*[6] is a Kamba one—and the tendency to blur these demarcations when talking of Kenyan delicacies, on the other hand. We were curious about the pupils' perceptions of these dynamics, as well as their views on the healthy—non-healthy juxtapositions, and we considered these adequate impulses for the pupils' engagement on the topic of food and the adjectives used to describe them. We chose adjectives that are comparable in English; sweet and delicious on one hand and sour, bitter, and hot on the other hand, with the objective of checking whether this differentiation also occurred in the pupils' repertoires.

Our sessions took place at 3:30 in the afternoon, to avoid the interruption of normal school operations.[7] I collaborated with the teacher of English,

---

[4]Literal translation from Kiswahili
[5]A boiled mix of white corn and beans
[6]A boiled mix of dehusked white corn and beans
[7]Many schools are hesitant to allow interruptions of the school program and would deny data collection that cannot run outside the regular hours.

Ms. Jane,[8] to develop and implement the session plan. In our discussions, we negotiated the balance of a conventional Kenyan classroom situation (which would, e.g., call for a strict English medium as well as 45-minute blocks) and the transition into our translanguaging experiment and developed the guide (Table 4.2) for our two sessions.

Execution: In the Classroom

Our sessions took place on Friday afternoons after regular classes. I worked with a group of twenty-one pupils of ages 10, 11, and 12. We met in their regular classroom with Ms. Jane present. She introduced me and explained the reason for my visit. The role of the teacher as the authority in the classroom lends the activity some legitimacy, in that the pupils are more inclined to cooperate and take the exercise seriously (Warren, 2021). Her presence, however, caused the pupils to remain fully in the "classroom mode"—and were, for example, hesitant to express themselves in non-Englishes, despite assurances that they were allowed and expected to. This however changed as soon as she left, and more pupils spoke up, striving primarily to retain an English matrix while embedding Kiswahili words as we discussed the worksheet (Table 4.1).[9]

We started off by discussing the notion of "mother tongue." The pupils told me that they learned about Indigenous languages (IL) in Social Studies.[10] They defined the ILs as "*language ya tribe yenu*" (the language of your tribe), and "*language ya ushago kwenu*"[11] (the language spoken in the village you come from) and the pupils identified themselves as belonging to the Luhya, Kikuyu, Kamba, Kisii, Giriama, Luo, and Somali communities and sat in their respective groups (Luhya-6, Kamba-3, Kisii-3, Kikuyu-3, Giriama-2, Luo-1, Somali-1). We then worked together to explore the various codes making up their linguistic repertoires by populating the table under task 1 (Languages you speak). The pupils quickly asked, "What if we mix [languages]?", to which I explained that they should write that down, indicating which languages they mixed and when they did so. Various responses to the question of the importance of the

---

[8]Pseudonym
[9]Approximate translations of the learners' expressions
[10]One of the eleven subjects taught in Kenyan schools at the primary level—All with an English medium, apart from Kiswahili
[11]There still exists the notion that Nairobi is a place we come to, that you have to have an *ushago* (Sheng for upcountry) where you come from. It is where people's roots are supposed to be. This is why people are taken "home" for burial after their demise, regardless of where they lived.

Table 4.2 Sessions Guide

Session 1	
Time	Activity
10 Min. (Plenary)	Introduction of the researcher, explanation of the session's activities and language use
5 Min. (Plenary)	Traditional v. junk foods • Pupils name the various traditional foods they know and the communities they are affiliated with • Pupils name the junk foods they know and compare them with traditional foods
15 Min. (Plenary)	Adjectives used to describe foods • Researcher introduces the worksheet (Table 4.1) and explains the activity • Researcher guides pupils through task 1 (Languages you speak) • Pupils check that they know the foods referred to in the worksheets • Pupils say what the adjectives used in the worksheets are known as in Kiswahili and their other languages
20 Min. (Group work)	Food adjectives in our languages • Pupils sit in their ethnolinguistically defined groups (which they identify with/as), discuss how they would say the listed phrases in their languages and write it down in the spaces provided.
10 Min. (Plenary)	Discussion • Pupils give feedback on the exercise • Researcher explains the homework (Worksheet, tasks 2 and 3)
Session 2	
5 Min. (Plenary)	Recap of the previous session
20 Min. (Group work)	Comparison • Researcher gives the pupils their worksheets from the previous session. • Pupils sit in their ethnolinguistically defined groups and compare their answers in the first session and the answers with their guardians' input.
20 Min. (Plenary)	Discussion • Pupils speak about their experiences, ask questions

ILs were tied to communication with relatives, especially grandparents, and playing with their cousins when they visited *ushago*.

The pupils' linguistic repertoire is summarized in Figure 4.1.

In sifting through their repertoires to identify the codes making them up, it was evident that the pupils' fluidity is inversely proportional to authority,

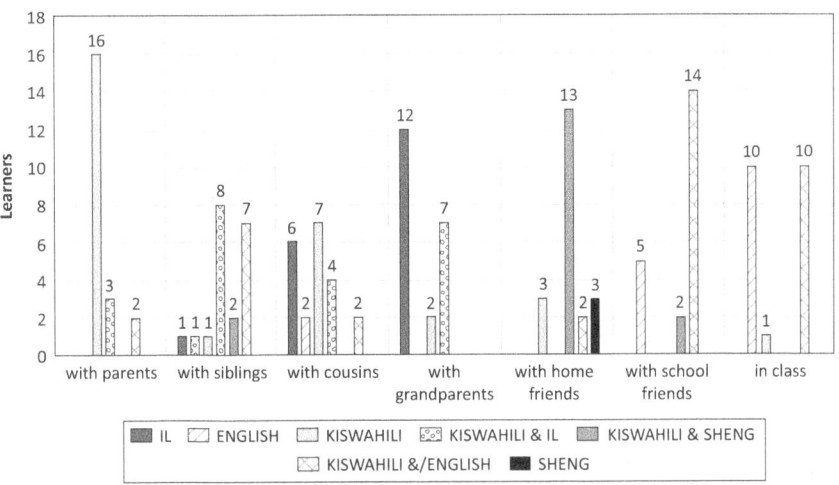

FIGURE 4.1 *Summary of Grade 5 pupils' linguistic repertoire.*

which includes grandparents, parents, and the school. Some pupils put down "English and Kiswahili" when it comes to interactions with siblings, cousins, and home friends, but "English or Kiswahili" in reference to interactions with parents, grandparents, and school friends, indicating their awareness of the nuances of fluidity depending on the situation and their interlocutors. Some pupils even qualified the Kiswahili they use in school as *sanifu* (standard), which highlights their awareness of the hierarchization of the Kiswahili varieties. Their reason for the cautious use of English and/or Kiswahili in school was that they would be punished if a teacher heard them use their other languages (here specifically ILs and Sheng). On the question why they mix languages, the responses included "When I don't know what something is in Kiluhya, I say it in Kiswahili," which reinforces the Ubuntu Translanguaging tenet of completion and interdependence, with the pupils' knowledge of both codes coming in to ensure that they (the pupils) are able to achieve communication.

Further explanation of the exercise involving the liberal use of their entire linguistic repertoire including their ILs was met with palpable excitement but also caution—perhaps due to fear of not being able to execute, as pupils raised their hands and said "But we do not learn ILs," "I cannot speak Kikisii,"[12] and "I know only a little Kikamba." I explained that the worksheet was not to test them but to help them learn from each other and from their guardians and relatives, and there was visible relief. There was also the concern that they did not know how to write in their languages, but we agreed that they

---

[12] Linguistic terminology: Ekegusii

would write as they speak; "like Kiswahili?", they asked—an indication of the learners' phonological awareness.

We then started off by skimming tasks 2 and (How would you say this in your "mother tongue"). The foods and their adjectives were familiar to the pupils, apart from the "black/African nightshade," which I explained is commonly referred to as *managu* in the environs of Nairobi, to which the Luhya and Kisii groups interjected *chimboka*, and *chinsagha*. The discussion on what the foods are referred to in the pupils' languages elicited laughter from some quarters, perhaps an indication of the socialization that our languages sound funny—a result of the comedy shows whose specialty is the caricaturization of the Kenyan and African languages and their accents in English and Kiswahili (Kasembeli, 2022). With this background, I chose to neither criticize nor forbid the laughter but quipped *tunacheka lakini tunasoma, sio?* (we laugh but also learn, right?) and they agreed *ndio!* This visibly lightened the mood and relaxed the pupils.

Despite clarification that the activities are group tasks, some pupils wanted to work by themselves, even hiding their worksheets from the others—pointing to the prevalence of an individualistic and competitive learning approach, which is characteristic of the examinations-oriented system (Mackatiani, 2017), as opposed to a cooperative approach in which community collaboration would be encouraged. In explaining to the pupils why it would be a good idea to consider working together, I called up proverbs in Kiswahili popular in the Kenyan space that encourage teamwork, by starting off *umoja ni*—and the pupils replied in an enthusiastic chorus—*nguvu!*[13] And *kidole kimoja*—and they chorused back—*hakivunji chawa!*[14] There was an evident shift in attitude and the pupils initiated changes in their sitting positions and formed small circles with their worksheets in the middle. The pupils from the Somali and Luo communities opted out of the exercise saying they did not know their languages and did not want to give it a try on their own. I let them be, since this was voluntary.

The ensuing discussions were vibrant, with snippets of *mtu husema aje* (how do you say . . . ?), *hiyo inaandikwa aje* (how is . . . . Written), *zii! Ni "i," sio "y"* (no, it is an "i," not "y"), *hiyo ni right kweli?* (Is that really correct?), and so on. audible from the various working groups. The conversations were largely in Kiswahili and Sheng, corresponding to their entries in Figure 4.1, also confirming how constricting the English-only medium is. None of the groups used their ILs for the discussions.

---

[13]Unity is strength.
[14]Literal translation: "One finger will not crush a louse."

Upon conclusion of the written group tasks, we had a discussion to reflect on the exercise. The pupils highlighted the following:

They were unsure about the spellings;
They had trouble differentiating between "sour", "hot", and "bitter" for the unripe mangoes, peppers, and black tea, as well as "sweet" and "delicious" for ripe bananas and meat.

Their observation set the tone for the "homework," which was an excerpt from the worksheet (Tasks 2 and 3). The instructions were to work with any people they knew who speak what they identified as their IL, including parents, guardians, siblings, relatives, family friends, and so on. Ms. Jane came back at this point to remind the pupils that this was homework and would be checked the following week. She collected the homework sheets on the following Monday after the weekend.

A week later, we had our follow-up session after school on Friday. After the preliminary conversation, the pupils sat in their ethnolinguistically defined groups and received their two worksheets, with the instructions to compare what they had written in class and what they wrote with the help of their community. Again, there ensued vibrant discussions in varieties of Kiswahili and Sheng.

While comparing the answers they got working with their home communities, the pupils discovered similarities and differences, some touching on dialects for example, some Luhya communities refer to the Black/African nightshade as *chinsaga* while others call it *lisutsa*. The Kamba community discovers that they differentiate between bitter and hot *(ndulu)* and sour *(ngaati)*, while the Kikuyu speaking group differentiates between delicious *(cama)* and sweet *(cukari)*.

After the group work, the pupils shared their experiences in a whole class discussion, and the following outcomes are highlighted:

- The role of community in (language) learning

    As mentioned, it took convincing and mobilization to get some learners to work with the others on the tasks. The observation, however, is how enriching the experience was when they collaborated on the tasks, as evidenced by their remarks like "I liked working with my friends." The change in attitude, from competition to collaboration, was evident as the pupils got engrossed in the group work. It was therefore not surprising to hear, "I learnt new words from my friends," as the pupils discovered and acknowledged that their classmates are also learning resources.

Additionally, the pupils reported enjoying working on the worksheet with their parents and guardians, as some talked of consulting their neighbors, friends, and even a grocery store owner/attendant. While it is common to have parents assist their children with their homework, studies have shown that due to their level of education, some parents, especially those from demographics similar to our pupils, face challenges related to inadequate knowledge and skills, which in turn hampers their ability to assist their children (Amunga et al., 2020; Dingili & Yungungu, 2023; Mwarari et al., 2020). Tasks in the ILs, in which the parents are experts, are a confidence booster for them.

- Linguistic awareness

This exercise got the pupils to reflect on the grammar and vocabulary of their languages as objects of study. In addition to differentiating the adjectives, the pupils, in working through the tasks with their classmates and home communities, make discoveries of some grammatical processes in their languages: "Depending on the fruit or thing, we say *ndulu*, or *malulu*, or *mishru*, just like in Kiswahili"; "When we are comparing things, we do it like in Kiswahili, instead of English, where we add 'er'." While they lack the metalanguage to describe it, they see the structural differences between their languages and English and similarities with Kiswahili. As they discover these similarities, they know that they can use Kiswahili (which is taught as a subject) as a reference for their languages. This sets the ground for the development of multilingual language learning awareness, which comes in handy as they expand their multilingual repertoires by learning foreign languages that are introduced in some secondary schools (Muchira, 2020).

- Appreciation for linguistic diversity

There was a marked curiosity for the languages represented in the classroom in the second session, with pupils asking each other how to say various things in their languages. Pupils expressed their desire to learn other languages so as to be included (*Rafiki zangu huongea Kikamba. Ningetaka kujua kuongea na wao*—My friends speak Kikamba and I would like to be able to speak with them) and to enjoy the cultural diversities that come with understanding a language (*Ningetaka kujua songs za Kisomali*—I would like to be able to sing Somali songs). It is evident that this exercise got the learners appreciative of the diversity made possible by the linguistic multiplicity in their classroom. This sentimental value might be the impetus to keep the ILs thriving in a society where their socioeconomic value is diminished.

Challenges

It is never an easy endeavor to include students' ILs in the classroom. The first hurdle is inclusion in a busy and demanding school schedule, where teachers are under immense pressure to cover the syllabus and prepare pupils for (national) examinations. Studies have described the Kenyan schools' programs as overwhelming for the teachers and learners, as the pressure to produce good results leads to cancellation of extracurricular activities and even enforcement of weekend and holiday coaching (Kipsang et al., 2016; Milligan, 2017). As a result, activities that are regarded as non-essential to academic excellence are sacrificed at the altar of preparation for examination. Unless the ILs are examinable, it is highly unlikely that schools would be inclined to create time for them, especially in the higher grades.

While teachers of English would be willing to integrate ILs in their classrooms, there are no materials available—despite curriculum requirements for their teaching in the lower primary grades. Teachers would have to develop these themselves, which is taxing for already overwhelmed teachers.

It is unlikely that parents would support an initiative to foster the inclusion of ILs in the English classrooms, and even the teachers fear that the parents would see it as a waste of time. Unless the parents see an educational value in the ILs, it is likely that they will reject repeated attempts to spend valuable school and homework time improving their children's mastery of their ILs.

Recommendations and Conclusion

Regardless of the likely challenges, improving the learners' IL is essential, given that it enhances their linguistic repertoires in their entirety, as explained by the Ubuntu Translanguaging tenets of interconnectedness and incompletion.

I therefore propose an approach of small-scale integration, one that does not require intensive preparation (for the teachers) and one that will not be regarded as "time wastage" by the school management and the parents. This could be in terms of simple verbal exchanges in the English language lesson, organized as casual and playful exercises, which include music and games, and are not examinable. By doing so, the English lesson becomes an arena for the exploration and discovery of multilingual fluidity. Teachers will also be encouraging and enforcing Ubuntu-collaborative learning, upon which intra- and extra-school community involvement is pegged.

The role of the teacher in promoting translanguaging practices in the classroom cannot be overemphasized, as they are usually the enforcers of the monolingual policies (Guzula et al., 2016). As our experiment shows, learners are hesitant to draw up their multilingual resources in the presence of the teacher—despite the reassurance that they are allowed to, and relax only when the teacher leaves. This underscores the fact that teachers have to be fully on board for translanguaging approaches of any kind to be effective.

Crucial to translanguaging efforts is the collaborative effort from all players within the school and beyond. It calls for the sensitization of, for example, the parents and guardians on the richness and versatility of the fluid multilingual repertoires of their children. It requires the legitimization of what are regarded as nonstandard varieties in the school environs. Additionally, there is a need to train teachers into multicompetent and multivocal actors (Makalela, 2018), equipped and empowered to innovate and implement translanguaging approaches in the classroom.

References

Amunga, J., Were, D., & Ashioya, I. (2020). The teacher-parent nexus in the competency based curriculum success equation in Kenya. *International Journal of Educational Administration and Policy Studies, 12*(1), 60–76.

Athiemoolam, L., & Kibui, A. (2013). 'An analysis of Kenyan learners' proficiency in English based on reading comprehension and vocabulary. *Journal of NELTA, 17*(1–2), 1–13.

Back, M. (2020). "It is a village": Translanguaging pedagogies and collective responsibility in a rural school district. *TESOL Quarterly, 54*(4), 900–924.

Banda, F. (2018). Translanguaging and English–African language mother tongues as linguistic dispensation in teaching and learning in a black township school in Cape Town. *Current Issues in Language Planning, 19*(2), 198–217.

Buregeya, A. (2006). Grammatical features of Kenyan English and the extent of their acceptability. *English World-Wide, 27*(2), 199–216.

Buregeya, A. (2013). Kenyan English. In B. Kortmann & K. Lunkenheimer (Eds.), *The electronic world atlas of varieties of English*. Max Planck Institute for Evolutionary Anthropology.

Carstens, A. (2016). Translanguaging as a vehicle for L2 acquisition and L1 development: Students' perceptions. *Language Matters, 47*(2), 203–222.

Cummins, J. (2019). Should schools undermine or sustain multilingualism? An analysis of theory, research, and pedagogical practice. *Sustainable Multilingualism, 15*(1), 1–26.

Dingili, R., & Yungungu, A. M. (2023). Parental involvement in grade four learners' take-home assignments in Vihiga County, Kenya. *Social Sciences & Humanities Open, 8*(1), 100589.

Githiora, C. (2018). Sheng: The expanding domains of an urban youth vernacular. *Journal of African Cultural Studies, 30*(2), 105–120.

GoK, MoE. (2018). Government of Kenya, and Ministry of Education. 2018. National Education Sector Strategic Plan 2018–2022.

Guzula, X., McKinney, C., & Tyler, R. (2016). Languaging-for-learning: Legitimising translanguaging and enabling multimodal practices in third spaces. *Southern African Linguistics and Applied Language Studies, 34*(3), 211–226.

Kanyoro, M. R. (1991). The politics of the English language in Kenya and Tanzania. In J. Cheshire (Ed.), *English round the world: Sociolinguistic perspectives* (pp. 402–419), Cambridge University Press.

Kasembeli, S. (2022). Stereotypes and the ambiguities of humour in Kenya: The churchill show. *Journal of African Cultural Studies, 34*(2), 173–185.

Kembo-Sure, & Ogechi, N. O. (2016). Literacy through a foreign language and children's rights to education: An examination of Kenya's medium of instruction policy. *Nordic Journal of African Studies, 25*(1), 15.

Kenya Institute of Curriculum Development. (2017). *Basic education curriculum framework: Kenya institute of curriculum development.* Retrieved from: https://kicd.ac.ke/wp-content/uploads/2017/10/CURRICULUMFRAMEWORK.pdf

Kim, S., Dorner, L. M., & Song, K. H. (2021). Conceptualizing community translanguaging through a family literacy project. *International Multilingual Research Journal, 15*(4), 293–316.

Kioko, A. N., & Muthwii, M. J. (2003). English variety for the public domain in Kenya: Speakers' attitudes and views. *Language, Culture and Curriculum, 16*(2), 130–145.

Kipsang, A., Saina, C., Kimurgor, J. B., & Taalam, B. (2016). Teachers' justifications for the need for school holiday coaching in Kenya: Syllabus coverage and other factors. *International Journal of Academic Research and Development, 1*(9), 61–68.

Kiramba, L. K., & Harris, V. J. (2019). Navigating authoritative discourses in a multilingual classroom: Conversations with policy and practice. *TESOL Quarterly, 53*(2), 456–481.

Krause, L. S. (2022). *Relanguaging language from a South African township school.* Multilingual Matters.

Louis Langdon Warren. (2021). The importance of teacher leadership skills in the classroom. *Education Journal, 10*(1), 8.

Macharia, P. M., Moturi, A. K., Mumo, E., Giorgi, E., Okiro, E. A., Snow, R. W., & Ray, N. (2023). Modelling geographic access and school catchment areas across public primary schools to support subnational planning in Kenya. *Children's Geographies, 21*(5), 832–848.

Mackatiani, C. I. (2017). Influence of examinations oriented approaches on quality education in primary schools in Kenya. *Journal of Education and Practice, 8*(14), 51–58.

Makalela, L. (2016). Ubuntu translanguaging: An alternative framework for complex multilingual encounters. *Southern African Linguistics and Applied Language Studies, 34*(3), 187–196.

Makalela, L. (2018). Teaching african languages the ubuntu way: The effects of translanguaging among pre-service teachers in South Africa. In P. Van Avermaet, S. Slembrouck, K. Van Gorp, S. Sierens, & K. Maryns (Eds.), *The multilingual edge of education* (pp. 261–282). Palgrave Macmillan.

Milligan, L. O. (2017). Education quality and the Kenyan 8-4-4 curriculum: Secondary school learners' experiences. *Research in Comparative and International Education, 12*(2), 198–212.

Muchira, R. (2020). Awareness of multilinguality and the resulting cross-linguistic influence of English and Kiswahili on German: A study of multilingual language learning awareness among Kenyan secondary school learners of German as a foreign language. Doctoral Thesis. Universität Leipzig.

Mwarari, C. N., Githui, P., & Mwenje, M. (2020). Parental involvement in the implementation of competency based curriculum in Kenya: Perceived challenges and opportunities. *American Journal of Humanities and Social Sciences Research*, *4*(3), 201–208.

Norro, S. (2022). Namibian teachers' practices in a multilingual context. *International Journal of Multilingualism*, *21*(1), 360–378.

Oduor, J. A. (2010). A SWOT analysis of the language policies in education in Kenya and Ethiopia. *The University of Nairobi Journal of Language and Linguistics*, *1*, 86–102.

Oduor, J. A. (2015). Towards a practical proposal for multilingualism in education in Kenya. *Multilingual Education*, *5*(1), 1.

Okombo, D. O. (2015). "My names are..." and other crimes. *Daily Nation*, June 2.

Omidire, M. F., & Ayob, S. (2022). The utilisation of translanguaging for learning and teaching in multilingual primary classrooms. *Multilingua*, *41*(1), 105–129.

Setyaningrum, R. W., Setiawan, S., & Anam, S. (2022). Translanguaging as a scaffolded practice in a primary school content and language integrated learning context during the Covid-19 pandemic. *European Journal of Educational Research*, *11*(4), 2043–2055.

5

Translanguaging Teaching Strategies in South Korea

Reframing EFL Elementary Classrooms as Multilingual Classrooms

Michael Rabbidge

Introduction

The language education context of South Korea (SK) exists within a society that traditionally self-identifies as Korean monolingual: one country with one language for one people. This entails a relationship to the English language summarized by terms like *outer circle country* (Kachru, 1985), *English as a Foreign Language* (EFL) context, and *non-native speaker teachers and students*. These descriptions, often originating in the discourses of English monolingualism, have not faced much resistance from within or beyond the peninsula; they are considered the norm, meaning English is not customarily considered an element of the Korean citizens' language identity (Park, 2009).

Nevertheless, the SK education sector strives to increase its competitiveness and relevance globally to attract international students as part of the SK government's efforts to address local concerns surrounding a decline in domestic student enrollment numbers due to dwindling national birth rates, a slowing economy, and a worsening employment market (Kim, 2019; Park & Song, 2013). The effect of this drive is that schools at elementary and secondary levels have now embraced language teaching ideologies that promote communicative language knowledge (Li, 1998; Park, 2009), and universities have adopted English as a Medium of Instruction (EMI) in lectures as part of larger efforts to compete globally for international students (Kim, 2019).

In 2001, the Teaching English in English (TEE) policy was enacted in South Korean public schools as part of a larger policy (Jee & Li, 2021) to improve English communicative proficiency in students. This was further supported in 2008 by the Lee administration. However, this policy led to a backlash from Korean English teachers and scholars alike (Li, 1998; Jee & Li, 2021). Research into teacher perceptions and practices regarding TEE has shown that Korean teachers generally perceive that the TEE policy is not being enforced, insinuating that Korean English teachers often work independent of standard policy and teach according to their own beliefs about effective practice (Rabbidge, 2019a, 2019b).

Despite the lack of adherence to government policy by Korean teachers (Rabbidge, 2019a, 2019b), the suggestion is that individual institutional educational policies that guide different curricula across different regions of the country continue to be dominated by traditional Second Language Acquisition (SLA) theories that favor monolingualism-influenced research (Jee & Li, 2021). Therefore, early in their careers, teachers may readily accept theories on language teaching and best practices that align with ideologies of native speakerism and standard English (Jee & Li, 2021).

Public school classrooms in South Korea, like others around the world, suffer from the influence of socioeconomic disparities between students that result in classrooms with students of different English language proficiencies. When confronted with classes of variable English proficiency, some teachers quickly realize that they need to employ their full linguistic repertoire (FLR) to ensure that students can participate in the learning process, while other teachers continue to persevere with excluding the Korean language (L1).

Although SK has not been understood as a multilingual context in traditional discourses, there is a growing call for SK to be reframed as a multilingual context to provide space for more positive language and identity growth (Rabbidge, 2019b; Turnbull, 2016). Reframing as a multilingual context opens spaces for new identity options that adhere to more inclusive ideologies of language use, such as emerging multilinguals (EMLs), and shifts the emphasis to how languages are used rather than if generalized language standards that are upheld by monolingual ideals are being met (Grosjean, 2013). Likewise, reframing as a multilingual context means discussions move away from the deficiency-oriented perspectives that have traditionally dominated research on such learners (Mahboob & Lin, 2016).

This inclusive understanding of language use reimagines language teachers as multilingual rather than non-native speakers of English (NNESTs), where multilinguals are defined as people who use at least two languages as part of their daily lives (Grosjean, 2013). Emerging multilingual education is therefore defined as a setting where more than one language is employed in the development of EMLs' linguistic repertoires.

The purpose of this chapter is to outline a set of general instructional guidelines, illustrated using translanguaging-in-action examples, to help language teachers reimagine classrooms as spaces that support heteroglossia perspectives on pedagogy. To help with this reimagining, observational data was collected on translanguaging pedagogical practices from experienced Korean elementary school English language teachers. The observational data reveals different strategies teachers use to ensure that teachers and students can align themselves with the more practical tenets of translanguaging, as outlined by García et al. (2017), namely the ability to participate and collaborate effectively to achieve student academic goals. Excerpts from these observations also illuminate how translanguaging, when employed inconsistently, may impede progression toward inclusivity, serving as a warning against ineffective pedagogical practices. Semi-structured interviews were conducted prior to and following the observations to provide more contextual information regarding the practices and decisions observed. In doing this, the discussed context is redefined as a multilingual context rather than its traditional designation, that of an EFL environment, to provide space for a more inclusive understanding of what Korean English language teachers may do in their classrooms.

Literature Review

Translanguaging Research in the Korean Context

Translanguaging research has tended to focus on European or American contexts, mostly because Asian contexts are hindered by monolingual ideological discourses dominated by terminologies such as EFL, non-native speaker/native speaker teachers, and similar others. Therefore, research focusing on translanguaging perspectives in SK is still relatively rare. In fact, research focusing on translanguaging in the Korean context either examines the translanguaging practices of Koreans abroad (Lee & Garcia, 2020; Song, 2015) or the perspectives of foreigners living in SK (Jang, 2022). For example, Jang's research (2022) examined the use of translanguaging of Uzbek students living in SK, revealing how student agency in the learning of English was influenced by a variety of contextual factors and often determined how well students' translanguaging practices could improve their developing linguistic repertoires. Studies that have focused on Koreans' translanguaging practices in Korea are rare. Rabbidge (2019a, 2019b) investigated the impact of translanguaging in Korean elementary schools, revealing how a lack of guidance and understanding by teachers in this context may negate the positive impact translanguaging can often have on student participation in language learning activities. Williams' (2023) research into undergraduate students' perceptions toward translanguaging in an EMI context built upon previous research in this context (Kim et al., 2017) that a translanguaging approach is needed to assist Korean students in overcoming constraints in learning that have been imposed by EMI. Ironically, the lack of focus on Korean teachers in Korea accentuates perspectives that Korean teachers in Korea are not considered viable subjects of multilingual or translanguaging research.

Translanguaging Stances

A translanguaging stance defines the philosophical belief system teachers draw on to guide their translanguaging in their classrooms (García et al., 2017). Implementing this translanguaging stance is influenced by a multitude of factors (Deroo & Ponzio, 2019), including but not limited to translanguaging's relative newness as a theory and language teachers' limited language learning and teaching experiences, the prevalence of monolingual ideology in school administrative systems that is influenced by standard English and its emphasis on a certain "correct" uses (Deroo & Ponzio, 2019).

Introducing translanguaging approaches to pre-service teachers has been shown to impact their assumptions regarding critical sociocultural understandings of language use and ideology in the classroom (Robinson et al., 2018). Research also highlights how some teachers struggle with certain incompatibilities between translanguaging and how language education has traditionally been framed in TESOL courses (Fallas-Escobar, 2020; Tian et al., 2020).

Resistance to implementing translanguaging pedagogies from those involved in language education is mostly underpinned by the ideology of monolingualism (Richards & Wilson, 2019), which prizes both a separation of languages in the learning process to theoretically maximize exposure to the target language as well as native speaker norms as a standard to be achieved in the learning process. A common cause of resistance to translanguaging is often seen in the guilt teachers have about using the L1 (Macaro, 2009; Wang, 2019). Other reasons regarding the decision to not employ translanguaging strategies are related to fears of students overusing the L1, as well as more macro concerns such as ideologies linked to language purism, language policies, and uncertainty on how to implement translanguaging due to a lack of support for teachers (Creese & Blackledge, 2011; Deroo & Ponzio, 2019; Wang, 2019; Wang & Kirkpatrick, 2012). Additionally, research into the perceptions of parents regarding the use of translanguaging shows that monolingual ideals still persist in parental thinking about language education (Wilson, 2021).

Pedagogical and Spontaneous Translanguaging

Pedagogical translanguaging combines pedagogical theories and practices realized in the classroom via instructional strategies that integrate two or more languages (Cenoz & Gorter, 2020). It focuses on the use of the EML student's FLR as an approach to ensure greater opportunity to comprehend educational content in the fostering of linguistic development (Flores & García, 2013).

Pedagogical translanguaging is a deliberate teaching action: it is planned with a pedagogical purpose (Cenoz & Gorter, 2020). Examples include the use of planned translanguaging practices to assist in the development of lexical and morphosyntactic knowledge, discourse-level knowledge, as well as pragmatic knowledge (Leonet et al., 2017; Rabbidge, 2019a). Importantly, pedagogical translanguaging empowers EML teachers and students to employ stronger linguistic elements to teach or learn new, or weaker, linguistic elements in a practical and efficient manner (Cummins, 2017).

Additionally, *pedagogical translanguaging* is often distinguished in scholarly works from *spontaneous translanguaging*, which is used to describe translanguaging practices outside the classroom that are considered fluid, dynamic, and contextually dependent (Cenoz & Gorter, 2020). Pedagogical translanguaging and spontaneous translanguaging are said to be on either side of a continuum that describes the multitude of choices and practices teachers have at their disposal while teaching languages (Cenoz & Gorter, 2020). Spontaneous translanguaging energizes teachers who choose to be unimpeded by outdated institutional policies that seek to confine the notion of education to what can be written out in policy documents.

Translanguaging-in-action

The observational data in this section discusses different translanguaging strategies that teachers have employed to improve students' participation in their classes. These excerpts highlight how translanguaging can remove ambiguity in the lesson, allowing students full access to the activities that are designed to help students develop their emerging English language repertoire.

From a translanguaging perspective, while giving instructions it is vital that teachers balance the different elements of their linguistic repertoires to ensure that students are both being exposed to the new language, in most cases English, but are also able to understand what it is the teacher requires of them as part of the learning process. Likewise, there exist practical concerns related to classroom management that teachers need to be mindful of when conducting class. These include elements such as time management and maintaining a level of control over the direction of the class. These are often overlooked in more theoretical discussions of translanguaging but are foundational to classrooms that involve younger learners.

The excerpts below come from a highly experienced elementary school English teacher with over fifteen years of experience in this context and who has participated in government-funded teacher training programs that espouse TEE approaches. In the excerpt, she is explaining a new activity to her students. Each line is numbered and designated as an *R for Response*, *I for Initiation*, or *F for Feedback*. This represents the most commonly occurring interaction pattern in language classrooms for younger learners around the world, the IRF interaction pattern. Ss stands for a group of students, S stands for a single student, and T stands for teacher.

Planning Is Important

This first discussion point highlights the value of planning for the teacher to achieve both translanguaging goals and address general teaching practicalities. The excerpts feature fifth-grade public elementary school students studying English as a mandatory subject in SK. The twenty-four students in the class displayed a mixture of English repertoire development. Development is employed here rather than the term proficiency to avoid the monolingual ideological connotations that accompany the term. Development is preferred as a term as it aligns with sociocultural-informed understandings of language acquisition.

In Excerpt 1, the teacher is preparing the students for a group running dictation activity that has students working in groups to gather sentences from around the room. Students must read a sentence, return to the group, and then say the sentence to another group member who writes the sentence down on a shared activity handout. During her interviews, the teacher explained that this is an activity that students have done before.

Except 1 shows a continuation of a much longer interaction. The teacher speaks to her students in English as she is confident the students can comprehend her linguistic choices. She calls out their group number, and the students give a physical response, showing comprehension that aligns with the teacher's language choice. She *Initiates* an interaction, the students *Respond*, often using the same linguistic choices as the teacher or in a manner that indicates a comprehension of the teacher, and she occasionally gives *Feedback* in reply to student responses.

Then, when she reaches a point of possible difficulty in explaining or understanding the instructions (turn 6), she employs her Korean repertoire to avoid ambiguity and ensure students know what to do in this situation, as this is the more developed area of the students' own emerging linguistic repertoire. This instructional translanguaging strategy embedded within a familiar interaction pattern sets students up for success in the following group activity and ensures they can achieve the academic goals of the lesson, which were to improve communicative competence in their emerging English linguistic repertoire by practicing using the assigned language structures within the lesson of the textbook. This was central to the school's English language curriculum and necessary for the teachers to complete by the end of the school year.

Excerpt 1

Turn	IRF	Actor	Interaction
1	R	Ss	(physical response—Students raise their hands.)
2	I	T	Four, four.
3	R	Ss	(physical response—Students raise their hands.)
4	I	T	OK, five.
5	R	Ss	(physical response—Students raise their hands.)
6	F	T	다섯 명이 없으면 모두가 말해요 (*if you don't have five, then all of you speak*).
7	I	T	OK, hands down. So first, number one in your team will go to one poster and remember the first sentence, like he has big brown eyes, and go back to your team and say the sentence to your team members . . .

In Excerpt 2, the teacher translanguages when concept-checking her student's comprehension of her instructions that she has given in Excerpt 1. In turn 10 she draws on her FLR to inquire if students understand what they should do during the activity she is setting up. Students respond (turn 11) to the teacher's FLR with Korean to confirm they understand, and the instructional interaction continues until the teacher is assured that the students are ready to start the intended activity.

Excerpt 2

Turn	IRF	Actor	Interaction
8	I	T	So, like this, it was team five's bandit, so you have to circle the right picture and circle team five, like this, so you have to find five bandits, how many bandits?
9	R	Ss	Five
10	F	T	Five bandits, 왜 다섯 개죠? 여섯 모둠인데? (*Why five? There are six groups* [of students]).
11	R	S	우리꺼 빼고요. (*We don't include our own*).
12	F	T	그렇죠 (*That's right*)
13	I	T	자기 거 빼고 몇 개 모둠을 찾으면 돼요? (*If you don't include your own, how many do you find?*).
14	R	Ss	다섯 (*five*).
15	F	T	다섯 모둠 것 찾으면 되겠습니다 (*You can find five*).
16	I	T	제일 먼저 누가 움직인다 구요? (*Which student moves first?*)

Instructional Guidelines from the Translanguaging Classroom

These excerpts provide insights into what can enable effective translanguaging in an EML context. Importantly, when asked about these exchanges, the teacher stated that she planned to employ her FLR as she felt students may become confused by the intricacy of the instructions if she were to only employ English. Therefore, this example of pedagogical translanguaging shows how, when a teacher is in the planning stage of a lesson, consideration of instructional language is important to ensure a level of continuity in the lesson. Likewise, time constraints in the class, a contextual issue often ignored in translanguaging research, meant she knew she would not have time to convey the complexity of the instructions by limiting herself to just English, so pedagogical translanguaging can allow teachers to address practical concerns related to classroom management.

Considering a generalized description of the classroom's FLR was an important element of the lesson's planning process and reveals the teacher's translanguaging stance. It allows her to demonstrate how she values the students' FLR as an important learning and teaching tool. This has a positive impact on the emerging multilingual identities, or EML identities, in this classroom as well. It also demonstrates her translanguaging design, as this planning ensured she was able to keep students engaged in the class content and set up an activity that allowed her students to develop their EML repertoires (García et al., 2017).

Critics may argue that she is sacrificing the amount of exposure students receive in the lesson by employing her FLR here, but exposure is irrelevant if it does not lead to comprehension, let alone acquisition. In this case, her predetermined decision to employ her FLR proved successful, as students were observed to complete the communicative language activity in English as intended. Additionally, the teacher was able to ensure that both languages were seen to have a valuable and positive role in the learning process, as well as expose students to a positive bilingual identity position in the classroom.

Guidelines for Improving Instructional Awareness and Applications

When asked if she explains to students why she uses her FLR the way she does, she replied that she did not do that. During our discussion, I suggested to her that there was potentially an opportunity for her to become more inclusive in her teaching practices by explaining to students how and why she chooses to use different elements of her linguistic repertoire in her classrooms. By helping students understand or even overcome potential influences related to monolingual ideals that tend to dominate the uninformed public's appreciation of effective teaching approaches, she can further educate students on potentially negative identity options that often implicitly infiltrate the language classroom. By providing her students with an emerging bilingual identity position, she may also improve motivational elements within the classroom.

Classrooms Are Dynamic by Nature

The next excerpts reveal how inconsistency when translanguaging can impact student willingness to participate in a lesson. Both excerpts come from the same teacher who had over ten years of teaching English teaching experience. In her current school, where she teaches fifth-grade students, teachers were expected to practice first-language (Korean) exclusion during English language lessons. Despite this institutional requirement, the teacher still chose to employ her FLR when she felt it was important to the learning process, revealing her translanguaging stance (García et al., 2017). However, the impact of the incongruencies between the teacher's stance and those of the school resulted in confusion during the lessons regarding repertoire use.

This could be a relatively common experience for language teachers in EML contexts, as at institutional and societal levels there remains a strong belief in first language exclusion as the best path forward for language education, which may often clash with practical applications and practices in the language classroom.

Excerpt 3 reveals the teacher interacting with her students, initiating responses via images of animals (turns 1–2). During the interaction, she employs English and expects students to respond accordingly. There comes a point when the picture is confusing, and this disrupts the flow of the interaction. She was pointing to a wolf and trying to elicit "fur" from students, but students responded with wolf, as seen in line 2. Realizing this confusion, she employs FLR so that the students know what she expects as a response. Students respond in their FLR (turn 5), seemingly following the teacher's lead. She then asks them to provide the English equivalent (turn 7), to which one student responds with the word "fur" (turn 8), meaning that they may have the word in their emerging English repertoire but also that other students in the group may not.

Excerpt 3

Turn	IRF	Actor	Interaction
1	I	T	Look at that, what's this? *Pointing to the screen*
2	R	Ss	Wolf!
3	F	T	In Korean, in Korean
4	I	T	This part 이부분을 뭐라고하지? *(What's this part called?)*
5	R	Ss	털(Fur)
6	F	T	Yes
7	I	T	In English
8	R	S	Fur
9	F	T	Fur, very good.

However, in Excerpt 4, a similar breakdown in lesson flow emerges (turn 2), and during this point, while some students say the word "eagle" in English, one student responds to the teacher's English initiation in Korean (line 4). Based on the previous excerpt, one would assume that this would be accepted by the teacher to maintain student engagement and that she would then try to elicit an English response from the student accordingly. However, the teacher chose to rebuke the student in turn five when she sternly asked the student who spoke Korean to only speak English. This intent was confirmed by the teacher in a follow-up interview about this interaction. This was observed to have negatively impacted the student's participation in the ensuing interactions.

Excerpt 4

Turn	IRF	Actor	Interaction
1	I	T	Do you know the name of any birds?
2	R	S	Huh?
3	F	T	Do you know any birds?
4	R	Ss	eagle (one student says 독수리 [eagle])
5	F	T	Eagle, right 친구야 지금 영어 센터 왔으니까 조금만 영어로 해줘 (friend, this is the English center, please use English)
			Teacher holds up a new card
6	R	Ss	Chicken

Instructional Guidelines from the Translanguaging Classroom

Excerpts 3 and 4 highlight the dynamic nature of language teaching, and how teachers need to be ready for the unexpected. They show what can happen when a teacher encounters a situation in which students' emerging English repertoires could impede classroom learning flow. The teacher's translanguaging acts here are more in line with spontaneous translanguaging, as the disruptions to the flow of the interaction were not foreseen by the teacher in the planning stage of the lesson. The first spontaneous translanguaging act in Excerpt 1 reveals how spontaneous translanguaging can allow for the maintenance of interactional flows that influence positive learning experiences. The teacher's use of her FLR facilitates the flow of the lesson and enhances access students have to the intended vocabulary item of the interaction. This instructional guideline implies that both Korean and English have value in the learning process, providing space for the continued development of the emerging bi or multilingual identities of the students and ensure participation is maximized.

However, Excerpt 4 acts as a caution to teachers who do not reflect upon the potential for disruptions to occur, and how negative teacher reactions can impact student participation negatively. The researcher witnessed the student who was told not to speak Korean stop participating in the class, and when asked about this in a follow-up interview, the teacher also confirmed the student's reaction, revealing how the teacher's inconsistency in allowing students to employ spontaneous translanguaging can negatively impact student participation. This instructional guideline is evident in Excerpt 4, when her spontaneous translanguaging is used to devalue student voice and repertoire choice, it had the opposite effect of her previous spontaneous translanguaging decision, which not only discouraged student participation but also adversely impacted their bi or multilingual identity development. This suggests an inconsistency and incoherence in the teacher's own stance toward spontaneous translanguaging practices.

Two Guidelines for Improving Instructional Awareness and Applications

During a semi-structured interview that was held as a follow-up to the observations, the teacher was asked about her two acts of spontaneous translanguaging and their contradictory nature. She replied that she felt institutional pressure to maintain student use of English as much as possible, and on this occasion, she did not appreciate the students accessing their Korean repertoire independently of her initiation.

This discussion on institutional pressure leads to how power and control are enacted in the language classroom, and how the maintenance of a teacher's power and control can impact student participation negatively (Rabbidge, 2019a). The teacher explained that on occasion her spontaneous translanguaging may present students with contradictions in her teaching practices, causing confusion and negatively impacting participation. It would seem then that raising teacher awareness on issues of power and control is vital to facilitate a level of consistency in their teaching and ensure that they do not trade inclusive translanguaging practices that encourage improved participation for the need to maintain a sense of control over the class. Inconsistencies in the valuing of languages or how student interactions are accepted in the flow of the class are small acts that have potentially large repercussions for language student development, as seen in the student who stopped participating in this excerpt.

To deal with this issue, teachers need to spend time discussing with students their intentions regarding full repertoire use. Class translanguaging guidelines should be put in place with students to guarantee they have an awareness of teacher intentions regarding language use and the impact that these intentions may have on student development. Classroom rules designed to guide student conduct are common enough, so extending such rules to include more linguistically inclusive practices may be included as part of this. There has been a lack of discussion on how teachers can develop student translanguaging stances by discussing with students' pedagogical aims appropriately framed that enable students to understand lesson purposes beyond just the supposed acquisition of linguistic features (García et al., 2017). When students can be shown their emerging or multilingual status, it can influence their relationship to language learning and challenge societal discourses that have tended to negatively frame language learning.

Signaling Intentions

This section discusses another equally experienced teacher who explicitly signals her intention to employ her Korean repertoire during her lessons. Like the other classes, this excerpt comes from a fifth-grade elementary school English lesson in a public elementary school in South Korea. The teacher stated that her translanguaging stance prioritizes the role of English in her lessons, yet also utilizes her FLR during moments when she feels her students' general English is not developed enough to understand important aspects of the lesson content.

Before the excerpt, she had elicited responses about the appearance of the students in her class as part of her focus on the language used to describe clothing. This followed the IRF routine seen in other excerpts. Then she moves on to language used to describe facial features. All interactions have been in English up to this point. When shifting to a focus on facial features, she explicitly tells her students that she will employ her FLR for a set period (turn 1) regarding the language expressions used to describe facial features. We can see in turns 6–9, the teacher elicits responses from her students about what she "is wearing" at the moment as a way to highlight the progressive structure—be verb +ing. This grammatical construction is focused on by the teacher because it is part of the teaching unit within the textbook that has been assigned for the English curriculum in the public elementary school she is teaching in.

Excerpt 5

Turn	IRF	Actor	Interaction
1	F	T	...Tall, long, pretty, handsome is like this, OK. Short, cap, glasses, earrings, OK, is wearing.
2	I	T	Ok I will speak, I will explain in Korean, for two minutes. OK, look at me
3	R	Ss	Look at you
4	I	T	우리가 외모를 설명 할 때는 얼굴에 있는 것들, 또는 이렇게 간단하게 생각을 해볼까? *(When we describe our appearance or things we have on our face or shall we simply think like this?)* 우리가 몸이야 몸이 있는데 근데 그몸에 귀가있고 입이있고 눈이 있어요 그러니까 뭐가 있는거야? *(Our body has ears, a mouth, eyes so what do you have?)* 있는 거죠 *(yes we have)* I have or he or she has 가지고 있어요 *(We have)* I have a nose, I have two eyes, I have two ears, I have... what? A beautiful mouth, like this 이렇게 할 수 있지만 우리몸을 전체적으로 한번 말해보자 어때요? *(We can say it like this but shall we talk about the whole body?)*
			Pretty 예뻐요 이건 형용사죠 예쁜 *(pretty is the adjective)*, ㄴ 으로 끝나는건 형용사라고 했죠? *(I told you when something finishes with ㄴ it's an adjective)* 동작을 나타내는 말을 만들려면 be 동사가 필요하다고 했죠? *(I told you if you want to talk about movement you need the be verb)* 그래서 *(so)* she is pretty, he is short. He is handsome 이렇게 표현합니다 그런데 우리가 입고있는 건 어떻게 할까? *(We express like this but how do you say it about what you are wearing?)* 입다 동사가 뭐야? *(What's the verb for wear?)* Wear 지금 현재 입고 있어요 *(I'm wearing now)*
5	I	T	OK, I am wearing something. I am wearing this coat, I am wearing blue jeans, I am wearing this shirt, I am wearing... what?
6	R	Ss	Earing
7	F	T	earrings 가지고 있는 것 *(something you have)*
8	I	T	I am wearing what?
9	R	Ss	Watch
10	F	T	Watch, OK good job 가지고 있는 것 입고 있는 것은 *(something you have or wear)* wearing be+~ing 몸 전체적으로는 형용사가 들어갈 때는 be 동사가 들어가서 *(when you talk about the whole body you need the be verb and the adjective)*

The excerpt demonstrates how the signaling of her linguistic intentions promoted a smooth transition that did not disrupt the flow of the class. It also reinforced the purpose of the class in prioritizing English as the focus of the lesson.

Instructional Guidelines for the Translanguaging Classroom

By explicitly telling students her intentions to employ her FLR, and briefly the pedagogical purpose behind this teaching decision, the teacher embraces the value that FLR use affords learning situations in emerging multilingual contexts. This highlights how making explicit to students the use of translanguaging strategies in the classroom can minimize disruptions to the flow of the learning situation. The extract highlights how her instructions do not just employ imperative linguistic constructions that require learners to be passive recipients of information, rather, they include interrogative linguistic constructions (turn 5) that create interactional sequences for the learners.

Guidelines for Improving Instructional Awareness and Applications

When asked about this, the teacher explained that she prefers to employ English as much as possible, but when she explains grammatical constructions to her students, she feels that employing her FLR is more beneficial as it allows her to ensure all students have access to the information, which in turn allows the students to participate in her lessons more effectively. It also has practical benefits in that it saves time and allows her to cover more of the content in the government-administered textbook, which makes up the curriculum of English classes in her school. During the discussion, I suggested that she could further develop this signaling by elaborating a little more on why she was choosing to employ her FLR, explaining the benefits of the teaching process to the students, as discussed above. This will potentially impact student awareness of the value of full repertoire use and develop students' emerging understanding of the relationship between the languages in their educational context.

Critics might argue that elementary school children are too immature to grasp concepts of inclusivity and positive language identity development, but they can definitely feel the impact of it. The dominant discourses of monolingualism often operate covertly throughout society and may negatively impact the emerging language identity options of students in traditional EFL contexts (Bhasin et al., 2023; Fallas-Escobar, 2020; García, 2009).

Discussing counter-discourses like translanguaging openly with students can offer alternatives to monolingual discourses and potentially liberate their perceptions of language learning (García, 2009; Wei, 2017, 2021).

Concluding Thoughts

The classroom excerpts shown in this chapter help suggest guidelines that teachers in EML contexts can adopt and adapt as part of their own efforts to implement a more inclusive translanguaging teaching approach in their classrooms. Guidelines by nature avoid being overly deterministic, and teachers are asked to reflect upon their own linguistic choices or practices and to consider that in each context, deciding what is effective for both them and their students is better than blind faith in guidelines that insist upon a singular course of action. The guidelines identify what teachers may do in the planning stage of lessons and during classroom interactions that arise spontaneously, as well as how teachers can be more transparent with their teaching intentions. Although represented individually, such guidelines should be considered interconnected by teachers when incorporating a translanguaging approach.

In the planning stages of a lesson:

- Plan for consistency in instructional language across and within lessons to avoid ambiguity.
- Employ pedagogical translanguaging to address practical concerns related to classroom management.

During interactions occurring in lessons:

- Employ spontaneous translanguaging to maintain interactional flows that influence positive learning experiences.
- Employ spontaneous translanguaging as a deliberate strategy to actively foster and enhance student participation.

Be more transparent with teaching intentions:

- Spend time discussing with students the teacher's intentions regarding full repertoire use.
- Make explicit to students that the use of translanguaging strategies in the classroom can minimize disruptions to the flow of the learning situation and raise their awareness about mobilizing their FLR for learning.

Although not exhaustive, the guidelines have emerged from real experiences that teachers have with their translanguaging practices. They consider practical teaching concerns and classroom management issues that teachers face daily and do not overly concern themselves with the more theoretical tenets of translanguaging. These guidelines provide a pathway for EML teachers to create positive EML identity development and instill a healthier relationship to language learning as part of their efforts to reimagine classrooms as spaces inclusive of translanguaging perspectives within contexts still dominated by monolingual restraints.

Reference List

Bhasin, A., Castro, M., & Román, D. (2023). Translanguaging through the lens of social justice: unpacking educators' understanding and practices. *International Multilingual Research Journal, 17*(4), (pp., 304–317). https://doi.org/10.1080/19313152.2023.2208510

Bilingual Education in the 21st Century: A Global Perspective O. Garcia Publisher: Wiley-Blackwell 2009.

Cenoz, J., & Gorter, D. (2020). Pedagogical translanguaging: An introduction. *System, 92*, 102269. https://doi.org/10.1016/j.system.2020.102269

Creese, A., & Blackledge, A. (2011). Separate and flexible bilingualism in complementary schools: Multiple language practices in interrelationship. *Journal of Pragmatics, 43*(5), 1196–1208. https://doi.org/10.1016/j.pragma.2010.10.006

Cummins, J. (2017). Teaching for transfer in multilingual school contexts. In O. García, A. Lin, & S. May (Eds.), *Bilingual and multilingual education, encyclopedia of language and education* (Vol. 3, pp. 103–115). Springer Cham.

Deroo, M. R., & Ponzio, C. (2019). Confronting ideologies: A discourse analysis of in-service teachers' translanguaging stance through an ecological lens. *Bilingual Research Journal, 42*(2), 214–231. https://doi.org/10.1080/15235882.2019.1589604

Dylan G Williams., (2023). Trust and translanguaging in English-medium instruction, ELT Journal, Volume 77, Issue 1, January 2023, (pp. 23–32). https://doi.org/10.1093/elt/ccac016

Fallas-Escobar, C. (2020). EFL Instructors' Ambivalent Ideological Stances Toward Translanguaging: Collaborative Reflection on Language Ideologies. In: Tian, Z., Aghai, L., Sayer, P., Schissel, J.L. (eds) Envisioning TESOL through a Translanguaging Lens. Educational Linguistics, vol 45. Springer, Cham. https://doi.org/10.1007/978-3-030-47031-9_15

Flores, N., & García, O. (2013). Linguistic third spaces in education: Teachers' translanguaging across the bilingual continuum. In D. Little, L. Constant, & P. V. Avermaet (Eds.), *Managing diversity in education* (pp. 243–256). Multilingual Matters.

García, O., Johnson, S. I., & Seltzer, K. (2017). *The translanguaging classroom: Leveraging student bilingualism for learning.* Caslon.

Grosjean, F. (2013). Bilingualism: A short introduction. In F. Grosjean & P. Li (Eds.), *The psycholinguistics of bilingualism*. Blackwell Publishing, 5–25.

Jang, J. (2022). Translanguaging as an Agentive Action: A Longitudinal Case Study of Uzbek EFL Learners in South Korea. Teaching English as a Second Language. *Electronic Journal (TESL-EJ), 26* (3). https://doi.org/10.55593/ej.26103a6.

Jee, Y., & Li, G. (2021). The ideologies of English as Foreign Language (EFL) educational policies in Korea: The case of teacher recruitment and teacher education. In K. Raza, C. Coombe, & D. Reynolds (Eds.), *Policy development in TESOL and multilingualism*. Springer, (pp 119–133).

Kachru, B. (1985). Standards, codification and sociolinguistic realism: English language in the outer circle. In R. Quirk & H. Widowson (Eds.), *English in the world: Teaching and learning the language and literatures* (pp. 11–36). Cambridge University Press.

Kim, E. G., Kweon, S. O. & Kim, J. Y. (2017). 'Korean engineering students' perceptions of English-medium instruction (EMI) and L1 use in EMI classes.' *Journal of Multilingual and Multicultural Development*. https://doi.org/10.1080/01434632.2016.1177061

Kim, H. S. (2019). Only 11 percent of graduating students have steady jobs to go to. *The Korea Herald*. Retrieved from http://www.koreaherald.com/view.php?ud=20190121000503

Lee, C., & García, G. E. (2020). Unpacking the oral translanguaging practices of Korean-American first graders. *Bilingual Research Journal, 43*(1), 32–49. https://doi.org/10.1080/15235882.2019.1703844.

Leonet, O., Cenoz, J., & Gorter, D. (2017). Challenging minority language isolation: Translanguaging in a trilingual school in the basque country. *Journal of Language, Identity & Education, 16*(4), 216–227. https://doi.org/10.1080/15348458.2017.1328281

Li, D. (1998). "It's always more difficult than you plan and imagine": Teachers' perceived difficulties in introducing the communicative approach in South Korea. *TESOL Quarterly, 32*(4), 677–703. https://doi.org/10.2307/3588000

Li Wei, Translanguaging as a political stance: implications for English language education, *ELT Journal, 76*(2), April 2021, (pp., 172–182). https://doi.org/10.1093/elt/ccab083

Macaro, E. (2009). Teacher use of codeswitching in the second language classroom: Exploring 'optimal' use. In M. Turnbull & J. D. O. Cain (Eds.), *First language use in second and foreign language learning* (pp. 35–49). Multilingual Matters.

Mahboob, A., & Lin, A. M. Y. (2016). Using local languages in English language classrooms. In H. Widodo & W. Renandya (Eds.), *English language teaching today: Building a closer link between theory and practice*. Springer International, 25–40.

Park, J. S.-Y. (2009). *The local construction of a global language: Ideologies of English in South Korea*. Mouton de Gruyter.

Park, S. H., & Song, Y. (2013). Internationalizing higher education in Korea: University and government responses. *Koreanische Zeitschrift für Wirtschaftswissenschaften 경상논총, 31*(2), 29–43.

Rabbidge, M. (2019a). The effects of translanguaging on participation in EFL classrooms. *The Journal of Asia TEFL, 16*(4), 1305–1322.

Rabbidge, M. (2019b). *Translanguaging in EFL contexts: A call for change*. Routledge.

Richards, J. C., & Wilson, O. (2019). On transidentitying. *RELC Journal, 50*(1), 179–187. https://doi.org/10.1177/0033688218824780

Song, K. (2015). "Okay, I will say in Korean and then in American": Translanguaging practices in bilingual homes. *Journal of Early Childhood Literacy, 16*(1), (pp., 84-106). https://doi.org/10.1177/1468798414566705 (Original work published 2016).

Teaching for justice: Introducing translanguaging in an undergraduate TESOL course E. Robinson, Z. Tian, T. Martínez and A. Qarqeen. *Journal of Language and Education* 2018, *4*(3), (pp., 77-87) DOI: doi: 10.17323/2411-7390-2018-4-3-77-87

Turnbull, B. (2016). Reframing foreign language learning as bilingual education: Epistemological changes towards the emergent bilingual. *International Journal of Bilingual Education and Bilingualism*, 1–8. https://doi.org/10.1080/13670050.2016.1238866

Wang, D. (2019). Translanguaging in Chinese foreign language classrooms: Students and teachers' attitudes and practices. *International Journal of Bilingual Education and Bilingualism, 22*(2), 138–149. https://doi.org/10.1080/13670050.2016.1231773

Wang, D., & Kirkpatrick, A. (2012). Code choice in the Chinese as a foreign language classroom. *Multilingual Education, 2*(1), 3. https://doi.org/10.1186/2191-5059-2-3

Wilson, S. (2021). To mix or not to mix: Parental attitudes towards translanguaging and language management choices. *International Journal of Bilingualism, 25*(1), 58–76. https://doi.org/10.1177/1367006920909902

6

A Critical Approach to Reading Assessment of Multilingual Language Learners

A Case Study of Translanguaging Pedagogies, Teacher Knowledge, and Know-How

Laura Ascenzi-Moreno and Jennifer Conte

> Am I able to adjust an assessment for my multilingual students?
> I know my multilingual students know more than what the assessment shows!

These two thoughts are illustrative of the narratives that exist for many elementary teachers of multilingual language learners (or students who use two or more languages in their daily lives and who are referred to here as MLLs). Many teachers are caught between the overarching framework that assessments should be administered "as is," and the knowledge that assessments should be adapted to better capture the skills and abilities of

MLLs (Ascenzi-Moreno, 2018). Moreover, as reading curricula become more scripted and AI (artificial intelligence) assistants "take responsibility" for assessment tasks, teachers are, more than ever, removed from classroom-based reading assessment processes (Klein, 2023). The message that assessments are for teachers to administer and not to tweak, regardless if they are attuned to students' profiles, is widespread. Yet, assessments have been created with monolingual students in mind, and require accommodation, so that teachers can truly ascertain what MLLs know and can do as readers (Ascenzi-Moreno, 2018; Schissel, 2020; Shohamy, 2011).

The goals of this chapter are twofold. It provides teachers of MLLs with the rationale of why assessments of MLLs may need adjustment to accurately capture what students know. The chapter also provides readers with practical know-how on what adapting reading assessments for MLLs can look like.

Why Should Educators Consider Assessing Multilingual Learners Differently?

Teachers may ask themselves, "Do I really need to adapt assessments for my MLLs? Why are the assessments I am asked to administer not adequately suited to evaluate MLLs' skills and abilities?" It is well known that the assessment of MLLs differs from the assessment of monolingual students (Abedi, 2011; Mahoney, 2017). When the language of the assessment is different from the language practices that students are familiar with and use, then both bias and inaccuracy can seep into the assessment process and yield results which do not truly describe the abilities of MLLs (Abedi, 2011; Mahoney, 2017; Valdés et al., 1994). At the core of this argument is that monolingual assessments are inadequate to capture the knowledge and skills of MLLs.

What Is Inaccuracy in Assessment?

First, let us tackle what we mean by *inaccuracy* in assessment. The message that assessments are neutral and valid regardless of the population they are implemented with is pervasive, so it may be easy to take for granted that assessment tools have limitations. These limitations are the result of being designed based on certain perspectives that are considered, "the norm." Take, for example, a math test that has questions about how many ounces are in a cup and how many pints are in a gallon. To many Americans who have spent their entire lives in the United States, this question seems straightforward.

However, the United States is one of the only countries in the world that continues to use the imperial system (cups, quarts, etc.). Therefore, a student from almost any other place in the world who answers questions about the imperial system of measurement would be disadvantaged because they understand measurement through the metric system (mL, L, etc.).

While the assessment described above is designed to gauge students' understanding of measurement, because this test item is intertwined with a cultural experience, the item *confounds* an understanding of measurement with the experience of learning about measurement through a particular system (Abedi, 2011). Educators viewing the results of this test item for students would not be able to identify the reason the student got the item incorrect—was it because the student does not understand general principles of measurement, or is it because they do not understand the imperial system of measurement?

This type of inaccuracy can show up in assessment in a variety of ways. For MLLs, test items can be inaccurate when language or when "normative" cultural contexts are proxies for knowledge (Shohamy, 2011; Solano-Flores, 2011). A student may possess the knowledge, but simply not have the language proficiency or the cultural knowledge to demonstrate that knowledge (Abedi, 2011). What is crucial for educators to consider is that, at times, test items may seem neutral, but may favor certain experiences, cultural knowledge, and language histories.

What Is Bias in Assessment?

When many or most of the assessment items and processes do not consider the multilingualism of students, then an assessment and its administration process can be *biased* (Mahoney, 2017). Take, for example, an assessment of reading that includes nonsense words. If a student reads the nonsense word, "zub," as, "zŭb," (with the u sounding like, uh), then it would conform to a pronunciation that is typical of English. However, if the student pronounces the nonsense word, "zub," as, "zyub," using their knowledge of the letter "u" sound in Spanish (in English referred to as the long u), then most teachers may believe that the student is reading the nonsense word inaccurately, when in fact, he or she is using knowledge of letter sounds in a different named language (Razfar & Rumenapp, 2014). When reading is equated solely with proficiency in English, then an assessment can be biased against MLLs.

Monolingual assessments do not accurately capture the skills and abilities of MLLs because MLLs always bring their dynamic and full linguistic repertoires to any literacy event, including assessment. When MLLs are expected to only provide answers in one bounded language, then MLLs are disadvantaged because they may not be able to fully express what they know (Schissel, 2020; Shohamy, 2011). Teachers may wonder why accommodations do not do the job of leveling the playing field for students. Most accommodations, such as extended time and monolingual translations, will not reduce the amount of error and bias because they do not eliminate bias and inaccuracy *for MLLs*. Namely, they do not shift the assessment to recognize and capture MLLs' linguistic assets and cultural resources.

For example, extended time, a common accommodation, presumes that MLLs will need more time to complete an assessment. For some students, this may be true. But if students need to draw upon their knowledge across languages, then extended time has no effect on their performance. Translations may be perceived as an adequate accommodation because they are linguistic in nature. However, since translations are also monoglossic in nature (or faithful to one named language), then they also do not account for MLLs' dynamic language practices. While translations may help students understand a given word, translations do not resolve the issue that cultural concepts may still be either unfamiliar or misunderstood. For example, students may know the words ounces or pints, but still have no idea as to what these refer in real life. Since most assessments suppose monolingualism as normative and do not incorporate opportunities for students to demonstrate what they know *through* their dynamic linguistic repertoires, an approach that centers MLLs' repertoires is necessary. Next, we turn to translanguaging as a critical lens to adapt assessment, so that elementary teachers can assess MLLs' reading abilities with precision and nuance.

What's Translanguaging?

First, it is important to define what translanguaging is to understand the heart of this chapter: "What is a translanguaging approach to assessment?" When first popularized, translanguaging theory was most commonly conceived as a theory that described the unitary linguistic repertoire of MLLs. Translanguaging theory signaled a significant departure from the idea that people act upon multiple, separate language systems to one in which people draw upon features from a unitary repertoire that is dynamic and emerging and thus focuses on "doing language" (García & Li Wei, 2014; Otheguy et al., 2015, 2019). While initially translanguaging referred primarily to MLLs' unitary linguistic repertoire, in this chapter we believe that an *expanded* definition of translanguaging is more suited to describe the type of translanguaging practices that are needed for assessment (Vogel et al., 2018). An expanded definition of translanguaging is based on the idea that people "do language," and includes not only language as traditionally conceived but also multimodal forms of language and people's sociocultural contexts.

Taking an expanded translanguaging lens on assessment allows researchers to consider the ways that assessment practices are situated within school contexts and how ideologies circulate around assessment (Ascenzi-Moreno & Seltzer, 2021). In addition, translanguaging theory can also be employed to analyze the ways in which assessment accurately captures the abilities of MLLs when enacted in classrooms (Ascenzi-Moreno, 2018; Grapin, 2023; Schissel, 2020).

Why a Translanguaging Approach to Classroom-Based Reading Assessments?

There has been an emergence of scholars who have taken up a translanguaging approach to assessments to accurately assess MLLs' reading (Ascenzi-Moreno, 2018; Bauer et al., 2018; Briceño & Klein, 2018; Kabuto, 2017, 2018). These promising approaches emphasize that without students' multilingual engagement, they are not actually demonstrating what they know as readers. This is because even classroom-based reading assessments are most often framed through the lens of monolingualism. For instance, when teachers ask students who have read a book in one language to respond in the same language as the book, their responses may not capture the entirety of their understanding of the text. For example, if a student reads a text in Spanish, but is able to respond in English about their comprehension, it is clear that the student understands the text, but may either not be able to or wish to communicate about it in the same language as the text.

A multipronged approach is necessary to combat a monolingual perspective on assessments. First, teachers should acquire assessment knowledge which enables them not simply to administer classroom assessments, but also to evaluate ways that assessments capture or do not capture MLLs' skills and abilities. Understanding the effect of assessments rooted in monolingualism on MLLs is a critical first step for teachers. Knowing that assessments which confound language proficiency with reading disadvantage MLLs is crucial because they position these students as either deficient or low-performing, which disenfranchises students from receiving the instruction that they need. Second, teachers can become familiar with approaches that shift assessments toward multilingual approaches.

Responsive adaptations are one way that the assessment process can be changed to account for students' multilingualism. Responsive adaptations are ways of tweaking assessments in favor of multilingualism through a translanguaging lens. Although covered at length elsewhere (Ascenzi-Moreno, 2018; Ascenzi-Moreno & Seltzer, 2021) responsive adaptations can take place before reading, during the assessment, and after the student reads the text. For example, at the end of text, teachers usually will ask comprehension questions of students to demonstrate their understanding. Typically, teachers ask questions given to them through assessment material. One way that teachers can bring a multilingual perspective to this aspect of the assessment is to change the language of the questions so that they are easier to understand and so they may be presented in a MLL's home language. In addition, students should be given a choice on how to respond and which language practices to incorporate into their response to teachers, including multilingual and multimodal expressions. It is important to remember that each MLL is unique and therefore should not be treated as a homogeneous group. Every MLL student has both strengths and weaknesses and thus needs different levels and types of scaffolding and support. It is critical that teachers have a nuanced understanding of their students so that they can encourage them to use their home language resources within assessment, when needed, to demonstrate their full abilities.

A Final Word on the Current Landscape for Reading Assessments

Reading is a complex task that involves decoding, comprehension, and fluency among other skills. It is important that whatever tools teachers use to assess students as readers are robust and provide a multifaceted view of reading. In other words, teachers need to know about students' prior knowledge, schema, decoding, fluency, and comprehension at multiple levels.

It is also important that teachers understand students as readers on an affective level—are students motivated? Are they engaged as they read? What kind of topics, themes, and genres are they drawn to? Lastly, even if educators assess the components of reading individually, it does not mean that students can orchestrate these different components together to read and comprehend. For this reason, teachers must be mindful that their assessments match the different purposes of reading and provide a holistic understanding of students as readers. For MLLs, this means that the classroom-based reading assessments that teachers administer must consider students' multilingualism and prior experiences. Therefore, regardless of the types of reading assessments teachers implement in their contexts, we hope that this chapter provides teachers with the analytical skills to analyze, question, and propose ways in which MLLs' resources and strengths can contribute to teachers' understanding of multilingual readers.

Who We Are

The co-authors of this chapter, Laura Ascenzi-Moreno and Jennifer Conte, have a history of working together on reading assessments with MLLs. Laura is a bilingual teacher educator who worked as a bilingual teacher in public schools in a large urban area. As a bilingual researcher and teacher educator, Laura studies translanguaging within literacy spaces. Jennifer is an ENL (English as a New Language) teacher in a dual-language bilingual public school in a suburban area. As an ENL teacher, Jennifer works in partnership with teachers to support students' literacy development. Both have experience working with Spanish-speaking MLLs. Laura's main research focus is translanguaging and literacy, while Jennifer is an expert practitioner with MLLs and reading. In the next section of the chapter, we focus on the concepts introduced at the beginning of this chapter from the perspective of a teacher.

From a Teachers' Perspective

In the dual-language, bilingual school where Jennifer works, all the kindergarten through fifth-grade students there are immersed and learn in an English Zone and a Spanish Zone classroom every other day. Some students' first language is Spanish, and some students' first language is English. As an ENL teacher, she works side by side with English Zone teachers during literacy. Jennifer believes that teaching students how to use all their language skills to best learn, express themselves, and show what they know, as well as encouraging them to do so, results in the best and most accurate instructional environment.

In what follows, Jennifer will describe her approach to reading assessment, first by analyzing the nature of the assessments she uses and then by describing how she administers these with MLLs. In this section, we take a conversational tone, hoping that readers will feel that they are in dialogue with us.

Knowing the Student: Before the Assessment

The first thing to consider when using most reading assessments with MLLs is that these assessments were created to be used with monolingual native speakers of English. Therefore, when teachers use these assessments with MLLs, they need to supplement the data they gather through additional probing during the session that is not included in the test manual directions. This additional information will allow teachers to get more complete and accurate data regarding students' reading ability and to understand the behaviors that demonstrate their abilities in both languages working together to help them as bilingual readers.

Gathering background information about students can help teachers learn more about their students holistically. Some of this information can be found on the school's intake forms. However, speaking with family members may be the most direct way to gather this information. If a teacher is not able to speak in the family's home language, community members are often willing and able to help translate. Knowing the language skills a student possesses in their first language and their schooling history provides the teacher with vital information. For example, if a student already knows how to read in one language, these abilities can be leveraged to read in another. The student will need to learn the "code" (letters and sound/symbol relationships) of the new language. On the other hand, students with inconsistent or minimal previous schooling will need more support during the transition to a new school. This information also supports teachers to understand their students' entire journey as a person and how this may impact their reading development.

The following are some categories of information teachers might want to learn about their students when they are first learning about their MLL students:

1. When did the student arrive in the United States (if they were not born in the United States)?

2. Did the student have prior education in their country of origin, or in the United States in a different school?

3. If so, what was the educational experience of the student? Did he/she attend school full or half days? Was attendance regular? What was taught academically in school? What was the language or languages of instruction?

4. Did prior schools express concerns about the student's learning? If yes, what were the concerns? Were special classes or help given to the student?

5. What traditions of literacy exist in the student's home?

6. Did the student experience a traumatic journey to the United States? If yes, it will be important to connect with building clinicians to best

plan for and understand how to support a student joining the school community with trauma.

These questions provide teachers with a general understanding of students' backgrounds, which can inform literacy instruction and assessment. Questions about readers' identities, like their interests and reading histories, can be asked at subsequent times. Now Jennifer will walk readers through the assessment process with one student.

Meet Veronica

I would like to introduce you to Veronica (pseudonym). She is a fourth-grade student who was born in Guatemala and enrolled in our school in first grade. Veronica has an older brother in fifth grade, and they are being raised by their mom. Veronica's family lives with extended family and is very involved in their church community. In their free time, some members of the family go fishing and to local parks. In New York State, every Spring students in public schools in grades K-12 who are identified as English Language Learners (ELLs) take a standardized test called the NYSESLAT (New York State English as a Second Language Achievement Test). This test measures students' progress in language acquisition across four areas: listening, speaking, reading, and writing.[1] Scores on this test determine the level of services students receive in a bilingual or stand-alone English as a New Language (ENL) program the following academic year.

Veronica's NYSESLAT level is Transitioning (Intermediate). At the beginning of the year, she completed the Teachers College (TC) Reading and Writing Project Assessment for Independent Reading Levels and scored at a Level G for instruction. By June, she progressed to an independent Level K. While both levels are below what is expected in fourth grade, they demonstrate Veronica's growth.

Now I will walk you through what she did during the assessments, and what I was thinking and documenting as I listened to her read. As an ENL teacher, my description of working with Veronica is focused on my listening to her read and speak about a book in English, but I insert some ways in which translanguaging can inform my knowledge of Veronica.

---

[1] The language proficiency levels a student taking the NYSESLAT can score are: Entering (Beginner), Emerging (Low Intermediate), Transitioning (Intermediate), Expanding (Advanced), and Commanding (Proficient).

Beginning the Assessment

The book Veronica read was *Bumpy the Frog* by Steven Beers. This book is about a young frog named Bumpy who gets hurt a lot while playing and trying to do the things his friends do. The teacher script prompts the teacher to give a brief introduction to the book that tells the name of the main character, Bumpy, and that he has many accidents and gets hurt a lot. During this section, I show students the name of the character in the text and have them repeat it orally. This additional move gives the students a preview of what the name of the character visually looks like on the page and allows them to practice pronouncing it before reading the text, like a little warm-up. The script also prompts the teacher to ask the students what they already know about the story based on what the teacher told them during the introduction. Veronica responded with one word, "Bumpy," but when probed with an unscripted follow-up question, "What will happen?" she responded, "He'll have many accidents." This follow-up question allowed Veronica to demonstrate what she recalled from the introduction, including the key word, *accidents*. Now she was focused on Bumpy having accidents and ready to read.

Reading the Text

While Veronica started reading, I drew scooped lines underneath the words and phrases she read together in the text. This practice became a record of her phrasing that I could look back at later when thinking about her reading fluency (see Figure 6.1). When she first started reading, Veronica read word by word, but after the first sentence, she read in longer phrases, although sometimes still word by word, and attended to punctuation. The first time she made a *language approximation* was when she read the word "scrape" as "scrap." When Veronica read this word, she was using her knowledge of Spanish to make meaning of the reading. This is called a language approximation. I noted in the margin that she will need instruction on vowel-consonant-e (VCe) words. Then she read "heal" as "health." I made a mental note to go back to those words later with Veronica to gather more information. As she continued reading, she made another VCe approximation with the word "outside," reading it with a short i instead of a long i. I noted this in the margin.

Notice on this page how I am scooping under the words as Veronica reads. This informs me about her fluency. I also write her word approximations above the actual word in the text. Later I go back and look for patterns and note them, like she needs to learn the VCe rule (vowel-consonant-e) and how to read the different sounds the "-ed" ending makes in words in the past tense in English.

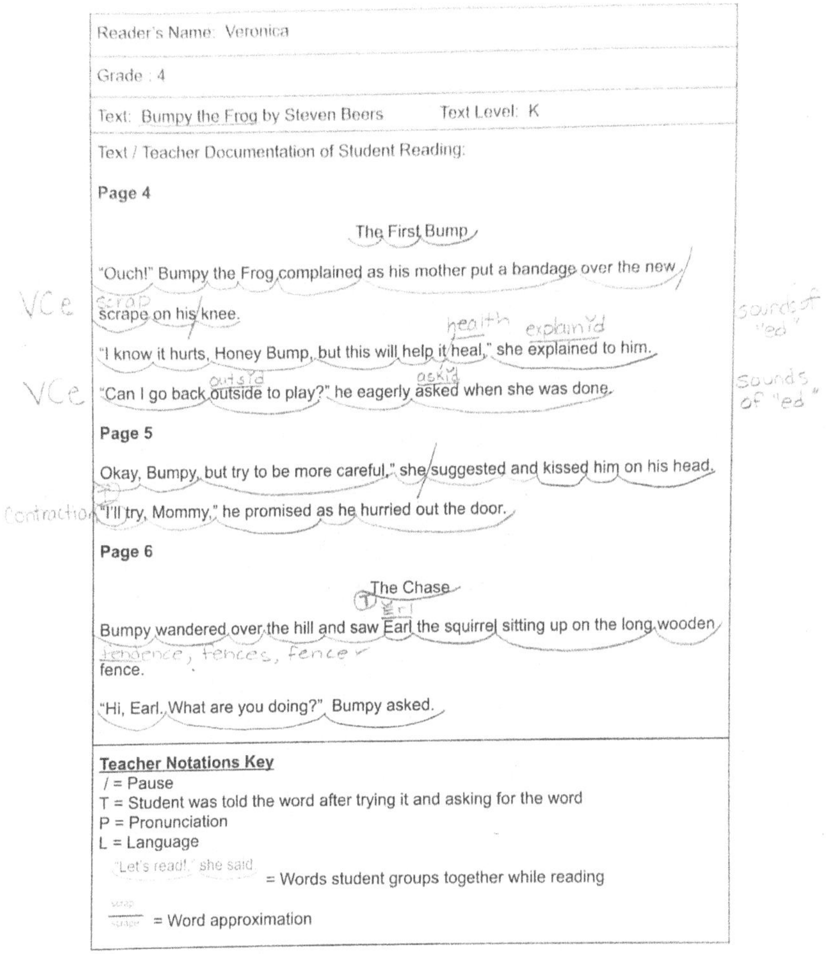

A CRITICAL APPROACH TO READING ASSESSMENT

> **Reader's Name:** Veronica
>
> **Grade:** 4
>
> **Text:** Bumpy the Frog by Steven Beers   **Text Level:** K
>
> Text / Teacher Documentation of Student Reading:
>
> **Page 4**
>
> ### The First Bump
>
> "Ouch!" Bumpy the Frog complained as his mother put a bandage over the new scrape on his knee. [VCe, scrap, sounds of "ed"]
>
> "I know it hurts, Honey Bump, but this will help it heal," she explained to him. [health, explain'd]
>
> "Can I go back outside to play?" he eagerly asked when she was done. [VCe, outsid, askd, sounds of "ed"]
>
> **Page 5**
>
> "Okay, Bumpy, but try to be more careful," she suggested and kissed him on his head.
>
> "I'll try, Mommy," he promised as he hurried out the door. [Contraction]
>
> **Page 6**
>
> ### The Chase
>
> Bumpy wandered over the hill and saw Earl the squirrel sitting up on the long, wooden fence. [fendence, fences, fencer]
>
> "Hi, Earl. What are you doing?" Bumpy asked.
>
> **Teacher Notations Key**
> / = Pause
> T = Student was told the word after trying it and asking for the word
> P = Pronunciation
> L = Language
> ⌢⌢⌢ "Let's read!" she said = Words student groups together while reading
> scrap/scrape = Word approximation

FIGURE 6.1 *Jennifer's documentation of Veronica's reading.*

Additionally, I notice where she is pausing to try to figure out words, and later, orally trying out different ways to read a word she sees that she is unsure how to read, like with the word "fence."

The Importance of Noticing Language Approximations

Another approximation pattern I noticed was that Veronica did not know how to read words that ended with the letter combination "ed." For example, she read "explained" as "explainid" and "asked" as "askid." I noted in the margins this future learning point, which is a common struggle for students learning English. The next struggle Veronica had was when she got to the word "I'll." The contraction threw her off. She did not know what to do with the apostrophe and asked me for help. I told her the word and made another note to myself that Veronica needed to learn about contractions. The final approximation Veronica made was when she came to the word "Earl," a character's name. She started to read it with a short e sound but knew that was not right and asked for help. I told her the name and moved on. I did not count this as an error since it was a name that did not follow the "rules" of phonics that she knew. To count this against her would be penalizing her for her developing language skills. She struggled once more before reading the one hundred words that I was documenting for the running record. When she came to the word "fence," she read it several different ways before self-correcting and reading the word correctly. It went like this: " . . . sitting up on the long wooden fendence / fences / fence."

Non-Scripted Moves

At this point in the assessment, I made another move the instruction manual does not instruct teachers to do. I went back to a few words that Veronica had approximated. I wanted to know if she could read them in isolation and if she knew what the words meant. The first word was "scrape." She still read it as "scrap," which confirmed she needed instruction for VCe words. When I asked her if she knew what it meant, she responded, "He hurts. When we fall, we get a scratch." Veronica's response told me that she knew what the word meant but did not know that exact word in English yet. I reinforced that she was correct about what the word meant and praised her. I told her, "This is how you read this word. Scrape. You say it now."

Next, I wanted to know more about the word "heal," which she had read as "health," which is visually similar. I asked her what she thought it meant, and she responded, "When you're hurt, and you put a Band-Aid and it doesn't hurt anymore." I told her, "Yes! That's what it means. The word is 'heal.' Now you try it."

Drilling down to investigate Veronica's approximations helped me learn that although she might not have the phonological skills in English to decode these words, she did have the vocabulary knowledge to know what they meant. This is important because it shows that the decoding approximations did not interfere with her being able to understand the story.

Lastly, I wanted to talk with Veronica about the contraction, "I'll." I explained that words that have this punctuation mark called an apostrophe are called contractions. Contractions are made from two words that are put together into one word in a shorter form. There is a whole group of words in English that are contractions. Today you saw "I'll." Then I jotted "I'll = I will, they'll = they will, I've = I have" on the paper. I told her, "The apostrophe goes in the place where the letters were taken away." Veronica repeated them orally after me. I gave her a paper to collect more contractions and bring them to me so we could talk about them.

A Translanguaging Approach to Retelling and Empowering Students to Demonstrate Understanding

Typically, once the reading portion assessment is completed, the student retells the story. The last part of a reading assessment involves teachers asking students several comprehension questions. To fully capture students' complete understanding of what they read, teachers invite students to respond in English, Spanish, or a combination of both, depending on which language best allows them to demonstrate what they understood. Students may use the book if they choose. My goal in this part of the assessment is to evaluate whether the student can accurately tell me the most important parts of the text in order, including important details, regardless of what language they use to do this. Veronica chose to retell the story entirely in English. However, I have had some students retell it completely in Spanish and others who retell it in a combination of Spanish and English.

Teachers might be wondering, if I do not understand or speak Spanish, how can I make this move? Fortunately, this can be accomplished in several ways. First, a Spanish-speaking staff member could join you for this part of the assessment and scribe the student's response in Spanish. After the student leaves, the staff member could translate the script into English so the teacher can evaluate it. Second, the teacher can record the student's response on a cell phone or computer. Later, it can be replayed and translated into English by a staff member. Third, the teacher can use a tool like Google Translate with the microphone enabled. Students can record their retelling while the app simultaneously translates it.

Scoring the Assessment

To determine a student's reading level, teachers are typically asked to score the student's accuracy, fluency, retelling, and response to comprehension questions. Regardless of the assessment that you are using, teachers are looking for students to read three-to-four-word phrases with good expression to be considered fluent at that level. For comprehension, if a student can accurately retell most or all of the text and answer most of the questions accurately, then they are considered to have a good comprehension of that text.

Veronica was able to give a sequential, accurate retelling of the story. She used language approximations in her grammar during the retelling, which I scribed as further data to inform my instruction with her (García et al., 2017). She was able to answer the comprehension questions accurately. I did not try a more difficult text with her since her reading fluency was not consistent in longer phrases yet.

Planning Next Steps

After I finished assessing Veronica, I needed to use the information I gathered to plan my next instructional steps for her (see Figure 6.2). First, I identified the language approximations that I noticed during her reading. These were: vowel-consonant-e words (VCe), the three sounds the letters "ed" make at the end of regular verbs in the past tense, and contractions, all indicative of her acquisition of English language conventions while learning to read. I decided to focus first on VCe word patterns. In Veronica's case, these skills were focused on acquiring language-specific knowledge related to English. To prepare for this work, I looked at my assessments and wrote down the names of other students who needed to learn to read VCe words so that I could pull them into a group with Veronica. Next, I looked for a text at Veronica's instructional level that contained a variety of VCe words to contextualize this skill. I made a list of these words so that I could highlight them with her on a word list before reading the text. Next, I prepared a list of single syllables (to start) VCe words that I could use to teach this phonics pattern. I grouped them by vowel sound and added picture clues next to each word so that my MLLs were not just learning a phonics pattern, but also growing their vocabulary. I also prepared my explanation of the rule to teach that skill and made extra copies of the list for students to use for practice and repeated reading.

While the skills that I identified were required to support Veronica's English language development alongside reading, they were done in context to support her reading overall. In addition, since Veronica demonstrated literal comprehension in the assessment, my next step in that area was to support her more nuanced understanding of text. Inferring character traits and finding evidence in the text to support or prove them is a skill from which she would benefit.

A CRITICAL APPROACH TO READING ASSESSMENT

Teacher move	Why is it Important?	How does this move support teachers' understanding of MLLs?
Before reading, show students the name of the main character(s) in the text and have them repeat it orally.	Precise reading of character names should not penalize MLLs.	Can the student hold onto this name or a close approximation to it?
Ask unscripted follow up questions when students' responses to scripted questions leaves you wondering if they understand.	MLLs might need additional prompts or follow up questions that are more specific to allow them to demonstrate their understanding.	When asked a more focused question, can the student show understanding of the key idea? Can the student hold on to key vocabulary?
Draw scooped lines underneath the words and phrases students read together in the text. This becomes a record of how they phrase text that can be looked back at later to analyze reading fluency.	Proficient readers understand how to group words and phrases together for understanding.	When students can read fluently, they are able to decode the text at a high enough level that they are not focused on the word level, but at the phrase and sentence level. This is a goal. If a student is not able to do this, explicit fluency instruction with a text that has fewer decoding challenges should be done during future instruction.
After completing a running record, go back to word approximations the student made or words they asked the teacher to tell them and gather more information.	Can the student read the word in isolation, but misread it while reading a larger text? Does the student know what the word means, but is not able to say it correctly in English yet? Is there a pattern related to words the student asked the teacher to tell them?	The student misread the word in context and in isolation. The student knows the meaning of the word, but needs additional explicit instruction in phonological awareness, which includes phonics, phonemic awareness, and sound production.
Identify next steps - What skills does the student need to learn next?	Teaching students responsively based on needs will help them progress in their ability to decode and/or comprehend texts of increasing difficulty.	When a student's performance reveals a need, that informs the teacher what to focus on next in a small group lesson or an individual conference with that student.

FIGURE 6.2 *Analyzing Jennifer's teaching moves and implications for future instruction.*

Implications

Our first goal in this chapter has been to provide teachers of MLLs with the rationale of why assessments of MLLs may need adjustment to accurately capture how MLLs read. MLLs are at a disadvantage when they are assessed with tools designed for monolingual students without any adjustments.

Multilingual and cultural frames are necessary to counteract this bias. Second, we gave a detailed account of Veronica's reading assessment and explained moves and adaptations that can be made for our MLLs. We hope that readers now have practical knowledge for application across contexts to allow students' entire linguistic repertoires to shine through. For all teachers who work with MLLs regardless of age, it is critical that they consider the ways in which assessments capture the abilities of students. In doing so, we send a message of valuing multilingualism and striving to remove barriers in assessments that were not designed for MLLs, making it possible for them to show their true abilities.

References

Abedi, J. (2011). Assessing English language learners: Critical issues. In M. del Rosario Baster, E. Trumbull, & G. Solano-Flores (Eds.), *Cultural validity in assessment: Addressing linguistic and cultural diversity* (pp. 49–71). Routledge.

Ascenzi-Moreno, L. (2018). Translanguaging and responsive adaptations: Emergent bilingual readers through the lens of possibility. *Language Arts, 95*(6), 355–369.

Ascenzi-Moreno, L., & Seltzer, K. (2021). Always at the bottom: Ideologies in the assessment of emergent bilinguals. *Journal of Literacy Research, 53*(4), 468–490.

Bauer, E. B., Colomer, S. E., & Wiemelt, J. (2018). Biliteracy of African American and Latinx kindergarten students in a dual-language program: Understanding students' translanguaging practices across informal assessments. *Urban Education, 55*(3), 331–361. https://doi.org/10.1177/0042085918789743

Briceño, A., & Klein, A. (2018). A second lens of formative reading assessment with multilingual students. *The Reading Teacher, 72*(5), 611–621. https://doi.org/10.1002/trtr.1774

García, O., Johnson, S. I., & Seltzer, K. (2017). *The translanguaging classroom: Leveraging student bilingualism for learning.* Caslon Publishing.

García, O., & Li, W. (2014). *Translanguaging: Language, bilingualism, and education.* Palgrave Macmillan.

Grapin, S. (2023). The complex terrain of equity for multilingual learners in K–12 education. *Educational Researcher.* https://doi.org/10.3102/0013189X231215345

Kabuto, B. (2017). A socio-psycholinguistic perspective on biliteracy: The use of miscue analysis as a culturally relevant assessment tool. *Reading Horizons, 56*(1), 25–43.

Kabuto, B. (2018). Becoming a bilingual reader as linguistic and identity enactments. *Talking Points, 29*(2), 11–18.

Klein, A. (2023, March 15). Measuring reading comprehension is hard. Can AI and adaptive tools help? *Education Week.*

Mahoney, K. (2017). *The assessment of emergent bilinguals: Supporting English language learners.* Multilingual Matters.

Otheguy, R., García, O., & Reid, W. (2015). Clarifying translanguaging and deconstructing named languages: A perspective from linguistics. *Applied Linguistics Review, 6*(3), 281–307. https://doi.org/10.1515/applirev-2015-0014

Otheguy, R., García, O., & Reid, W. (2019). A translanguaging view of the linguistic system of bilinguals. *Applied Linguistics Review, 10*(4), 625–651. https://doi.org/10.1515/applirev-2018-0020

Razfar, A., & Rumenapp, J. (2014). *Applying linguistics in the classroom: A sociocultural approach.* Routledge.

Schissel, J. L. (2020). Moving beyond deficit positioning of linguistically diverse test takers: Bi/multilingualism and the essence of validity. In S. Mirhosseini & P. I. De Costa (Eds.), *Sociopolitics of English language testing* (pp. 91–108). Bloomsbury Publishing.

Shohamy, E. (2011). Assessing multilingual competencies: Adopting construct valid assessment policies. *Modern Language Journal, 95*(3), 418–442. https://doi.org/10.1111/j.1540 4781.2011.01210.x

Solano-Flores, G. (2011). Cultural validity in assessment: Addressing linguistic and cultural diversity. In M. del Rosario Bastera, E. Trumbull, & G. Solano-Flores (Eds.), *Cultural validity in assessment: Addressing linguistic and cultural diversity* (pp. 49–71). Routledge.

Valdés, G., & Figueroa, R. A. (1994). *Bilingualism and testing: A special case of bias.* Ablex Publishing.

Vogel, S., Ascenzi-Moreno, L., & García, O. (2018). An expanded view of translanguaging: Leveraging the dynamic interactions between a young multilingual writer and machine translation software. In S. Ollerman & J. Choi (Eds.), *Plurilingualism in learning and teaching: Complexities across Contexts* (pp-89-106). Routledge.

PART III

Translanguaging Practices in Secondary Classrooms

7

Translanguaging as a Decolonial Option

Exploring Curricular Cracks for Critical Literacy in EFL Classrooms

Phelippe Oliveira and Sunny Man Chu Lau

Introduction

In this chapter, we describe three vignettes based on a unit on globalization in an English as a foreign language (EFL) classroom in a secondary school in Brazil. We came together through our shared interest in exploring the pedagogical contributions of translanguaging (TL) scholarship to English language teaching and learning and critical literacy education. The vignettes were taken from an action research study by Phelippe (Author 1) conducted in his Grade twelve EFL classes (see Oliveira, 2023) with the aims to promote critical literacy and language learning. The study was a response to the challenges posed by the political crisis in Brazil and the government's adoption of a neoliberal and ultraconservative agenda that dehumanizes education and eliminates the critical component of language and literacy education (Dardot & Laval,

2019). As a fellow critical literacy advocate and translanguaging researcher, Sunny (Author 2) has offered an insightful perspective into Phelippe's study, particularly its pedagogical implications for second/foreign language teaching that support critical literacy. As an English second language (ESL) learner and later a teacher in British colonial Hong Kong, she experienced and fully understood how enduring monolingual ideologies and English hegemony impacted the education system. These experiences have fueled her commitment to decolonizing ESL/EFL and supporting minoritized students' education as she became a language teacher educator in Canada.

In this chapter, we illustrate how teachers can explore *curricular openings or cracks* in commonly used ESL/EFL textbooks and harness these opportunities to engage students in critical inquiries. By tapping into the pedagogical contributions of TL, students' transdisciplinary and outside-school knowledge can be spotlighted and mobilized for greater critical discussions, repositioning them as agents of their learning process instead of passive consumers of other people's discourses and beliefs. Further, the teaching and learning activities described here also aim to demonstrate how critical literacy practices can be designed and implemented despite curricular constraints and thus present themselves as a decolonial option in language education in the Global South.[1]

The School Context

In order to understand the broader context of the study, we elaborate on a few important political events that took place in Brazil in the past decade. In 2011, Dilma Rousseff, a former Minister of Energy and then Chief of Staff for the government led by the Workers' Party, became the first woman voted in as president of the country. However, far-right party politicians soon attempted to undercut her authority during her two terms of presidency by linking her office with corruption scandals. The Vice President Michel Temer, a politician from the centrist party Brazilian Democratic Movement, participated in a coup orchestrated by Eduardo Cunha, former president of the Chamber of Deputies, which had Rousseff impeached in April 2016, and removed from office later that year. These series of political upheavals led to the election of far-right candidate Jair Bolsonaro, who became president from 2019 to 2022. Bolsonaro's term in office was deeply marked by his advancement of a neoliberal and ultraconservative agenda, including issuing recurring

---

[1] Global South refers to a "geopolitical space of marginalization" (Makalela & Silva, 2023, p. 1) which is created and perpetuated by the different domains of coloniality (i.e., coloniality of power, being and knowing) (Quijano, 2005).

misogynistic, LGBTQ-phobic, and hateful public statements, as well as his deliberate neglect and denial of the outbreak of coronavirus in Brazil, which caused the deaths of more than 700,000 people. In addition, Bolsonaro's presidency deeply impaired the educational policies. Among other initiatives, his government endorsed movements, such as *Novo Ensino Médio* (New High School) and the *Escola Sem Partido* (Apolitical School), in the name of "depoliticizing" education while implementing the ultraconservative and neoliberal agendas at both private and public schools. Inevitably, such initiatives produced very palpable consequences in schools, and language education was equally impacted. Prior to the New High School project, for instance, Spanish could be offered as a foreign language in public schools, which represented an important step toward political integration between Brazil, the only Portuguese-speaking country in Latin America, and its neighbors. However, the New High School Project made English the only mandatory foreign language at the secondary level. The "National Textbook Program," an important educational policy from the previous federal government that had researchers/professors from public universities to write textbooks for use in public schools, was also under attack during Bolsonaro's regime. Those textbooks were criticized by the more radical supporters of the government as "ideologically biased," "leftist," and "excessively progressive" as they included Brazil-specific social issues, such as promoting affirmative action for Black and Indigenous peoples, questioning patriarchal values and traditional role of women in society, among others. Eventually, these textbooks were discontinued for use in some public schools. The government's constant strikes on critical education reverberated with a wider global movement of anti-intellectualism and skepticism toward science, which gained momentum with Trump's election in 2016 and had become even more evident during the Covid-19 pandemic.

Given these complex, precarious sociopolitical circumstances, Phelippe was eager to explore how he could engage his EFL learners in critical literacy education through a TL lens that helped bring students' cultural identities and broader sociolinguistic repertoires in learning English. Using action research methodology (McNiff & Whitehead, 2010), the study was carried out with his EFL classes based on this research question: In what ways does TL scholarship support a more critical and decolonial teaching and learning of English in a Brazilian public school as a counterpoint to the neoliberal and ultraconservative project put in place? This chapter aims to share practical insights from the study through three teaching vignettes, with the hope to inspire other teachers facing sociopolitical challenges alike to explore the critical and decolonial potential of the translingual turn in EFL teaching.

Translanguaging and Its Decolonial Potential

TL scholarship has gained special attention in Applied Linguistics in the past fifteen years. Originally conceived as a scaffolding strategy to support bilinguals' development (Williams, 1994), TL has been conceptualized also as "multiple discursive practices in which bilinguals engage in order to make sense of their bilingual worlds" (García, 2009). Premised on dynamic understandings of language, TL pedagogy leverages students' multilingual and multicultural repertoires to make meaning and to learn language and content (García et al., 2017). It also underpins an educational movement that invites teachers and students to adopt a more critical view of the sociolinguistic differences between their languages and English. It aims to bring forth language practices and knowledge that are traditionally considered illegitimate or nonstandard into heavily surveilled and regulated learning spaces in order to challenge established knowledge, language boundaries, and hierarchies (Li Wei & García, 2022) which are steeped in colonial histories of nation building and governance (Flores & Rosa, 2023).

In Brazilian EFL classrooms, there has been a long, sustained tradition of adopting a monolingual orientation toward English language teaching and learning, treating language as a monolithic set of grammar rules endorsed by an idealized native speaker (Canagarajah, 2013). Monolingual standards have informed mechanical approaches to language teaching, focusing on language norms and, quite often, serving as a vessel for cultural imperialism. Considering the growing diversity in Brazilian classrooms, such as Spanish-speaking immigrant learners from neighboring countries (e.g., Venezuela, Bolivia, Paraguay, etc.), the adoption of monolingual approaches could be harmful as it prevents students from drawing on the entirety of their complex semiotic and sociolinguistic repertoires when participating in language classes. The adoption of a TL pedagogy in that sense is to disrupt the colonial patterns inherent in monolingual teaching methods and offer a "resistance practice" to the oppressive discourses and abyssal differences prevalent in the Brazilian EFL context (Rocha & Megale, 2023). Windle and Possas (2023) stress also how TL contributes to the development of an affective bond between EFL teachers and learners and creates opportunities for critical language awareness, which is essential in destabilizing hegemonic discourses around the English language and power asymmetries established by colonial relations.

Mignolo (2018) defines *colonialism* as the historical situation in which Europeans invaded territories and dominated other peoples. It originated from a set of discourses, including Western Christian humanism and its correlated notions of science, economic progress, and democracy, which were used to justify domination and cognitive superiority. Along with capitalism and patriarchy, it has imposed global patterns of power relations along racial/ethnic lines. White, Eurocentric culture, knowledge, and languages (Quijano, 2000) are deemed essential for progress and humanization. Despite the end of political colonization, such discourses have been naturalized by most people in former colonies, including teachers, educators, parents, and learners alike. Its lingering effects are what the term *coloniality* refers to, a hidden and more obscure side of modernity, which continues to operationalize colonial difference through "culture, labor, intersubjective relations, and knowledge production" (Maldonado-Torres, 2010, p. 97) until today.

Decoloniality, in turn, emerges as a response to the pair modernity/coloniality, and denotes alternative ways of thinking, knowing, being, and doing. Even though decolonial studies have only gained more academic momentum over the past twenty years with the modernity/coloniality project led by scholars such as Aníbal Quijano (a Peruvian sociologist), Ramón Grosfoguel (a Puerto Rican sociologist), Walter Mignolo (an Argentinian anthropologist), Catherine Walsh (an American scholar in Latin-American cultural studies), Arturo Escobar (a Colombian-American anthropologist), and Maldonado-Torres (a Puerto Rican philosopher), among others, the decolonial struggle originated long ago with the concrete acts of resistance of the colonized, especially Indigenous peoples.

In more practical terms, the first step toward decoloniality is what Thiong'o (1986), a Kenyan novelist and critic, calls "decolonizing the mind," a process in which colonial alienation is interrupted, and critical attention is drawn to how "the choice of language and the use to which language is put [a]s central to a people's definition of themselves in relation to their natural and social environment, indeed in relation to the entire universe" (1986, p. 4). In this sense, the TL scholarship offers a powerful framework to disrupt colonial discourses around language not dissimilar to the critical literacy (CL) tradition. As Sunny (Lau, 2019) explains,

> both CL and translanguaging espouse an inherent critique of what language and literacy mean and what counts as legitimate knowledge and knowledge-construction processes, with an aim to enact border-crossing and boundary-breaking language and literacy practices to valorize marginalized identities and cultures (p. 77).

From a pedagogical standpoint, both frameworks allow for the disruption of deficit discourses surrounding language learners and might reposition them as more active, creative agents in the learning process who engage in multiple literacies and language practices to construct knowledge, meaning, and their own identities. In the Brazilian context, more specifically, Makalela and Silva (2023) highlight TL's decolonial potential as a theoretical and pedagogical practice that sits at the center of decoloniality and transformation for the Global South's ways of acting, knowing, and being. Based on this, the pedagogical implications of TL scholarship could potentially create opportunities for teachers and students to identify dominant and hegemonic discourses established by modernity/coloniality, which are still frequently endorsed in EFL classrooms. Additionally, the very notion of homogeneous linguistic competence as the desired outcome can be actively challenged when students engage in critical literacy work. The pedagogical dimension of TL, in this way, can be understood as a potentially *decolonial option*, which, as Mignolo (2018) argues, offers concrete opportunities to delink language and knowledge from the colonial matrix of power.

Exploring Curricular Cracks for Critical Literacy through TL

The unit plan presented in this chapter was based on a research study with four groups of Grade 12 students (107 in total) in a federal public school in Juiz de Fora, a mid-sized city located in a state in the southeast of Brazil. Secondary education comprises Grades 10 to 12, and English language teaching is only mandatory after Grade 6. Each thirty-student group had two EFL periods each week totaling eighty minutes. In-person classes had to pivot to online meetings due to the Covid-19 pandemic for one and a half years, including the period in which the following activities took place.

Interested in understanding his predominantly Portuguese-speaking students' experience with EFL learning as well as their self-perception of language proficiency, Phelippe conducted an online survey with them. The results showed that over half of them reported only having formal English instruction after joining this high school. One-third considered themselves EFL beginners, around half were intermediate, and about one-fifth were of advanced level. These numbers reflected a wide range of abilities, which is common in Brazilian public schools serving students with a mix of socioeconomic backgrounds. Eager to engage students in critical literacy work, Phelippe explored what Duboc (2012) calls *curricular cracks* in his EFL classes, that is, emerging opportunities in the teaching practice which result *in* and *from* the friction arising from different ways of knowing and being. When planning lessons, teachers might anticipate curricular cracks and, in turn, prepare additional resources or adjustments to the curriculum in actual lesson delivery. Equally important, if not more so, are the opportunities that emerge from spontaneous responses from students or unanticipated student-student exchanges. Nevertheless, it still remains in the hands of the teacher to seize those opportunities and harness their potential as curricular cracks in engaging students in more critical and complex learning.

Phelippe engaged in action research cycles of planning, implementing, evaluating, and reflecting to develop, adapt, and seek alternative critical teaching and learning options which were based on a textbook unit from *Access 3* (Barros, 2016). The class worked on a unit titled *It's a Small World*, which revolved around the theme of globalization. Curricular cracks were explored to deepen students' understanding of its dominant discourses and associated asymmetric power relations. Throughout the unit, students examined critically, from a decolonial perspective, the role played by the English language in constructing or maintaining current globalization patterns. Illustrating the unit and lesson steps in this chapter, our goal is to inspire fellow teachers to find and explore curricular cracks through the TL lens. In the next three subsections, we discuss three main curricular cracks harnessed in the unit and how TL contributed to students' critical literacy engagement.

Provoking Friction

Most textbook's warm-up activities tend to be rather impersonal and formulaic, focusing mainly on the mechanical and cultural dimensions of literacy, while critical literacy activities are usually presented at the end of units and are frequently skipped by teachers for several reasons: time constraints, lack of engagement on the students' part, or political reasons, as discussed earlier in the chapter. The unit *It's a Small World* starts with a section called *Engaging* which features an image of a ball of yarn with the globe on it and three thought-provoking questions:

1. *What analogy is made in this image?*
2. *What comes to your mind when you hear the word globalization?*
3. *Do you think people around the world will ever be unified into a single society? (Barros, 2016, p. 49)*

Such questions were designed to briefly elicit oral production and introduce the topic of globalization. To engage students in deeper discussion, Phelippe looked for potential curricular cracks for critical literacy and translingual practices. He hence designed an additional activity to expand their thinking, particularly about Question 2.

He asked students to type in words associated with globalization on an online interactive platform (*mentimeter.com*) using their mobile phones. As students entered their contributions, a word cloud was generated in real time, with words changing in sizes as more entries of the same terms were inputted. Students could see these instantaneous changes on the screen.

Figures 7.1–7.4 (below) show the word clouds created by Phelippe's four EFL classes.

After the word cloud was finalized, Phelippe posed further questions to invite the class to share and elaborate on their thinking behind their contributions:

i. What word(s) is/are more or less frequently used? Who contributed those words? What did you have in mind when you wrote them?

ii. Did you notice words that seemed to represent very different values/opinions associated with globalization? What do they suggest?

Before this project, Phelippe would not have allowed his students to use other languages in the EFL classes but, this time around, aiming to decolonize his teaching practice, he welcomed his students' responses in other languages. We see an entry in Portuguese, that is, *ONU* (Figure 7.2), the acronym of *the United Nations—Organização das Nações Unidas*. Another example is the Japanese kanji expression 人類補完計画 (Figure 7.4), which refers to the *Human Instrumentality Project* (n.d.), a notion developed in a Japanese anime called *Neon Genesis Evangelion*. The anime describes a hypothetical future when all human beings are interconnected as part of one single consciousness. This shows the contributor's awareness of a positive configuration of globalization with its potential of bringing people together. Another entry from the same class was the term *telefone sem fio* (Figure 7.4), meaning "wireless telephone" in Portuguese. The term can also refer to the children's game called "Chinese whispers" in which a message is whispered from ear to ear and often gets distorted as it is passed around. The student who had submitted this entry explained its double entendre as both a signal to underscore technological advancements and also as a metaphor to highlight possible misunderstandings in global-scale communication and transmission of information.

The flexible use of linguistic resources had also prompted students to engage in the discussion in a more critical manner, shifting their focus from language learning per se to more meaningful debates and thinking. One entry was the name *Milton Santos* (Figure 7.1), who was a Black Brazilian geographer and scholar pioneering work in critical geography. Santos (2001) discusses globalization from three overlapping views: (1) the *fable* of the "inevitable" movement for economic prosperity, scientific growth, and cultural interconnectedness; (2) the *perversity* which produces and sustains socially unjust colonial relations; (3) and the *possibility* of a new discourse of globalization that favors *sociodiversity* and puts technological advancements to the actual use of people (Santos, 2001, p. 21). During the class discussions, the students who had submitted the entry of Milton Santos explained that they had learned about Santos' work in their Geography classes and were familiar with his proposed reconfiguration of globalization. Taken together,

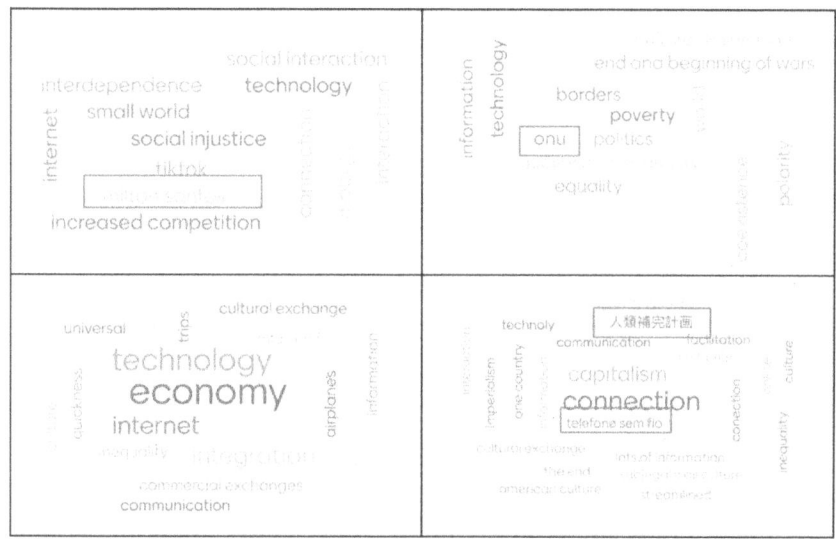

FIGURES 7.1–7.4 *Word clouds from students in Groups 1–4 (from top left to bottom right).*

these translingual practices allowed the teacher not only a glimpse into the students' rich semiotic and linguistic repertoires but also a more accurate understanding of their wide critical repertoire and transdisciplinary and outside-school knowledge. These dynamic language practices also pointed to emerging curricular cracks in which Phelippe later engaged his students for further inquiry into the issues of globalization. An English-only approach would have filtered out these rich learning opportunities for students to demonstrate their prior knowledge in a multimodal manner.

Regarding the last question about different opinions on globalization, students pointed out, on the one hand, the prominent use of words such as *technology* (Figures 7.1–7.4), *connection* (Figures 7.1 and 7.4), *internet* (Figures 7.1 and 7.3), *mobility* (Figure 7.1), *information* (Figures 7.2, 7.3, and 7.4), *cultural exchange* (Figure 7.3), *integration* (Figure 7.3), and *no frontiers* (Figure 7.4). On the other hand, some less frequent entries such as *social injustice* (Figure 7.1), *poverty* (Figures 7.2 and 7.3), *subjugate all culture* (Figure 7.4), *imperialism* (Figure 7.4), and *inequality* (Figures 7.2–7.4) helped Phelippe draw students' attention to divergent views. Students were able to distinguish opinions that largely reflected a more mainstream positive discourse about globalization from those that were more critical about its potentially harmful aspects. As the word cloud was shown on the screen in real time, students' instantaneous entries could have inspired or challenged their own thinking, allowing them to see the discordant ideas and reflect on those differences. Their diverging views also signaled a potential crack for further critical dialogue about the real impact of globalization on their lives, which informed subsequent activities. When looking for curricular cracks, these are crucial moments in which to engage students for more meaningful discussion/reflection.

Cracking the Textbook Open

After the *Engaging* section, the textbook featured a *Reading Practice* segment. In this unit, the focal texts are four email exchanges between Michael Elliott, a journalist and an executive for *Time Magazine*, the *Economist*, and *Newsweek*, and Colin Hines, political advisor, co-founder of the Green New Deal Group, and former Greenpeace member. The messages are grouped under the title *Globalization: Villain or Hero*, which suggests two strongly polarized positions on the topic. Before reading the emails, there is a skimming and scanning task for students to determine their text types and content and to focus on the pre-underlined words and phrases to guess the main purpose of the messages. There is also a vocabulary exercise for students to match the definitions to the five words/expressions from the context—*income, job loss, living standards, trade, and wealth*. The final task is a multiple-choice comprehension with four questions on each author's main and supporting ideas. Once again, these activities focused mainly on the more mechanical aspects of language learning and superficial comprehension of basic information. The After-Reading sections (i.e., Language Practice I and II) in this unit mainly focus on formal aspects of the language (i.e., the use of phrasal verbs and passive voice). There is no real engagement with the main texts, and students are not encouraged to formulate their opinions about globalization or position themselves in relation to it.

Despite these more mechanical and surface-level language exercises, some students took on a more critical stance in reading the article and opined that the two authors' arguments were very much dichotomized and, in some instances, hyperbolic yet reductive. They pointed out, for example, that Elliott described globalization in an overly idealized way, highlighting quotes such as "*it reinforces human freedom,*" "*increases income everywhere,*" "*gives us the chance to establish 'one world',*" and so on. Hines, on the other hand, criticized how unilateral Elliott's viewpoints were, mentioning job losses and disparities in wealth accumulation as drawbacks of globalization. Though Hines's position seemed more sensible to how people in less privileged countries experienced the phenomenon, the discussion was in general broad and at times hypothetical, which was questioned by the students. To harness students' emerging critical resources, Phelippe designed an additional activity on the class's *Moodle* course (Figure 7.5) as an extension.

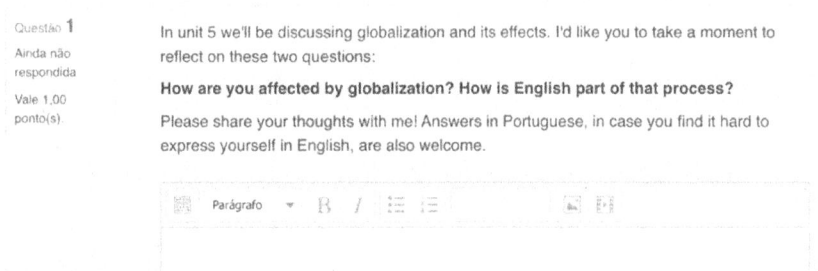

FIGURE 7.5 *Moodle activity.*

The task prompted students to think about the impact of globalization on their own lives, particularly reflecting on how English language learning constituted part of this process, as a way to disrupt language and knowledge colonialities. The teacher also welcomed student responses in Portuguese to create opportunities for their engagement with their embodied knowledges and experiences as learners from the Global South.

Close to a hundred responses to the assignment were posted, showing students' active participation in this task. Students' contributions once again illustrated their critical thinking with much affective intensity toward the topic of globalization. Their responses showed mixed and different perspectives on globalization. Below are two examples of answers which conveyed more positive views of globalization and mainstream discourses on the role played by the English language in the process (all underlined responses are our added emphasis):

> *English has become* an important part of this process, *because it* facilitates communication *between people who do not speak the same language.* (Flora[2])
>
> *A nice perspective about globalization is that you will always see quotes on T-shirts written in English no matter where you are from or you will notice that everyone knows at least one English song. I would say then that* English is the language of globalization, *because you will always see something related to it.* (Marcia)

Other students shared a more skeptical attitude toward the impact of globalization, such as cultural homogenization, social injustice, and inequality, views that were expanded from some of the previous entries from the word clouds:

---

[2]All student names are pseudonyms.

> On another hand, sometimes the globalization can erase the national culture, making people wanna know more about other countries and forgetting about their own history *(Ronald)*
> It's obvious that everyone is affected by it, but people suffer different consequences because of it. This is one of the reasons why I believe globalization is also about inequality. *(Martha)*

Some students also submitted their responses in Portuguese (around 30 percent), some of which also reflected a more ambivalent attitude toward globalization. For example, Layla wrote about " . . . *a desvalorização da cultura local, e nos impulsiona a pensar que os filmes, músicas e tradições próprias do Brasil são inferiores*" highlighting how globalization might devalue local culture, leading people to think that Brazil's own traditions are inferior.

The added Moodle discussion task opened up a space for students to read against the texts, question dominant discourses, and reposition themselves as protagonists of the narratives on globalization to think through its impact on their lives. An example of how dynamic language practice favors a more active and critical attitude toward the discussion can be found in Yara's bilingual entry shown below:

> English: "*[T]his occurs through* American, *Japanese and Chinese products that I consume, for example*"
> Portuguese: " . . . *e isso ocorre por meio de produtos* estadunidenses, *japoneses e chineses que eu consumo, por exemplo, e quando percebo a importância de aprender outros idiomas além do português*"

In the Portuguese version, she used the adjective "estadunidense" (i.e., people who are born in the United States specifically) to stand in for the adjective "American" used in the English version. In Portuguese, the word "American" can refer to anyone born in the Americas. By choosing to use "estadunidense" instead of "americano" or "norte-americano," which are both more general adjectives to refer to people born on the American continent, the student showed her awareness of the meaning nuances in what these adjectives signal. This was particularly pertinent in light of the current attempts in Brazil to decolonize the Brazilian Portuguese by replacing words (such as "americano" or "norte-americano") which discursively perpetuate colonial asymmetries or differences. Interestingly, after Yara's English version and before her Portuguese answer, she added a commentary in parentheses: "*(para o caso de eu não ter, em inglês, me expressado como eu gostaria),*" meaning "*in case I haven't expressed myself in English the way I wanted to.*" This demonstrates Yara's metalinguistic awareness as well as her agentic attempt to negotiate for the teacher's focus on the nuanced meaning she would like to express, rather than on the English grammatical mistakes she could have made (which often prevents teachers from fully appreciating the content of students' responses). Ronald, who had submitted his response in English critiquing that globalization could possibly lead to cultural erasure, did something similar and included the following remark for the teacher at the end of his answer:

> *If I did some english mistake, pretend that I didn't pls :) (Ronald)*

Similar to Yara, Ronald reminded his teacher to focus on his ideas and not on potential grammatical mistakes, underscoring the first and foremost importance of meaning-making in English language learning. Besides, he ended his answer with the *emoticon* :) which added an affective layer to his message, indicating a friendly attitude toward the teacher. This example shows that students also draw on multiple semiotic resources that have been incorporated into their repertoires, especially those frequently used on the internet, when interacting with their teachers and peers online, and exemplifies their complex languaging practices. From a pedagogical stance, this is an important dimension of translanguaging to be discussed and considered in EFL teaching/learning since most students are frequently in contact with English on the internet and other online resources. Another example is from Laura's translingual response:

> *Em contrapartida e consoante o livro "Por uma outra globalização", de Milton Santos, é preciso interpretar esse fenômeno de maneira crítica e pontuar seus aspectos negativos: os países menos desenvolvidos, como o Brasil, retornam à condição de colônia, exportando matéria-prima; ocorre a obsolescência programada (as mercadorias são programadas para durarem pouco) e, por fim, a padronização cultural, em que somos meras cópias do "american way of life" e perdemos nossas raízes culturais. Em suma, só teremos o "Brasil brasileiro" e uma aldeia global se houver uma fusão de culturas, sem desprezar nenhuma manifestação. (Laura)*

Laura, citing Milton Santos, argued for a more critical interrogation of globalization, drawing attention to its "negative aspects" that reproduce colonial conditions, including the "exportation of raw materials, planned obsolescence and cultural homogenization" produced by capitalism. She stressed that people copying the "american way of life" [from the original text] could only lead to the loss of their cultural roots. She strongly argues for the existence of a *"Brazilian Brazil",* which would only be possible when different cultures in a globalized world are respected without the subjugation of any cultural manifestation. The concept of *"Brasil brasileiro"* has been made famous by a samba song, *Aquarela do Brasil*, which pays tribute to Brazilian traditions by acknowledging key elements of the national identity. This concept was also used in her answer to juxtapose the notion of "american way of life" with the word *"american"* in small letters. Her intentional use of lowercase could be due to an overgeneralization of capitalization rules for adjectives in Portuguese. However, considering the fact that Laura was a very strong and careful writer in both English and Portuguese, the choice of the word "american" in small letters could be interpreted as a decolonial gesture as it symbolically diminishes the importance of North American culture. In sum, these students' responses in two languages demonstrated complex translingual practices that went beyond mere translation to articulate a more critical and decolonial stance, which also reflected their strong affective investment in the task.

Expanding the Cracks to Assessment

Teachers who are willing to explore critical literacy in their classes might dismiss the crucial role of assessment in the process, believing that assessment is only useful to evaluate students' linguistic progress. Creating a space for students to take stock of their development of critical literacy and disposition could inform more continuous engagement in critical literacy work. To this end, Phelippe adopted a portfolio assessment to better capture students' development in language learning and critical literacy throughout the year. Students included their work from the unit on globalization, for example, their written productions on the Moodle task (Figure 7.5) and other units, some textbook exercises, and a final self-assessment questionnaire through which students could critically reflect on their linguistic development and their attitude toward language learning. Additionally, students could also revisit some critical discussion points, reconsider their views after the classes, and reflect on their own development in critical literacy. To do this, Phelippe invited students to reflect on this question: *Do you think English is the most important language to learn? And why (not)?*

Even though most students' responses to the question were affirmative, the reasons they provided reflected a critical, balanced, and even decolonial stance. Interestingly, several students who had previously aligned themselves with more mainstream discourses on the importance of English learning submitted their answers with critical nuances:

> *Because* all languages are important, *be one of the most spoken language it doesn't mean that is the most important to learn (Mary)*
> *Although English is a fundamental language these days, I think* the most important language to learn is our mother tongue *(Lydia)*

Several answers also showed a critical attitude toward the global status of English. For example, Eddie had previously agreed with it in his Moodle answer, saying, "English is fundamental *in the today's world for information and communication*." In the year-end self-assessment questionnaire, he addressed the issue from a more complex and balanced viewpoint:

> *It's difficult to discuss this. Globally, [English] may be the most important language (no wonder it's called the universal language); but the fact we live in a country that speaks portuguese makes* English a secundary priority (although portuguese is natural to learn how to speak, it's not that easy to master how to write correcly, thinking in college entrance exams). There is a *lot of factors to consider before difining one language as the most important to learn (Eddie)*

Similarly, June, who had described English as an "essential tool" for communication in her Moodle activity, adopted a more critical tone in her final self-assessment questionnaire:

> *I don't think it would be fair to say it is* the most important, *because that depends on the contexts [. . .], people from* different nationalities *use it to* speak their minds, *that's why I think it's* crucial

These examples illustrate that, at the end of the year, not only did the students adopt a more balanced, non-dichotomous position toward globalization, but they also came to question the superior status of English. It is important to mention that students' development of critical disposition was not limited to the activities or the assessment tasks in this unit about globalization. For the rest of the year, Phelippe continued to engage students in critical conversations about various social issues that emerged through other textbook cracks. This is to say that critical literacy work is never a one-off attempt, but rather built on a continuous basis, with assessment as an integral part of the instruction *for* and *as* learning of not only the linguistic aspects but also students' critical disposition.

Concluding Thoughts

In this chapter, we illustrated how an EFL teacher, by adopting a TL lens, managed to explore curricular cracks or openings in the adopted textbook which was designed mainly for discrete language learning and surface-level comprehension. We bring this chapter to an end by offering a few pedagogical insights in exploring TL for critical literacy and its decolonial potential in language education in the Global South.

Our first suggestion is that teachers, even in the face of curricular constraints, can use the textbook to their advantage by searching for cracks (or creating their own!) where critical literacy can be made possible. In sociopolitical contexts where curricular material that promotes critical literacy is not always available, teachers can engage students in challenging social assumptions and dominant discourses endorsed in textbooks and the curriculum itself. EFL materials, especially those produced by the dominant publishing companies in the Global North, seldom reflect the social issues or struggles experienced by teachers and learners from the Global South. Teachers should also attend to students' reactions in class to look for curricular cracks for more critical engagement.

Our second suggestion is related to TL's decolonial potential. English language education in Brazil, as in other parts of the Global South, is usually marked by a deficit-oriented discourse. English "competence" is often measured against a standard set by the inner circle, reflecting a dehumanizing act of positioning local students as deficient and non-competent (Flores & Rosa, 2023). TL pedagogy can offer an alternative to promote more equal/ socially just teaching/learning opportunities in which students can display fully their transdisciplinary and out-of-school knowledge for in-depth learning and critical discussions of important issues that matter to their lives (García, Johnson, & Seltzer, 2017; Lau, 2019). The unit described in this chapter shows that students' translingual practices not only offered a glimpse into their semiotic and linguistic repertoires but also enriched the teacher's understanding of their wide critical repertoire, which helped signal emerging curricular cracks that could be harnessed for further inquiry into the issues of globalization.

This brings us to our third suggestion about the need to engage students on both the cognitive and affective levels. When teachers strictly adhere to surface-level comprehension questions based on the textbook, they often simply get their students to go through the motions of completing their reading comprehension tasks, rather than drawing on their embodied experiences and knowledges to make meaning for themselves. It is students' affective investment in the learning process that supports more critical participation in language classes as it creates opportunities for them to reshape the colonial narratives that were told in their English language learning process in the Global South. Spinoza (2009) argues that *affection* is a notion that straddles the relationship between the mind and the body without positioning them as opposites, but as parts of a continuum, instead. For the Dutch philosopher, the greater our power to be affected, the greater our power to act, which means that an increased awareness of how we are affected by the world around us results in an increased power to act upon it (Spinoza, 2009).

And lastly, we encourage teachers to expand their views of assessment as a critical literacy resource. Alternative assessment methods such as portfolios or self-assessment tasks provide important spaces for students to reflect on and take stock of new or emerging viewpoints or perspectives they encounter during the learning process. Assessment that harnesses students' translingual practices can constitute a powerful resource in itself to help teachers identify assumed beliefs and values held by students, as well as their prior knowledge and critical repertoires, which often are not accessed if tasks are to be accomplished in English only. Having a fuller picture of students' prior knowledge and critical repertoires is key to exploring possible curricular cracks for further critical literacy engagement. Inviting students to reflect on not only their language development but also their relationship with English so as to set their individual goals for learning is a more humanizing act, disrupting the reification of "homogeneous language competence" (Flores & Rosa, 2023) that traditional assessment upholds.

To conclude, this chapter showcases how the pedagogical dimension of TL can support critical literacy work, repositioning students as knowledge makers instead of passive consumers of other people's language and discourses, or distant spectators of Eurocentric conversations. Mobilizing students' prior linguistic knowledge and experiences as equally valid and important in their own knowledge-making process constitutes a powerful decolonial option in English language teaching/learning.

References

Barros, L. O. (2016). *Access 3*. Moderna.

Canagarajah, A. S. (2013). *Translingual practice: Global englishes and cosmopolitan relations*. Routledge.

Dardot, P. and Laval, C. (2019). A anatomia do novo neoliberalismo. Revista Instituto Humanitas Unisinos. https://www.ihu.unisinos.br/categorias/591075-anatomia-do-novo-neoliberalismo-artigo-de-pierre-dardot-e-christian-laval

Duboc, A. P. M. (2012). Atitude curricular: letramentos críticos nas brechas da formação de professores de inglês. Doctoral dissertation, Repositório da Produção USP, Universidade de São Paulo.

Flores, N., & Rosa, J. (2023). Undoing competence: Coloniality, homogeneity, and the overrepresentation of whiteness in applied linguistics. *Language Learning*, *73*(S2), 268–295. https://doi.org/10.1111/lang.12528

García, O. (2009). Education, multilingualism and translanguaging in the 21st century. In T. Skutnabb-Kangas, R. Phillipson, S. P. Mohanty, & M. Panda (Eds.), *Social Justice through Multilingual Education* (pp. 140–158). Multilingual Matters.

García, O., Johnson, S. I., & Seltzer, K. (2017). *The translanguaging classroom: Leveraging student bilingualism for learning*. Calson.

Human Instrumentality Project. n.d. Academic dictionaries and encyclopedias.

Lau, S. M. C. (2019). Convergences and alignments between translanguaging and critical literacies work in bilingual classrooms. *Journal of Translation and Translanguaging in Multilingual Contexts, 5*(1 [Special Issue] Positive synergies: Translanguaging and critical theories in education), 67–85. https://doi.org/10.1075/ttmc.00025.lau

Makalela, L., & da Silva, K. A. (2023). Translanguaging and language policy in the global south: Introductory notes. *Revista Brasileira de Linguística Aplicada, 23*(1), 1–4.

Maldonado-Torres, N. (2010). On the coloniality of being: Contributions to the development of a concept. In W. Mignolo & A. Escobar (Eds.), *Globalization and the decolonial option* (pp. 94–124). Routledge.

McNiff, J., & Whitehead, J. (2010). *You and your action research project* (3rd ed.). Routledge.

Mignolo, W. D. (2018). The decolonial option. In W. D. Mignolo & C. E. Walsh (Eds.), *On decoloniality: Concepts, analytics, praxis* (pp. 105-244). Duke University Press. https://doi.org/10.1215/9780822371779

Oliveira, P. (2023). *Translanguaging pelas brechas: práticas de letramento crítico-decolonial em tempos pandêmicos*. Doctoral dissertation, Universidade Federal de Minas Gerais. http://hdl.handle.net/1843/62860

Quijano, A. (2000). Coloniality of power and Eurocentrism in Latin America. *International Sociology, 15*(2), 215–232. https://doi.org/10.1177/0268580900015002005

Quijano, A. (2005). Colonialidade do saber: eurocentrismo e ciências sociais. Perspectivas latino-americanas. In *CLACSO, Consejo Latinoamericano de Ciencias Sociales* (pp. 117–142).

Rocha, C. H., & Megale, A. H. (2023). Translanguaging and boundary crossings: About conceptual understandings and possibilities towards decolonizingcontemporary language education. *DELTA: Documentação de estudos em linguística teórica e aplicada, 39*(2), 1–32. https://doi.org/10.1590/1678-460X202339251788

Santos, M. (2001). *Por uma outra globalização: do pensamento único à consciência universal*. Record.

Spinoza, Benedictus de. (2009). *Ethics*. The Floating Press.

Thiong'o, Ngũgĩ wa. (1986). *Decolonising the mind: The politics of language in African literature*. James Currey.

Wei, L., & García, O. (2022). Not a first language but one repertoire: Translanguaging as a decolonizing project. *RELC Journal, 53*(2), 313–324. https://doi.org/10.1177/00336882221092841

Williams, C. (1994). Arfarniad o ddulliau dysgu ac addysgu yng nghyd-destun addysg uwchradd ddwyieithog. Doctoral dissertation, University of Wales.

Windle, J., & Possas, L. A. (2023). Translanguaging and educational inequality in the global south: Stance-taking amongst Brazilian teachers of English. *Applied Linguistics, 44*(2), 312–327.

8

Translanguaging in Action with Youth from Refugee Backgrounds

Saskia Van Viegen

Introduction

Students in K-12 education who have experienced forced migration and displacement face formidable challenges of resettlement in host countries, underscoring the strong need for schools to identify the most effective educational programs and social supports. These efforts are critical, given that the number of global refugees, including internally displaced persons and asylum seekers, is higher than at any other point in human history. In 2022, this number was 35.3 million[1] people, with a disproportionate share (76 percent) hosted in low- and middle-income countries (UNHCR, 2024). Whereas most displaced persons remain within their region of origin, staying close to home in neighboring countries, third country resettlement provides a secure and stable solution for refugees to integrate and participate in the economic and social life of host countries. These circumstances have significant implications for education, requiring culturally responsive educational programming and instruction to support displaced people, children and youth among them.

---

[1] This number refers to refugees; however, the number of forcibly displaced people worldwide was estimated at 108.4 million, including refugees, asylum seekers, internally displaced people, and other people in need of international protection (UNHCR, 2024).

Addressing these considerations, this chapter explores how translanguaging (TL) pedagogies, envisioned as not only an instructional approach but a philosophical orientation and mindset (Li, 2024; Li & García, 2022), can engage refugee students' experiences and identities in a transformative way, for an affirming and healing approach to language and literacy instruction. TL pedagogy stands in contrast to the narrow, monolingual orientations of English language teaching, upholding students' multilingual capabilities as resources for learning rather than language practices in need of remediation when compared to dominant Standard English norms (García et al., 2021). Importantly, TL pedagogy involves teachers' flexibility and willingness to embrace students' TL practice, a belief in the value of students' TL for language and content learning, and efforts to develop creative and strategic learning opportunities that engage TL (García et al., 2017; Tian & Shepard-Carey, 2020).

The chapter dives into recent literature from language and educational researchers across diverse global contexts to identify how TL pedagogies have been used to support refugee students' transition and educational integration (e.g., Mary et al., 2021; Symons & Ponzio, 2019; Stolk et al., 2025; Van Viegen, 2020 among others). Across these contexts, similar benefits have been identified; namely, opportunities to valorize students' linguistic capabilities, expand language learning and sense-making, promote inclusion, and support participation in a new social and educational context. At the same time, this research highlights challenges that persist in supporting students' socioemotional needs, countering the effects of trauma, poverty, and low literacy, and developing students' learning strategies, agency, and resilience in school (Dryden-Peterson, 2016; Stewart et al., 2019). The chapter then provides concrete examples of translanguaging-in-action, illustrated with examples from classroom practice gathered from an empirical study with youth and their teachers in one Canadian secondary school. These examples illustrate TL as dynamic flows across languages and modes to support learning and communication, cultivating students' self-expression, sense of belonging, and agency.

Recent Key Studies

Research in education has drawn attention to the needs of students from refugee backgrounds, emphasizing the sociopolitical realities of global conflict (Dryden-Peterson, 2016; Miller et al., 2018; Nelson & Appleby, 2015; Patel et al., 2018; Stewart, 2019). While experiences of displacement are unique and diverse, circumstances can include fleeing dangerous and violent environments, often separating or losing family members, and living with financial hardship and inadequate access to the necessities of life including food, shelter, and healthcare. Upon arrival in host countries, families may subsequently navigate temporary housing, altered family circumstances, precarious migration status, and limited employment. Importantly, studies in this domain underscore the significant effects of forced displacement and migration, including socioemotional stressors and experiences of trauma. This research uniformly identifies schools as critical supports for students and their families in resettlement and educational integration, for learning new knowledge and skills, and developing relationships and community ties that refugees need to flourish (Patel et al., 2017).

A common theme among these studies is the critique of English language and literacy instruction that is envisioned as uniform for all English learners (ELs), often without accounting for the varied access to formal education that encounters students from refugee backgrounds. Students may be referred to as low- or late-to-literacy learners, or students with limited or interrupted formal education (SLIFE), for whom literacy in their home language or English may be an obstacle to curriculum learning. Although schools may provide English as a Second or Additional Language (ESL/EAL) and literacy learning programs, refugee students can benefit from support that extends beyond language. Schools and school districts may not be prepared to meet the full range of students' needs, and teachers may struggle to identify appropriate instructional strategies. Studies conducted over the last ten years have highlighted pedagogies that counter traditional monolingual English approaches to language and literacy teaching, engaging students' full linguistic repertoire as a resource for learning and creating inclusive and equitable spaces for students from refugee backgrounds to thrive.

Shapiro and colleagues (Shapiro, 2018) showcase empirical work with students from refugee backgrounds, illuminating the complexity of students' identities and experiences and diverse approaches to meet their needs. Chapters illustrate how students themselves transcend deficit orientations to the refugee label, thereby informing pedagogies that focus on student agency, funds of knowledge, and resistance. The volume underscores that literacy cannot be taught or learned outside of the social context of the refugee experience. Researchers explored pedagogies to engage students' knowledge and build on their linguistic strengths (e.g., Nakutnyy & Sterzuk, 2018; Omerbašić, 2018; Park & Valdez, 2018). They also connected language and literacy teaching with trauma-informed pedagogies. For instance, Montero (2018) created digital stories with a group of Rohingya youth in Canada to promote their self-healing and resilience, and Papa (2018) used youth participatory action research and photovoice methods with Cambodian and Guatemalan students in the United States to make their perspectives visible to schools and policymakers. Taken together, the studies showcased in this volume illustrate the importance of connecting teaching and learning with students' socioemotional needs, translocal knowledge, and lived experiences.

Working with high school students who are resettled refugees in New York, US, Bartlett et al. (2017) describe practices that supported students' academic success, social and cultural integration, and well-being. They emphasize the importance of centering the refugee experience and cultivating a relational model of trust between teachers, students, and their peers. They argue that understandings of educational integration should incorporate a dynamic sensibility, rejecting static notions of language and culture that function as limiting ideologies. They synthesize recommendations for teaching from a stance that engages students' home language as a resource for learning English and invites students to learn using all of the languages in their repertoire, particularly with peers (Mendenhall & Bartlett, 2018).

In the Canadian context, Stewart et al. (2019) focus on Syrian children and youth refugees in two cities, identifying three layers of trauma that students face, first in their country of origin, then during transition, and finally upon resettlement. They found that students felt powerless and isolated in school, often struggling with feeling behind their same-age peers in curriculum learning. At the same time, teachers reported feeling unprepared to address these circumstances, including understanding students' backgrounds, mental health needs, and knowledge of trauma-sensitive pedagogies. They conclude that English language comprises a significant barrier to student learning, captured by one student's reflection, "I do not exist without the language" (p. 63). In response, the researchers developed a peer-to-peer program between English-speaking Canadian students and Arabic-speaking Syrian students to engage in shared social and extracurricular activities. The program resulted in language learning for both groups of students, across Arabic and English.

Koyama and Kasper (2022) conducted a case study in Arizona, US, with resettled refugee students and families from Congo, Somalia, and Nepal, examining pedagogical practices and students' social and academic identities. They found that teachers and students resisted English-only policies and practices, engaging in translanguaging using their shared semiotic resources and affective sensibilities to make meaning and participate in learning tasks. Students engaged in what the researchers called "transworlding," that is, making sense of their knowing and learning across the spaces and cultures that they had previously inhabited yet remained connected to and continued to access, creating a "multi-vocal learning environment." As one teacher reflected, "They still speak Somali and sometimes other languages. I'm not supposed to let them, but I know it helps them progress and I don't believe in English only." (p. 7). Teachers' translanguaging pedagogy supported students to bring their full, complex identities to the classroom, wherein English monolingual pedagogy was not only impractical, but impossible.

Connecting translanguaging pedagogy with arts-based practice, Burton and Van Viegen (2021) used multilingual spoken word poetry to support students to voice their perspectives and memories, not only to be heard by others but also to support their own process of negotiating the changing realities of resettlement and integration. Spoken word activities evoked an affective response, combining poetry, voice, movement, and gesture for students' creative self-expression and performance of their multilingual lives and identities. They concluded that creative and expressive approaches to translanguaging pedagogy comprise critical educational practices to support youth in their transition to the Canadian learning context.

As these studies illustrate, education of students from refugee backgrounds requires a pedagogical approach that not only engages students' language practices as a resource for language and literacy learning, but also encompasses inclusion and social justice aims (Lau & Van Viegen, 2020; Paulsrud et al., 2021).

Translanguaging-in-action

Illustrating translanguaging-in-action with students recently resettled as part of Canada's rapid response to the global refugee crisis, I share insights from a case study (Duff, 2018) conducted at one school with students and their teachers as part of a larger, multi-site study (2017–21) across secondary schools in two Canadian provinces. The broad purpose of the study was to determine the unique teaching and learning needs of youth refugees in secondary schools and to understand their everyday and school-based language and literacy practices. At the time the study was conducted, Canada had resettled more than 40,000 Syrian refugees as part of a special initiative (Government of Canada, 2024), many of whom were school-aged children and youth. The high volume and speed of the resettlement effort demanded culturally responsive educational programming to support families and youth, including English language and literacy programs and settlement workers in schools.

Together with a team of multilingual, multicultural graduate student researchers, we engaged a collaborative approach, working with participating teachers and youth as co-researchers to generate data from field work, observation, and pedagogical documentation of student learning. We also gathered perspectives from teachers, settlement workers, and administrators through interviews, focus groups, and an online survey.

To construct insights from these data, we engaged thematic analysis (Clarke & Braun, 2017), focusing in particular on teacher instructional practices, attitudes and beliefs, classroom interactions, and student language and literacy practices. We drew on a translanguaging (TL) theory of language, to recognize students' complex, dynamic language practices and functionally integrated language repertoires. Providing a dynamic and expansive view, a TL perspective illuminated how learners make meaning with the range of available multilingual, multisemiotic, and multimodal resources at their disposal (Li, 2018; Tian & Shepard-Carey., 2020), helping us to recognize the "assemblage of diverse material, biological, semiotic and cognitive properties and capacities" (Thibault, 2017, p. 82) orchestrated for communication and meaning-making in the classroom.

Teaching and Learning Context

Located in a large suburban metropolis, the school comprised a rich linguistic ecology, wherein students and staff had a wealth of language resources. Most students at the school identified as multilingual, with 76 percent reporting a first language other than English (Ontario Ministry of Education, 2023) and Punjabi, Urdu, Arabic, Gujarati, and Hindi among the most common languages of the community. The school staff involved in the project were from a range of backgrounds, some of whom were racialized migrants themselves and spoke languages shared by students, and some of whom were White, monolingual English speakers. Working with youth recently resettled from Syria, Iran, Iraq, Congo, Palestine, El Salvador, and Colombia, our project took place across six classes, including four Grades 9–12 language and literacy, math, and art classes for students aged 13–18, and two accelerated credit language and literacy classes for students aged 19–21. The accelerated program was a locally developed model that enabled the older group of learners to extend their education in high school rather than enroll in adult education, which the school deemed more appropriate for students who had had limited opportunities for formal education, allowing greater time for academic socialization in the high school setting. Below, I elaborate on teacher- and student-directed translanguaging practices that the team documented in the classrooms.

Identity-affirming Practice

Giving attention to students' experience, teachers recognized that school played a key role in students' transition to life in Canada, providing stability and serving as a hub for community-based support and integrated settlement services. One administrator described this as a "wrap-around approach," inclusive of supports, structures, and strategies for both students and their families (Administrator Survey, 12/11/2017). This approach was critical as many students had experienced hardships before or after their arrival in Canada. An educator noted, "It can be most challenging for families to adjust to having left their loved ones in their home country where daily survival is questionable . . . Though that is a situation we have no control of, there are things we can do here to support families living with trauma. Giving families a voice, addressing needs simultaneously, acknowledging challenges and offering support in a meaningful way are key to stabilization and growth." (Educator survey, 11/30/2017). Teachers recognized this vulnerability and saw the importance of fostering a sense of safety and security. As one teacher shared, "You need to know, as their teachers, to watch out for signs in the classroom. You wonder why one day, today I had a student who just lost a cousin . . . now I can understand why you're down and you're not able to focus" (Teacher interview, 05/25/2018). Such observations alerted teachers that students' experiences were very different from their same-age peers born in Canada. For instance, one seventeen-year-old student from Syria had spent two years living alone in Sweden before being reunited with his family in Canada, and an eighteen-year-old student had moved to Lebanon with her family at thirteen, working along with her family in tobacco fields for five years before arriving in Canada. To address the socio-emotional needs related to these experiences, teachers engaged in various identity-affirming activities to connect with students' lives, and using students' full linguistic repertoire facilitated this effort.

As an example, Ms. Lightheart's grade ten class completed a poetry unit, exploring poems and songs from different cultural contexts and then writing their own dual-language "Where I am From" poems. Ms. Lightheart was a qualified and experienced ESL teacher and monolingual English speaker who didn't speak the languages of the students in her class. However, she made an effort to learn some words in Arabic to use in her teaching. For instance, in speaking with her students, she said, "Write a <ARA> jubla [sentence] about your house. Do ten <jublas>. Write the <jublas> here." And reflected, "<ARA> Jubla, loopda [period]. It's a joke with us but also a reminder." (Teacher interview, 11/25/19). Ms. Lightheart learned these grammatical terms to not only convey instructions but also to connect and build rapport with her students.

To support students to write bilingually, Ms. Lightheart asked students to use Google Translate or work with peers and family members to write in both English and their home language. Reflecting on her observations of students' the writing process, and their challenge of writing in just one language, Ms. Lightheart shared, "I feel like their level of English would inhibit them. They have so much more that they want to express than they can express in English. But then they're also self-conscious about their first languages so that piece is hard too" (Teacher interview, 02/06/20). Using both languages, students' poems were expressive and meaningful, articulating references to home, family, relationships, and memories. In Excerpt 1 below, a grade ten student from El Salvador writes in English and Spanish about his grandfather and his old neighborhood, invoking a sense of inner strength and resilience:

Excerpt 1

I am from the things my grandfather always told me was that I never stop fighting for what I want/ Soy de las cosas que mi abuelo siempre me decía que nunca dejó de
pelear por lo que quiero
I'm from my grandfather saying was that I never give up/ Soy de mi abuelo diciendo que nunca me rendiría
I am from my place of birth is in El salvador/ Soy de mi lugar de nacimiento es en El salvador
From my neighborhood with all my friends/ De mi barrio con todos mis amigos
See my grandparents live again/ Ver a mis abuelos vivir de nuevo

The poem in Excerpt 2, written in English and Arabic by a student from Syria, referred to the consequences of war, the importance of helping others, and the unity she finds in friendship.

Excerpt 2

I am from Arabic song that talk of sadness and talk about the reason/
[Arabic] أنا من غنية عربية بتحكي عن الحزن وبتعبر عن السبب
I am from respect for parents and respect for others and the elderly and to help someone/
أنا من الاحترام وبعني فيه احترام الوالدين وكبار السن وغيرون ، وبنندم المساعدة إلهن.
I am from sad like girl lost her family in the war, I am from my best friends are the one for everything/
أنا من الحزن متل صبية فقدت عيلتها بالحرب، أنا أحسن وحده برفقاتي واللي هن كل شي بحياتي.

Students' poems were an expression and projection of their identity into the school space, fostering inclusion and creating a counter-discourse that elevated their language practice and lived experience as important for language and curriculum learning. Expanding the activity to include students' home languages, even though the teacher didn't speak them, sent a positive message about the value of their language practice to learning.

Student Self-directed Multilingual Learning Strategies

Students in the project demonstrated significant use of multilingual learning strategies to support meaning-making and communication using a rich range of strategies and semiotic resources across languages and modes. Teachers observed and documented this strategy use to reinforce students' engagement and effort. The image shown in Figure 8.1 below illustrates how Ahmed,[2] in his grade ten language and literacy class, used a collection of multimodal and multilingual resources, including a teacher-created graphic organizer, English picture dictionary, iPad with a map and images, and translation software on his phone to complete an activity about community resources. Notably, this student was in school for the first time in his life and did not write in Arabic, so the digital resources and text-to-speech translation app supported him in mediating meaning in both English and Arabic, across oral and written texts.

Like Ahmed, students frequently searched for and found translations for English words independently, consulting with peers and using their personal smartphones to access online dictionaries or translation applications. In a further move, students verified their translations using Google Images and showed these images and the translations they found to their teachers, often spending several minutes teaching these words to their teachers or debating word choices and their meanings with classmates.

Mobilizing their translanguaging for learning, these efforts were strategic and purposeful, supported and encouraged by peers and teachers alike. While these efforts were spontaneous rather than planned, they set the expectation that students' linguistic resources were welcome in the classroom. Aligned with this practice, students sometimes opted to complete classwork in a language other than English, without prompting from their teacher. For instance, Fida, in her Grade 9/10 language and literacy class, completed a vocabulary task using both English and Arabic, adding translations in Arabic to support her learning.

Reflecting on this evidence of students' strategy use, their teacher shared, "It doesn't all have to be, like, I don't need to have control over all movement and utensils of learning, tools of learning, right?" and another teacher added, " . . . kids would like to freely use the whiteboard, like if they were trying to work something out. I've seen it in your classroom and then mine, like they just go up and you know like we'll translate something or draw a diagram of something or something like that and just like how they would initiate on their

---

[2] All names have been changed to pseudonyms to maintain confidentiality.

FIGURE 8.1 *Ahmed mediating communication across Arabic and English with oral and written texts.*

own, you know, using the resources in the classroom" (Teacher focus group, 06/02/2020).

These are but two illustrations of the ways in which students mobilized their own resources for learning, creating supports and scaffolds to assist them in accomplishing curriculum tasks. We documented and discussed these observations with teachers to discuss ways to expand and enhance instructional tasks to incorporate the practices and promote these kinds of strategies in a broader range of teaching and learning activities. Teachers continued to make various technology supports available in the classroom and ensured that students knew how to use them to support their learning, such that they could choose when, how, and whether to use language supports and resources in self-directed ways.

Developing Language Awareness

Students' languages served as a scaffold for learning and communication. Observing classroom interactions, students frequently negotiated meaning and understanding of key words and concepts, and this process often engaged the teacher and their language resources. For example, Mr. Gill, an experienced teacher who spoke English, Punjabi, Urdu, and Arabic, involved his Grade 10/11 English for Literacy Development (ELD) class in reading an adapted version of Jack London's story, *The Call of the Wild*. The purpose of the activity was to develop reading comprehension and strategies to build vocabulary. While reading an excerpt, Mr. Gill prompted students to confirm their understanding. He highlighted key words and supported students in using contextual cues to help them identify main ideas and summarize the text orally, using both English and other languages.

Working with a small group, Mr. Gill helped students use word recognition strategies across the languages they shared. Drawing from his own linguistic repertoire, he modeled the identification of cognates, language families, and intercultural dimensions of language use. This is illustrated in Excerpt 1 below, which illustrates discussion between the teacher and two students, along with a digital photograph of the teacher's accompanying board work ("ARA" for Arabic, "PUN" for Punjabi) (Figure 8.2):

Excerpt 1

Mr. Gill: How do you say "paw" in Syrian?
Amar: <ARA>Dalsart. It's hard to say in Syrian. I'll try to find an easy word for you Mr. G. [Student uses Google translate then checks translation using Google images on phone] <ARA>Qadam. You can write qadam.
Mr. Gill: No, it's <PUN>khur. In my language, Punjabi, it's <PUN>khur. The languages are all derived from one. We use <ARA>kitab in Persian, Urdu, Arabic. [Writes words on board]
Amar: <ARA>Kebab is barbecue. It's the same, Mr. G., language. My people it's the same.
Yaser: No, it's meat.

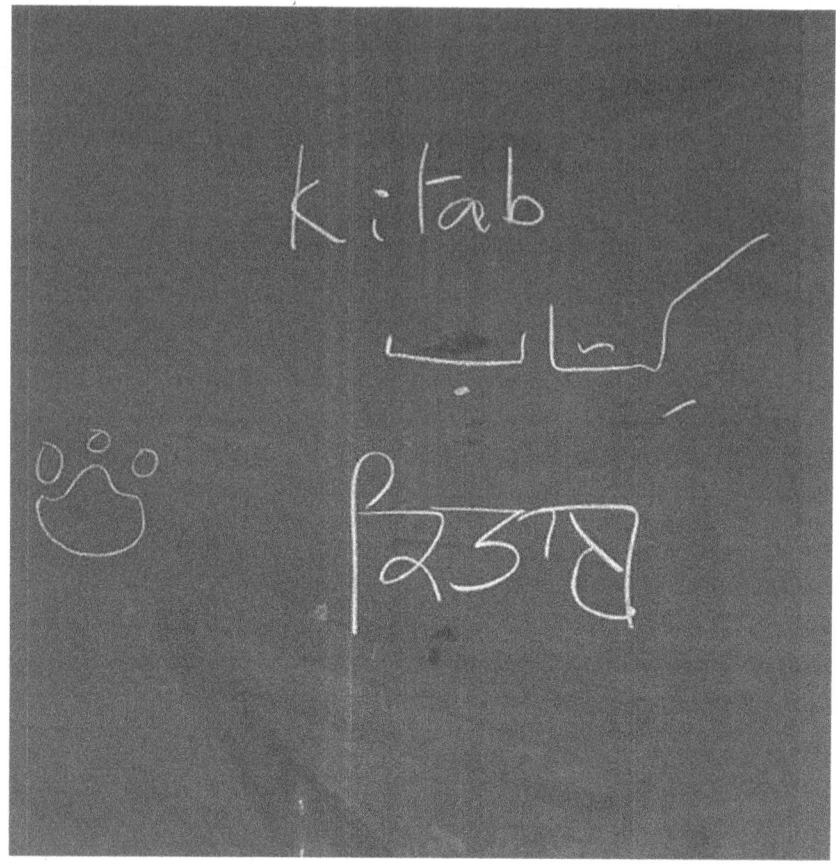

FIGURE 8.2 *Mr. Gill's translations. (Grade 10/11 ELD class)*

Amar: No, it's barbecue
Yaser: Barbecue is same.
Amar: <ARA>Kitab is closer to <ARA>kitaba. Is writing.

This excerpt illustrates how the students and their teacher engaged multiple languages in a chain of meaning-making in Arabic *[kitab-kitaba]* and across languages (English, Arabic, Persian, Punjabi, and Urdu) and modes (oral, written) which facilitated language awareness and translingual and trans-semiotic vocabulary building strategies.

Reflecting on his approach to this instructional strategy, Mr. Gill's explanation went beyond a technical or instrumental use of students' language(s), elaborating a fundamentally asset-oriented lens to students' plural competencies. He explained that all of students' linguistic resources were a valuable resource for learning, and he described the importance of promoting positive affect, student self-efficacy and self-regulation:

Otherwise a kid who does not feel encouraged, who feels discouraged, will not pick up anything. Make them express themselves the way they want if they have some questions. To be bilingual, or trilingual or multilingual I feel it's the expertise or the knowledge which kids already have it, that adds to the learning, quick learning, if not they can figure out what is that, what is this, if they're able to get some language support in terms of learning a new language. (Teacher Interview, 06/27/19)

Viewing multilingualism as the norm, Mr. Gill's comments and actions suggest a belief that teachers and students should be free to use their linguistic resources as they wish, unrestricted. Reflecting on the documentation of this kind of spontaneous, teacher-led translanguaging practice, we discussed the artificial divide between in- and out-of-school language practices, which may be unhelpful and potentially marginalizing for youth from refugee backgrounds who need to make sense of and engage with curricular concepts in a way that builds on their funds of knowledge, including their conceptual knowledge connected to other language(s). We discussed whether and how teachers might address these considerations more purposefully in teaching and learning activities. We wondered how students might respond and feel about seeing their language(s) included in a greater range of classroom materials and/or instructional tasks and hoped that such efforts would contribute to students' agency and sense of inclusion in the school.

From a monolingual paradigm, such practice is often understood as a form of language contact and often seen as interference or deficit; however, viewing multilingualism as the norm, this practice can be seen as legitimate and unrestricted: students are free to use their linguistic resources as they wish.

Translanguaging in Math Learning

Teachers in two math classes incorporated students' language(s) into a variety of teaching and learning tasks. Importantly, their efforts illustrate how teachers engaged in multilingualism not only for language and literacy learning, but also to build conceptual knowledge and disciplinary skills in curriculum subject areas. Figures 8.3 and 8.4 present a series of images connected with a collaborative hands-on task designed to promote number sense, reasoning, and financial literacy, skills critical to students' resettlement and social integration needs. For instance, a common activity in several language and literacy classes at the school was taking students on a field trip to a local bank and teaching them how to use automated teller machines (ATMs). Teaching math through a discovery model, students were assigned a project to build a

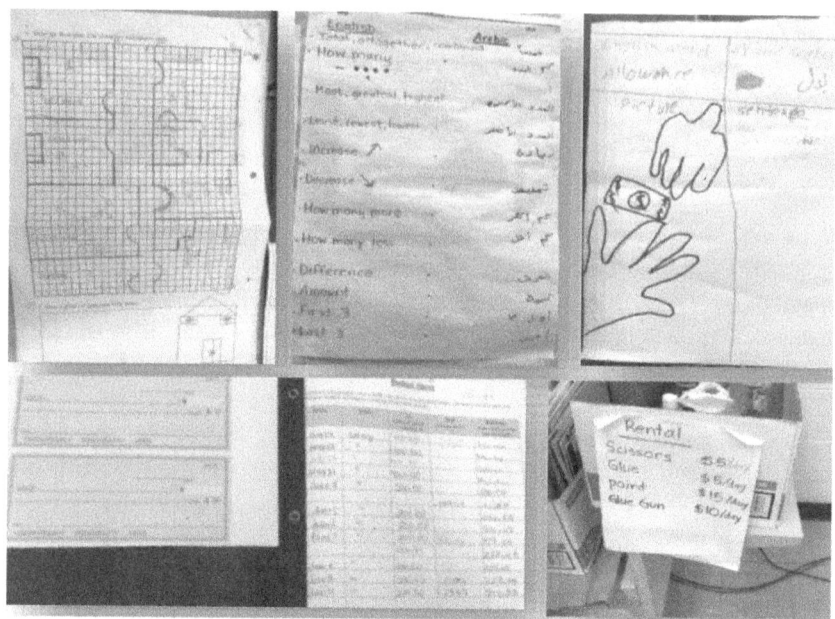

FIGURE 8.3 *Financial literacy activity (Class observation, Grade 10/11 ELD Math).*

FIGURE 8.4 *House building activity (Class observation, Grade 10/11 ELD Math).*

house; however, to do so, they were required to work together and cooperate to purchase arts and crafts supplies and rent tools to build the house from their teacher. The teacher provided them with a daily allowance using checks, and students had to record their spending against their budget and balance their bank account. Together, the teacher and students created a bilingual anchor chart with key mathematical concepts, and the students completed a dual-language vocabulary placemat activity to support meaning-making of these concepts.

Similar to the house building activity, Figure 8.5 comprises images of a problem-solving task designed to teach and practice formulas, equations, and critical mathematical thinking.

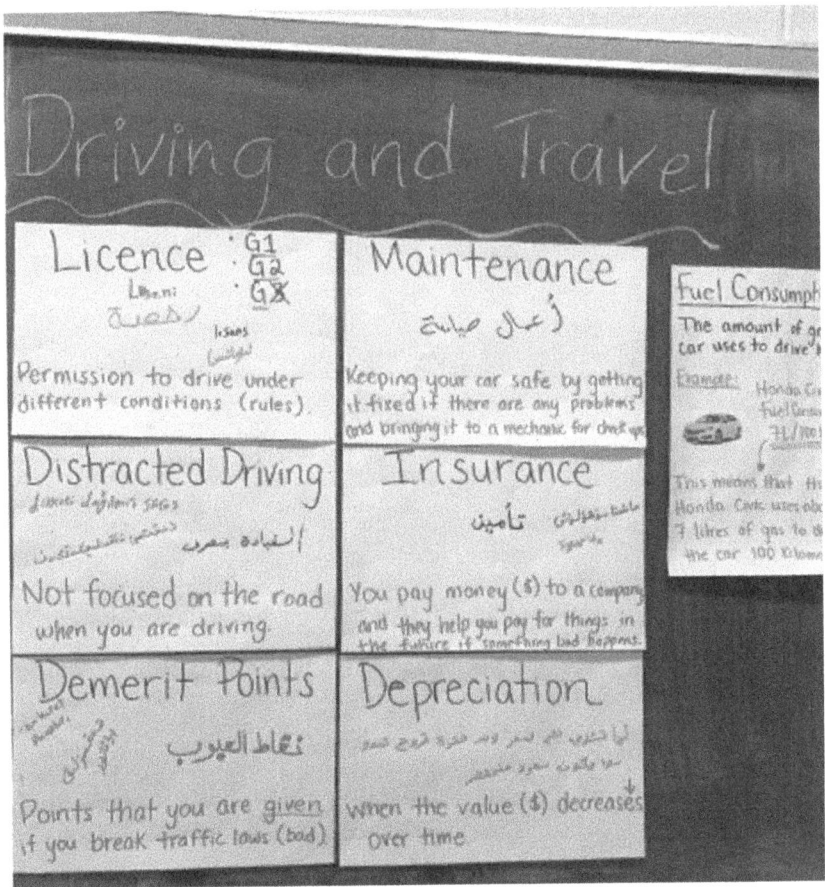

FIGURE 8.5 *Teaching mathematical vocabulary (Class observation, Grade 11/12 ELD Math).*

Students were assigned a project to plan a trip and calculate the cheapest and most efficient way to travel to their selected destination with a partner, during which they actively negotiated with one another using all of their shared language resources. To scaffold students' completion of the assignment, the teacher, Ms. Nowak, presented key vocabulary words and mathematical concepts, as shown in Figure 8.6, which the students discussed and translated into Arabic. Ms. Nowak prompted students' use of other language(s) by making space on the graphic organizer, see Figure 8.6, for students to identify key words in their first language to scaffold completion of the task for assessment and evaluation purposes.

Taken together, these examples illustrate how teachers promoted and supported students to use their full linguistic repertoire for math teaching and learning by including and encouraging students to use their shared languages in whole-class activities, in individual written work, and in active, collaborative learning tasks. Reflecting on the design and implementation of these tasks with the teachers, we noted that these kinds of examples illustrated purposeful and intentional use of students' linguistic repertoires rather than in-the-moment, ad-hoc improvisation. By planning in advance strategies to

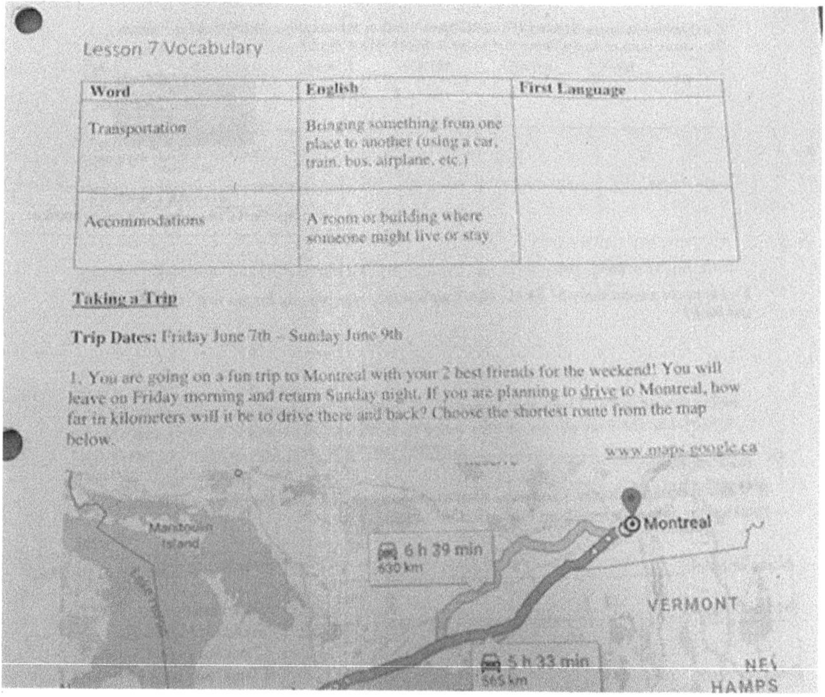

Lesson 7 Vocabulary

Word	English	First Language
Transportation	Bringing something from one place to another (using a car, train, bus, airplane, etc.)	
Accommodations	A room or building where someone might live or stay	

Taking a Trip

Trip Dates: Friday June 7th – Sunday June 9th

1. You are going on a fun trip to Montreal with your 2 best friends for the weekend! You will leave on Friday morning and return Sunday night. If you are planning to drive to Montreal, how far in kilometers will it be to drive there and back? Choose the shortest route from the map below.

www.maps.google.ca

FIGURE 8.6 *Teaching mathematical formulas (Class observation, Grade 11/12 ELD Math).*

prompt students' translanguaging, these activities were teacher-initiated rather than student-initiated. Moreover, the tasks engaged students' linguistic repertoire as a resource for developing mathematical concepts and skills, not as a mere scaffold for English teaching and learning.

Potential Challenges

Although educators adopted and implemented strategies to engage students' linguistic repertoires for teaching and learning, bringing multiple languages to the classroom environment, these efforts were largely inconsequential in challenging the social and educational circumstances of schooling for youth refugees and ongoing challenges related to resettlement. Often focusing on basic language and curriculum, not all language and literacy activities built upon students' complex, critical thinking and lived experiences. Finally, the sheltered instruction model for language and literacy programming exacerbated these circumstances, as the ESL/EAL classes separated the youth from their same-age peers, creating obstacles to full access to and participation in school life, including interaction and potentially friendship.

Concluding Thoughts

Whereas language education for refugee students often remains oriented toward teaching English to support students' acculturation and social and educational integration as quickly as possible, teachers were able to invite students' complex, multi-voiced, and unique semiotic resources into the classroom. As the examples show, TL can play an important role in supporting this aim. Teachers mediated students' use of other languages in the classroom by modeling, prompting, and encouraging, or during planned and strategic tasks and activities. While some teachers shared students' home languages and were able to engage in TL to provide instructions, explain concepts, or manage classroom activities, teachers who were monolingual English speakers also made purposeful efforts to learn and use students' home languages. As one teacher shared, "I use my 'broken Arabic' to connect with students" (Teacher interview, 11/25/19). For students who have had little opportunity for formal education, this small move shows students that they and their languages belong in school. Moreover, in a school community where English is dominant, this also sends a message that TL practice is welcome in learning.

While the examples provided above illustrate how teachers and students moved between languages in the classroom, it is important to understand these practices as more than translation or code-switching. When students access their home languages for learning, the meanings and understandings they already have are unlocked and mobilized in the construction of new knowledge. Moreover, the use of other resources adds to this process of meaning-making, including the use of digital devices, visual images, and classroom artifacts. For instance, Ahmed used the translation app on his mobile device along with digital images on the classroom tablet and visual prompts in the picture dictionary to build his understanding of urban spaces. Mr. Gill's students connected word knowledge in three languages and visual prompts on the blackboard to support reading comprehension of their classroom novel and to build metalinguistic awareness of the relationships between different languages and cultures. Additionally, students in the math class engaged English and their home languages during an experiential learning activity to develop mathematical thinking and promote financial literacy.

These examples illustrate that TL comprises a continuous flow of meaning-making, supporting students to add new understandings to what they already know. As Lin and He (2017) write, there should be no separation of languages in student learning, underscoring "the inseparability of elements (both physical and symbolic) involved in the speech/action events and the futility of isolating languages into distinct systems (or codes) and stipulating which languages are legitimate or illegitimate to use" (p. 237). From this perspective, the nature of TL is envisioned as a dynamic activity flow in which languages and modes, along with the affordances of technology tools and digital translation apps, can and should be intertwined to facilitate student learning and connection to knowledge they bring from their homes, cultures, and lived experiences. For refugee students, who may have gaps in their schooling, such pieces of knowledge comprise a foundation or bridge to schooling in host countries, fostering feelings of inclusion and belonging in their new community and educational setting. From this stance, TL pedagogies are co-facilitative, providing access to the dominant language without reifying English monolingual ideologies or reinforcing social and linguistic hierarchies (Cenoz & Gorter, 2015; Lau et al., 2017). By contrast, when multilingual students' linguistic capabilities are evaluated according to narrow definitions of language, students themselves may be seen as deficient, their language practice in need of remediation when compared to dominant monolingual language users (García et al., 2021).

Finally, while TL comprises both a pedagogical scaffold and resource for learning, it also facilitates opportunities to affirm student identities and cultivate connections between students and teachers. For students from refugee backgrounds, such aims are critical as part of a trauma-informed pedagogy that brings sensitivity to and awareness of students' experiences before, during, and after migration. As one teacher shared, "I'll sit down with the student and find out what's going on. You develop a relationship, a rapport with students . . . you have to reach out, you have to do something, you can't leave them there" (Teacher focus group, 05/25/18). With this kind of understanding in mind, Ms. Lightheart planned the poetry activity to engage students in sharing memories of traditions, relationships, and the homes they left behind. Inviting students to use their full linguistic repertoire along with English sent a message about maintaining their funds of knowledge and adapting to new ways of communicating. At the same time, the content of students' poetry contributed a counter-narrative to negative discourses that might circulate about refugees.

Broadly, TL comprises a pedagogical approach for teaching students from refugee backgrounds that involves more than just strategies; it encompasses a transformative and critical mindset and an explicit connection to social justice and inclusion (Li, 2024). Recognizing students' identities together with their language practices and countering the persistence of monolingual policies and practices (García et al., 2021; Li & García, 2022), students and teachers alike can expand equitable access to and participation in their multilingual worlds and school communities.

References

Bartlett, L., Mendenhall, M., & Ghaffar-Kucher, A. (2017). Culture in acculturation: Refugee youth's schooling experiences in international schools in New York City. *International Journal of Intercultural Relations, 60*, 109–119.

Burton, J., & Van Viegen, S. (2021). Spoken word poetry with multilingual youth from refugee backgrounds. *Journal of Adolescent & Adult Literacy, 65*(1), 75-84.

Cenoz, J., & Gorter, D. (Eds.). (2015). Multilingual education. Cambridge University Press.

Clarke, V., & Braun, V. (2017). Thematic analysis. *The Journal of Positive Psychology, 12*(3), 297–298.

Dryden-Peterson, S. (2016). Refugee education: The crossroads of globalization. *Educational Researcher, 45*(9), 473–482.

Duff, P. (2018). Case study research in applied linguistics. Routledge.

García, O., Flores, N., Seltzer, K., Wei, L., Otheguy, R., & Rosa, J. (2021). Rejecting abyssal thinking in the language and education of racialized bilinguals: A manifesto. *Critical Inquiry in Language Studies, 18*(3), 203–228.

García, O., Johnson, S. I., & Seltzer, K. (2017). *The translanguaging classroom: Leveraging student bilingualism for learning* (pp. v–xix). Caslon.

Government of Canada. (2024). Retrieved from https://www.canada.ca/en/immigration-refugees-citizenship/services/refugees/about-refugee-system/welcome-syrian-refugees/looking-future.html

Koyama, J., & Kasper, J. (2022). Transworlding and translanguaging: Negotiating and resisting monoglossic language ideologies, policies, and pedagogies. *Linguistics and Education, 70*, 101010.

Lau, S. M. C., Juby-Smith, B., & Desbiens, I. (2017). Translanguaging for transgressive praxis: Promoting critical literacy in a multiage bilingual classroom. *Critical Inquiry in Language Studies, 14*(1), 99-127.

Lau, S. M. C., & Van Viegen, S. (2020). Plurilingual pedagogies. *Springer International Publishing, 10*, 978–3.

Li Wei, Translanguaging as a Practical Theory of Language, Applied Linguistics, Volume 39, Issue 1, February 2018, Pages 9–30, https://doi.org/10.1093/applin/amx039

Lin, A. M., & He, P. (2017). Translanguaging as dynamic activity flows in CLIL classrooms. Journal of Language, Identity & Education, 16(4), 228-244.

Li, W. (2024). Transformative pedagogy for inclusion and social justice through translanguaging, co-learning, and transpositioning. *Language Teaching, 57*(2), 203–214.

Li, W., & García, O. (2022). Not a first language but one repertoire: Translanguaging as a decolonizing project. *RELC Journal, 53*(2), 313–324.

Mary, L., Krüger, A. B., & Young, A. S. (Eds.). (2021). Migration, multilingualism and education: Critical perspectives on inclusion (Vol. 91). Multilingual Matters.

Mendenhall, M., & Bartlett, L. (2018). Academic and extracurricular support for refugee students in the US: Lessons learned. *Theory into Practice, 57*(2), 109–118. https://doi.org/10.1080/00405841.2018.1469910

Miller, E., Ziaian, T., & Esterman, A. (2018). Australian school practices and the education experiences of students with a refugee background: A review of the literature. *International Journal of Inclusive Education, 22*(4), 339–359.

Montero, M. K. (2018). Narratives of trauma and self-healing processes in a literacy program for adolescent refugee newcomers. In *Educating refugee-background students: Critical issues and dynamic contexts* (pp. 92–106). Multilingual Matters.

Nakutnyy, K., & Sterzuk, A. (2018). 5 Sociocultural Literacy Practices of a Sudanese Mother and Son in Canada. Educating Refugee-background Students: Critical Issues and Dynamic Contexts, 59.

Nelson, C. D., & Appleby, R. (2015). Conflict, militarization, and their after-effects: Key challenges for TESOL. *Tesol Quarterly, 49*(2), 309-332.

Omerbašić, D. (2018). Girls with refugee backgrounds creating digital landscapes of knowing. Educating refugee-background students: Critical issues and dynamic contexts, 59.

Ontario Ministry of Education. (2023). *School information finder: Secondary school profile.* Queen's Printer for Ontario. https://www.ontario.ca/page/find-your-school

Paulsrud, B., Tian, Z., & Toth, J. (Eds.). (2021). *English-medium instruction and translanguaging* (Vol. 126). Multilingual Matters.

Papa, E. L. (2018). 10 using photovoice with Cambodian and Guatemalan youth to uncover community cultural wealth and influence policy chan. In *Educating refugee-background students: Critical issues and dynamic contexts* (p. 59).

Park, K., & Valdez, V. E. (2018). Translanguaging pedagogy to support the language learning of older Nepali-Bhutanese adults. Educating refugee-background students: Critical issues and dynamic contexts, 49-65.

Patel, L. (2018). Immigrant populations and sanctuary schools. *Journal of Literacy Research, 50*(4), 524-529.

Shapiro, S., Farrelly, R., &and Curry, M.J. Educating Refugee-background Students: Critical Issues and Dynamic Contexts, Bristol, Blue Ridge Summit: Multilingual Matters, 2018, (pp. 159-176). Multilingual Matters. https://doi.org/10.21832/9781783099986

Stewart, J., El Chaar, D., McCluskey, K., & Borgardt, K. (2019). Refugee student integration: A focus on settlement, education, and psychosocial support. *Journal of Contemporary Issues in Education, 14*(1), 55–70.

Stolk, Y., Kaplan, I., & Szwarc, J. (2025). Majority language acquisition by children of refugee background: a review. *International Journal of Inclusive Education, 29*(5), 619-642.

Symons, C., & Ponzio, C. (2019). Schools cannot do it alone: A community-based approach to refugee youth's language development. *Journal of Research in Childhood Education, 33*(1), 98-118.

Thibault, P. J. (2017). The reflexivity of human languaging and Nigel Love's two orders of language. Language Sciences, 61, 74-85.

Tian, Z., & Shepard-Carey, L. (2020). (Re) imagining the future of translanguaging pedagogies in TESOL through teacher–researcher collaboration. *TESOL Quarterly, 54*(4), 1131–1143.

United Nations High Commission on Refugees. (2024). Global trends report, 2022. Retrieved from https://www.unhcr.org/global-trends-report-2022

9

Aware-Explore-Apply Strengths Model

Translanguaging and Transknowledging for Critical Embodied Engagement

Joanna Rowe and Sunny Man Chu Lau

Introduction

This chapter describes an interdisciplinary project that aims to strengthen multilingual students' sense of self while promoting their learning of English as a second language (ESL). As long-term language teachers and educators, we both believe in contextualized, meaningful language education that supports not only students' language attainments but more importantly their sense of self and self-efficacy as the engine of an autonomous, joyful learner. Without self-efficacy, a human being simply cannot operate. For language-minoritized students, their full repertoire of languages, cultures, and identities needs to be recognized, acknowledged, and valued to support a firm ground for their sense of self. And when people feel they can be present with all of themselves, not just the piece working in the target language, great things happen. The road to equity in the classroom will be much smoother. The interdisciplinary translanguaging project described in this chapter was conceptualized by Joanna

(Author 1), who has worked on it with multilingual students in Germany before applying it to the Indigenous context in Kuujjuaq, where she is now working as an educational consultant. Kuujjuaq is the gateway hub of the region of Nunavik in North Quebec. It has a population of approximately 14,000 people, most of whom are of Inuit origin. The educational context is highly complex and multi-layered, with an interplay of three languages—Inuktitut, English and French in the community. The provisions of the 1975 North Quebec and James Bay Agreement[1] (Turcotte, 2019) allow the local school board to stipulate that the first language of instruction at school is Inuktitut, the language of the Inuit in Nunavik and Nunavut. When children move into Grade 3, parents decide whether their children will learn English or French as a second language (ESL or FSL). Depending on their choice, students will learn all academic subjects in the second language and continue their learning of Inuktitut in separate language and culture lessons.

The lesson concept outlined in this chapter is envisaged for use in a typical Nunavik multi-level class of Grades 9–11 students (ages from 15 to 21). Since 2022, Sunny (Author 2) has been invited as an external consultant to give advice on proposed changes in the language programs with a view to supporting students' maintenance and mastery of Inuktitut and a second language across the grade levels. Her contribution to the discourse around translanguaging and transknowledging (García & Li Wei, 2014; Heugh, 2021) has been important in shaping teaching practices in the educational environment of Nunavik.

Colonialism affected—and continues to affect—many Inuit adversely. The brutal legacy of residential schools (when Indigenous children were forced to leave their homes to go to boarding schools run by churches, see Truth and Reconciliation Commission of Canada, 2015) continues to haunt the Indigenous communities. In Kuujjuaq, the community at large is still in the process of healing and taking back control of their lives. While these afflictions are gradually easing and healing, and people are finding new confidence in a renewed sense of identity, many students continue to feel the pressure to conform to an education format that is alien to them, delivered by teachers who may not understand well the language and cultures of the Inuit. In this learning context, raising self-efficacy among students hence becomes a prerequisite for student success. Self-efficacy in learning of any kind rests on a strong sense of self. One important way to build a sense of self in the learning environment is to give space to all the language and cultural repertoires students bring to the classroom. The unit plan at hand is a practical offering

---

[1] The agreement between the Indigenous peoples of North Quebec and James Bay and the Provincial Government of Quebec was a seminal moment in reconciliation and set a precedent in Canada for many subsequent negotiations about regional autonomy and land claims.

inspired by interdisciplinary research and practice in Positive Psychology and the pedagogical practice of translanguaging and transknowledging. The lesson plan outlined in this chapter leverages students' knowledge, allowing inclusion of different worldviews in the experience of strength-based reflection on life situations and how to tackle them. In this chapter, readers will be offered a brief overview of the theoretical background to the character strengths on which the lesson plan is centered, as well as the connections between the Positive Psychology tools to build (emotional) literacy in language learning and the concepts of translanguaging and transknowledging as featured in the unit plan.

Translanguaging as Transknowledging for Decolonization

Translanguaging pedagogy underscores the value of multilingual students' diverse languages and cultural resources in teaching and learning. Instead of dismissing students' home language(s) as "interference" (Derakhshan & Karimi, 2015), they are mobilized to support target language learning. Numerous research studies have shown that learners' home or previously learned languages can have a positive influence on their target language learning, including stronger metalinguistic awareness, reciprocal use of literacy-related skills and strategies, greater comprehension, and a stronger sense of self (Cummins, 2017; García & Kleifgen, 2020; Lin, 2015). Learners are constantly comparing new language features with ones they have learned in other languages, whether they are allowed to do so or not (Bérubé & Marinova-Todd, 2012; Dmitrenko, 2017). Forcing them to adhere to one language in learning squanders their prior knowledge and cultural experiences anchored in languages they have learned (Cummins, 2021). This also marginalizes multilingual voices and multicultural identities (de los Rios & Seltzer, 2017), framing them as inadequate. Indigenous students particularly face stigma regarding their languages and worldviews, which continues to imperil their vitality and survival (Ball & McIvor, 2013; Sterzuk, 2020). In modern education, minoritized languages/varieties, including Indigenous languages, continue to be positioned as irrelevant and valueless (Makoni & Pennycook, 2007), which reflects a long-standing history of colonialism and nation building that promotes an idealized and pure form of the dominant language.

Translanguaging pedagogy aims to not only recover subjugated languages under monolingual discourses but also to reclaim their associated knowledge bases that are deemed "uncivilized" or "non-scientific" based on Western-centric values (Canagarajah, 2023). Heugh (2021) argues that the recent efforts in the recovery and recognition of multilingualism in the Global North should give more attention to the "fundamental differences in faith, culture and knowledge systems," all of which, however, tend to be "(conveniently) subsumed under or hidden by differences that relate to language" (p. 39). To Heugh, the valorization and mobilization of linguistic diversity in education should go hand in hand with the reclamation of alternative ways of knowing (epistemology), being (ontology), and believing (cosmology) (Heugh, 2017). Similarly, Makoni and other scholars (Antia & Makoni, 2023; Makoni et al., 2023) have been calling to "Southernize" Applied Linguistics and language education, meaning to expand the intellectual repertoires to include minoritized and Indigenous perspectives and to address global inequalities in knowledge production dominated by the North. Here, the Global North-Global South divide is a metaphorical rather than a geographical description to refer to the significant economic and social disparities that exist in societies and communities around the world. Heugh (2021) argues that translanguaging practices and pedagogies can help reduce sociolinguistic inequities in education, but more importantly, it can create spaces to maximize exchanges of knowledge (i.e., *transknowledging*) among students from linguistic and cultural backgrounds. For example, the core Indigenous values of communality as well as care and responsibility for all human and nonhuman living beings and environment conflict with the neo/colonial education systems that prioritize individualism. For education to be truly inclusive and ethical, it is crucial that these alternative worldviews and student voices are included and empowered to counterbalance the hegemonic Northern epistemologies. When teachers open up spaces for languages other than the target language, they are also inviting linguistic, cultural, cognitive, and emotional connections among these languages, supporting reciprocal exchanges of knowledge.

Responding to the Truth and Reconciliation's Calls to Action (2015), Abe (2017, August), a Beothuk ESL instructor and curriculum developer, argues for the Indigenization of ESL as a first step to decolonize English education, aiming to "promote the balancing of Indigenous and Western worldviews, values, and ways of knowing as an act of Reconciliation" (p. 30). Abe further argues that teachers also need to change their teaching processes to prioritize experiential learning that engages students in experiencing, reflecting, analyzing, and applying the learned knowledge in real-life situations (See also Battiste, 2013). Kanu (2011) added that the infusion of Indigenous cultures and knowledges in the curriculum should be embedded within a critique of the enduring harmful impact of colonialism on contemporary Indigenous communities. Kanu's (2011) vision of curriculum is one that is "livable and imbued with human dignity" (p. 204) for the empowerment of Indigenous learners. The lesson unit described here is to showcase how translanguaging practices can support transknowledging to decolonize ESL teaching and learning in an Inuit school and to reiterate the message that teaching and learning a new language is not to forget or erase learners' other languages and knowledges, but rather to integrate them for a more holistic and critical education for their development as responsible caretakers in the human/nonhuman world.

The PERMA Model of Well-being and Multilingual Students' Different Worldviews

Joanna's training in education and psychology had inspired her interest in an interdisciplinary project focused on the concept of PERMA, an acronym for Martin Seligman's (2011) theory of well-being, which stands for Positive Emotion, Engagement, Relationships, Meaning, and Accomplishment. Anchored in the field of Positive Psychology, Peterson and Seligman (2004) constructed a "common language" of character strengths that denotes all that is best in human beings (See Table 9.1). These strengths were adopted and operationalized in the coaching contexts by Ryan Niemiec, who devised the AEA coaching model (2014), that is, Aware-Explore-Apply, to support participants to identify and harness their twenty-four strengths for sustained efficacy and well-being. During the Aware Phase, participants take a survey (see VIACharacter.org), indicating how well various statements represent their practices and approaches in daily life situations. These statements reflect the twenty-four strengths of the "common language," and the survey results help narrow down to five signature strengths with which the participants associate the most. Then, in the Explore Phase, participants are invited to reflect on the different domains of their lives where they utilize their strengths and values. Finally, in the Apply Phase, participants analyze how they could utilize their signature strengths in future endeavors and possibly in other domains of life in order to make the best possible use of their signature strengths.

Using PERMA in educational contexts has been shown to promote self-efficacy, a core element for developing *grit* in transcending challenges and pursuing life goals. According to Duckworth (2016), grit encompasses self-efficacy and is the added layer over perseverance that enables a student to power through challenges. Four key traits of grit include *practice*, *interest*, *purpose*, and *hope*. It is that perseverant, effortful thinking that is needed to master a math problem or a piano piece after sustained practice, for instance. To get to that kind of deep thinking and commitment, students need to be emotionally in a place where they believe deep down in themselves. Without grit, they may become distracted when the hill of achievement is steep and may give up entirely.

One challenge for educators everywhere is to offer opportunities for students to develop grit, which is so inextricably linked to their self-efficacy and ability to recognize and name their emotional experiences. Thus, the

Table 9.1 Classification of Peterson and Seligman's (2004) 24 Strengths and Virtues from ViA Institute on Character

Strength identifying: Aware phase—24 character strengths in six categories					
Virtue of Wisdom	Virtue of Courage	Virtue of Humanity	Virtue of Justice	Virtue of Temperance	Virtue of Transcendence
Creativity	Bravery	Love	Teamwork	Forgiveness	Appearance of beauty and excellence
Curiosity	Perseverance	Kindness	Fairness	Humility	Gratitude
Judgment	Honesty	Social intelligence	Leadership	Prudence	Hope
Love of learning	Zest			Self-regulation	Humour
Perspective					Spirituality

motivation to transpose the PERMA model into the language-learning context is to create an opportunity for learners to explore the interconnections between language, emotions, and identity to support *all* students, particularly language-minoritized students, in finding their own self-efficacy in the process of learning a second language.

Despite the educational potential of the PERMA model, a generally perceived limitation of the theory of well-being (and other psychological concepts in intercultural contexts) is the tendency to understand human beings as actors with universal traits. Is there really a common language shared among cultures to identify human strengths? One interesting finding from a PERMA project in 2017 with Business Psychology students in Germany showed otherwise (Turner et al., 2019). The study findings showed that many German heritage language or first language speakers believed that for the character strength "hope" (in the Transcendence category—see Table 9.1), it should be translated as "*Optimismus*" (i.e., optimism) rather than "*Hoffnung*" (i.e., hope). The German speakers argued that the "optimism" suggested an intellectual choice, a cognitive, rational processing of possible responses to a situation, and that such a choice had almost a moral quality. In contrast, "hope" conveys an inherent, emotional disposition and hence is not a quality of Transcendence like "optimism." This understanding of Transcendence may reflect a core value in German culture as part of the Enlightenment process based on individuals' reason and moral choices.

Later when the project was carried out in 2018 with South Asian students studying Business Administration, the students found, when discussing the character strengths in the column Virtue of Humanity, that the notion of involvement was not a positive attribute for actors and stakeholders. Rather, they saw *involvement* as synonymous with *attachment*, which in their cultural frames of reference was viewed as highly undesirable as a foundation on which to base knowledge and decisions. The South Asian students, drawing on the philosophy school Vedanta, explained that *sattvik* knowledge—and the action based on it—is free from attachment and therefore based on one's obligatory duty and responsibility. This knowledge does not have the "I-am-the-doer attitude." And it contrasts with the knowledge and action *rajasik* that is desire-ridden and attached to outcomes. With this thought process, the Southeast Asian students found the twenty-four character strengths devised by Peterson and Seligman (2004) to be too self-referenced, desire-ridden, causing strains on the doers. The differences in cultural perceptions became evident in these projects, with most international student respondents maintaining that the naming and classification of strengths and values in the PERMA model as being mostly US-centric and thus restrictive in some instances. Joanna's involvement in these two studies (2017 and 2018) also led her to design learning activities that support multicultural learners' vocabulary knowledge about character traits while engaging them in critical dialogues and explorations of common and/or unique notions of strengths and values in English and in other languages and cultures. Drawing on students' home languages and worldviews in English language learning also increases their willingness to take risks in learning tasks, raises their metacognitive and metalinguistic awareness, and most importantly, reinforces their sense of self.

At the time of writing, there is no research yet around PERMA as a tool with Indigenous or Inuit students. The lesson concept proposed here for Inuit ESL learners aims to draw on the Nunavut *Inuit Qaujimajatuqangit* Education Framework (i.e., Inuit traditional knowledge framework), which structures the core curriculum into four "strands": *Nunavusiutit* Principles (heritage and historical events), *Aulajaaqtut* Principles (wellness, one's place in society), *Iqqaqqaukkaringniq* Principles (problem solving, analytical and critical thinking), and *Uqausiliriniq* (relationships and communication). These four strands encompass key Inuit societal values that guide all aspects of social life (see Table 9.2). The teaching opportunity offered by the lesson concept at hand lies in engaging Inuit ESL learners in reflecting on the similarities and differences between cultural references of strengths and values in English and in Inuktitut

Table 9.2. *Nunavut Inuit Qaujimajatuqangit Education Framework, Integrated Curriculum Content Strands* (Nunavut Department of Education, 2007, p. 48)

1. *Uqaujjusiaminik Malingniq* **(discipline, learning from mistakes)** 2. *Piusirsusiarnik Ikpiniarniqatsiarniq* **(having the right attitude)** 3. *Saimaniup Pimmariuninga* **(importance of harmony)** 4. *Ujjirusutsiarniq* **(having awareness)** 5. *Piniarnikkut Ilitsiniq* **(learning to do)** 6. *Upalungaijaqsiminaq* **(having a plan)** 7. *Ilagiiniq/tuqsurausiit* **(relationship/kinship)**	1. *Uqumaittunik isumaksaqsiurniq* **(heavy thinking)** 2. *Qaujimajumaniq* **(curiosity)** 3. *Uukturarniq* **(experimentation)** 4. *Sivuliqsiniq* **(leadership)** 5. *Ilittiniq tammaqtarnikkut* **(learning from mistakes)**
1. *Inuuqatiqarunnaqsivallianiq* **(building relationships)** 2. *Suusutsasiarniq Inuuqatiminik* **(respecting others)** 3. *Sanatunirmik tukisiniarniq* **(thinking creatively and seeking to understand)** 4. *Pivallianirmik ullumi sivuniksaqatsiarnirmut* **(improving on the present and building strength for the future)**	1. *Saimaniq* **(harmony)** 2. *Pijatsaqarniq* **(responsibility)** 3. *Tatittusainiq* **(discipline)** 4. *Silatuniq* **(wisdom)**

and in evaluating what is applicable to their own life situations as they navigate their intercultural worlds.

Promoting Learners' Sense of Multilingual Self Using the PERMA Model of Well-being

In this section, we offer a unit plan designed for a high school ESL class (Grades 9–11) in Joanna's current educational context in the region of Nunavik, North Quebec, where students have varying degrees of Inuktitut and English. We envisage a four to five-period sequence (40–45 mins each) over a week or so. The lesson sequence broadly adapts the Aware-Explore-Apply coaching model (Niemiec, 2014) where students get to learn the vocabulary describing character strengths, then identify and explore how their strengths (and values) are connected with past achievements (or triumphs over adversity), and lastly, think ahead to action planning and to leveraging their strengths and values in various domains of their life. Students are invited to discuss how they differ (or are similar) and how this might change or add to their goals for themselves. Students are encouraged to use their full linguistic repertoires to translanguage for meaning-driven discussions.

Lesson 1 (Aware Phase)

Learning Goals: Get in touch with the strengths at the core of who you are
   Procedures:

1. The teacher introduces the notion of character strengths using Table 9.1 which should be pinned up or shown on a display board. The teacher introduces the virtues one by one, focusing on pronunciation and asking students if they know the meaning in English or in Inuktitut. If students call out a strength listed, the teacher can illustrate with a situational example, such as: "*Well, 'Prudence' . . . that would be when you are careful and cautious with spending money, or with doing something risky . . . .*" Alternatively, the teacher can assign each group a column of virtues and have them predict or look up the meanings of each virtue, encouraging students to use English dictionaries or English-Inuktitut online translation tools, then come back as a whole class for discussion.

2. Assigning one group to one cluster of virtues, the teacher can ask each student to choose one strength to comment on and explain to

the group why this particular character strength belongs to this cluster of virtue. The teacher models an example: "*Gratitude belongs to the Virtue Transcendence because being grateful (thankful) for your life and what you have helps you overcome/transcend challenges or difficulties you encounter.*"

3. Each group will have 5–8 mins for one Virtue column; then, when the time is up, they have move to the next column. Depending on how much time the class has, each group can cover 2–3 columns. Encourage students to translanguage between English and Inuktitut to focus on meaning construction.

4. Students return to the whole class and participate in a final sharing of the choices they have made in their small groups and what they have found out. The teacher also uses this opportunity to teach (or review) the vocabulary from the twenty-four strengths and values table.

5. Students go to ViAcharacter.org or VIA Youth Survey to complete a survey on their character strengths. The survey statements are straightforward; they are about everyday life and have been adapted for youth. Students can look up words from an online dictionary (English or English-Inuktitut) or ask the teacher to clarify. The teacher reassures students that the results of the survey are not for evaluation.

6. The survey will identify one "signature strength" for the respondent. The teacher gives each student five cue cards and asks them to write down the signature strength together with four other strengths they consider important to them. Students are encouraged to use their own wording (in English and/or Inuktitut) to represent these signature strengths.

7. Teachers can get them into small groups to share their thoughts and feelings (translanguaging is encouraged) about the results, using these question prompts:

    - Do you find the results accurate in reflecting who you are?
    - What is surprising and what is expected?
    - Why is the word "signature" used to describe the top character strengths?

8. The teacher brings students back for a whole-class discussion, inviting them to share what their top strengths are and other interesting thoughts they have had during the group activity.

Alternatives or Extensions

- Instead of showing students Table 9.1 with all the character strengths pinned to the six categories, the teacher initially leaves the columns of the twenty-four strengths table blank and gives out individual character strength cards to students. The teacher asks students to classify the strengths into each category of virtue, as they see fit, and then discuss.

Lessons 2 (Explore Phase)

Learning Goal: Tying character strengths to past achievements and challenges in life

Outline of activities:
1. Students get out their five signature strengths, and on the desk or wall, they can place them in order of "most powerful" strength. If time allows, students can exchange with a partner about their list of top five strengths (translanguaging is encouraged).
2. The teacher has put up a poster-sized target on one wall of the classroom (Figure 9.1). The target has been divided into quadrants by the crosshairs that run through the middle. Quadrants signify life

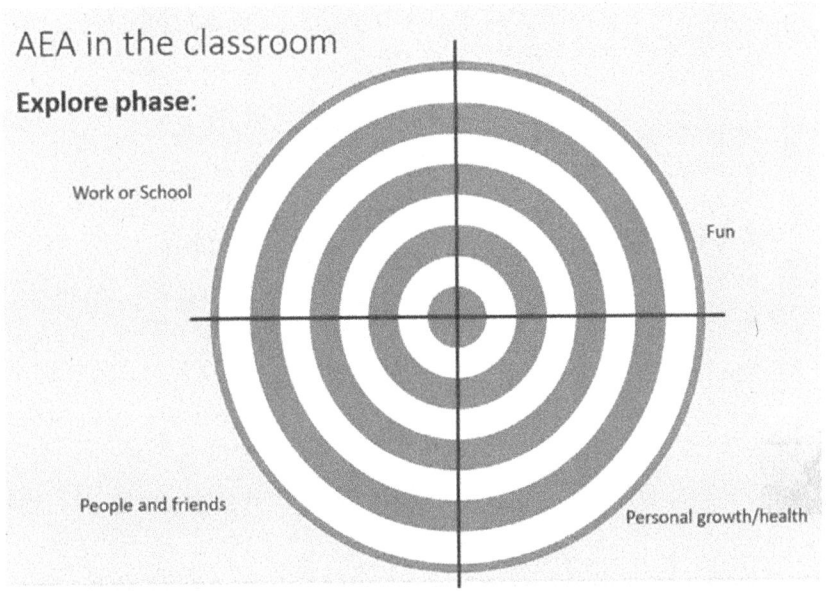

FIGURE 9.1 *Target for Explore phase.*

domains and are labeled "School/Work" "People and Friends," "Fun," and "Personal growth/health".

3. Students are asked to think about their everyday lives. The goal is for students to think of situations and achievements in the life domains shown on the "target" and reflect on how these achievements might have something to do with their signature strengths.

4. Teacher invites students to make links with questions such as: *When you think about things that worked out for you or when you were successful in the past, which strengths were you using? Which strengths came into play?*

5. Students can jot down some notes, and/or share with a partner (translanguaging is encouraged).

    To reinforce the process, teacher models an example sentence:

    Yesterday I was feeling nervous about asking permission from a new teacher to leave class early because of a family commitment. So I had to use my bravery to overcome my nerves. In fact, I was surprised how kind and helpful the new teacher was to me.

    Teacher then puts the card "Bravery" on the life domain of "People and friends," as this demonstrates the speaker's signature strength in talking to strangers or people in authority. Depending on whether "Bravery" is a top signature strength or not, one can place the card closer to or farther from the bullseye.

6. Teacher then invites students to pin/stick their five signature strengths to the areas of their lives where they leverage most of these signature strengths. The teacher reminds students that if a character strength is stronger for them, they can put it closer to the bullseye of the target.

7. The quadrants of the target will become plastered with strengths that the students currently put to good use in their everyday lives.

8. Teacher takes a picture or screenshot of the target pinned with strength cards. Figure 9.2 is an example of what it might look like when the students have finished this part of the AEA model.

9. Students share in groups which strengths have been pinned to which life domains, where they coincide with other group members and where there are differences (translanguaging is encouraged). Here are some question prompts:

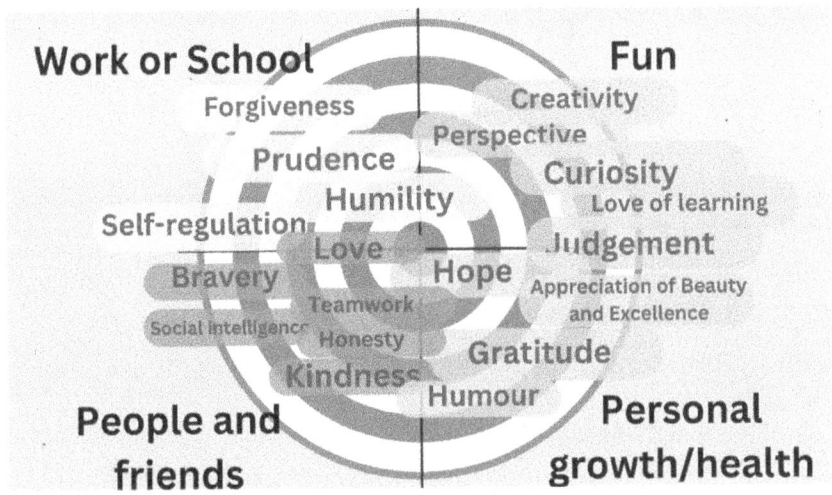

FIGURE 9.2 *Target after Explore phase with "shots."*

- What do you notice about how the cards are distributed across the life domains?
- Are there character strengths that are not being used?
- Why is that?
- Are there strengths that were used but were not noticed before?
- Who put a new strength—one they hadn't thought they had before—on the life domain of _____? Why is it important to you?

   Students come back to share as a whole class.

10. Wrap up—This can be followed up by a writing exercise, for example, writing sentences (with prompts that go back to the example at the beginning of the lesson—"*When I [event or action] . . . , I use my signature strength X to . . .*":

   e.g., When I <u>do a challenging assignment,</u> I use my signature strength <u>of perseverance</u> to follow through the task and make sure it is done.

Alternatives or Extensions

The teacher provides students with a template for a weekly journal with prompts, such as

- "*On Monday evening I did. . . . When I do X, I use my signature strength Z.*"
- "*When I feel bored/down/excited, I remember my superpower e.g., humor/. . .*"

This weekly journal will be used as a tool for students in the following, more complex lessons.

Lesson 3 (Apply Phase)

Learning Goal: Think about the strengths that you can use to get closer to your goals.

Outline of Activities:

1. The teacher brings back the screenshot of the target from the last lesson, which is filled with students' strengths. The students and the teacher take a moment to recap and call to mind the connections between their signature strengths and the domains of life where they use them.

2. The teacher has prepared a worksheet with a picture of the target filled with strengths on one side and a new, empty target on the other. The empty target is labeled "Future."

3. The teacher invites students to think about their future goals. The teacher can help students visualize by asking questions such as: *Which of your signature strengths would you like to work on? Where could you imagine that your signature strength would be most powerful?*

4. Teachers can share their own examples of a present target and a future target to model.

5. The teacher invites students to reflect for themselves and to fill in the part of the worksheet with the future target. Then, students get into small groups and brainstorm some goals and aspirations that they have (translanguaging is encouraged).

6. With the whole class, the teacher places two large targets side by side: one from the previous class that represents students' current everyday life, and the second is a clean target ready for students to fill with their signature strengths connected to future goals and challenges that they anticipate. The teacher invites students to come up to the "Future" target and pin their strength cards to the right spots and then share their future goals, for example:

I would like to join the stand-up comedy club. And I can imagine that my signature strength Humour would work well for me, if I joined the club.

7. The teacher can now introduce a final task and present a writing challenge to the students—an expressive writing task: *Imagine you are yourself in the future. Write a letter to yourself as you are now.* Invite students to reflect on these questions as they brainstorm for ideas: What does that (particular) strength mean to you? What's good about it? What is the win?

The teacher goes over the letter format with the class, eliciting ideas on how to start and end a letter and organize the body paragraphs. It will help if the teacher brainstorms with the class some ideas as they read the sample below and pinpoints the use of tenses to describe past and future events.

Dear Self,
    Now that you're a world-famous stand-up comedian and performer, you must be grateful to your former Self! Just think how your signature strengths **have helped** you achieve success!
    It was thanks to your <u>humor</u> and your <u>bravery</u> that you **managed** to get up on stage that very first time.
    And these two signature strengths, along with your <u>perseverance</u>, **made** all the difference when you **went** through hard times. At the beginning of your career, you certainly **had to struggle** to make ends meet—and to make your way in the competitive world of actors and performers.
    Finally, your <u>teamwork</u> and <u>social intelligence</u> **enabled** you to create shows with others.
    You have a wide circle of friends who love and support you and celebrate who you are. So, when you use your strengths, you **will** always **count** on great friends to walk with you on your journey.
    Well done, Self!

Encourage students to use translanguaging in their drafting process.

Alternatives or Extensions

a. Students in pairs write and enact an interview with Self, starring the peer in the main character role.

b. Students read/re-read an exciting passage from a novel or film and put themselves in the protagonist's role. How does Self tackle the issue in the plot? Which signature strengths will Self utilize?

Lesson 4: Rethinking PERMA through Different Eyes

Learning Goal: Hone critical thinking and intercultural competence through examining how character strengths are valued, conceptualized, and named differently in different cultures and how they represent different worldviews

A note about the *Inuit Qaujimajatuqangit* Education Framework: *Inuit Qaujimajatuqangit*, or Inuit Traditional Knowledge, can be literally translated as "that which we have always known to be true," a knowledge system celebrated and championed by researchers such as Marianne Stenbaek and Nunavik leader Minnie Grey.[2] Engaging students in examining their strengths and values through their own Indigenous cultural lens allows them to reclaim their Indigenous value systems (i.e., transknowledging), and thus decolonize English language learning, making it culturally meaningful and relevant to their life goals. Table 9.2 is taken from the Nunavut *Inuit Qaujimajatuqangit Education Framework* (Nunavut Cross-competency Curriculum, Content Strands, 2007, p. 50) and sets out notions of character strengths according to Inuit traditional knowledge. For this lesson plan, it is the perfect tool to offset the twenty-four strengths the students have already been working with and to allow deeper examination of PERMA through their own cultural frame. Since students have already built up some familiarity with the three phases of the Aware-Explore-Apply model in the previous classes, it will be easier for them to engage in the process again, this time examining their character strengths through a fresh lens of their own language and culture.

Outline of Activities

1. Before class, the teacher has pinned/put up the table of twenty-four strengths for review (Table 9.1). Students can get out their cards with their five signature strengths.

2. Teacher invites students to share whether anything has changed for them since they started thinking about the twenty-four strengths. For example, if they have used a particular strength more or tried using a strength they had not been aware of before. Students can think about this individually and/or speak with a partner.

---

[2] More information about *Inuit Qaujimajatuqangit* can be found in the article "Future Ready" (*ttps://www.mcgill.ca/research/article/that-which-we-have-always-known-be-true*).

3. While students are thinking and working, the teacher pins/puts up the *Inuit Qaujimajatuqangit*[3] "principles" on a big poster (Table 9.2), displayed in a prominent place so that students can focus on this. Table 9.1 (with the original PERMA twenty-four strengths) and the target filled with students' strengths (e.g., Figure 9.2) should be visible somewhere in class.

4. By now, students should be familiar with the five character strengths they have already chosen from the twenty-four strengths table. The teacher invites students to study the *Inuit Qaujimajatuqangit* strengths and values as displayed and to choose five signature strengths from the *Inuit Qaujimajatuqangit* table (Table 9.2).

5. The teacher distributes five blank cards for each student and asks them to write the five *Inuit Qaujimajatuqangit* strengths and values on the cards.

6. The teacher puts students in groups and asks them to share their five *Inuit Qaujimajatuqangit* strengths and values and discuss these questions (translanguaging is encouraged):

   - Which five strengths did you choose and why?
   - How do your strengths according to *Inuit Qaujimajatuqangit* compare to the five signature strengths you chose from the twenty-four strengths in the previous lessons?
   - Are there different qualities in the two lists, qualities that are not directly comparable?

7. The teacher brings students to a whole class discussion, particularly inviting comparisons between the two lists (i.e., PERMA strengths and *Inuit Qaujimajatuqangit* strengths and values). The teacher shares two examples:

   Example 1: In a project on PERMA (Yasmin & Khan, 2017), some South-East Asian students expressed that the way they viewed transcendence differed from the way Peterson and Seligman (2004) define it. In the terms of reference of the South-east Asian students, transcendence is a general aspect of well-being and comprises meeting and acquiescing to expectations of family and

---

[3] With grateful thanks to Nunavik elder and Education Consultant, Lizzie Airo, who advised on the terms used in this lesson for the strengths and values as conceived by *Inuit Qaujimajatuqangit*, or Inuit Way of Knowing, and who adapted the Nunavut dialect in some cases so as to be understood by and familiar to speakers of Inuktitut in Nunavik.

external community, rather than the more self-referenced notion of a virtue.

Example 2: In Peterson and Seligman's 24 strengths, we find "love of learning" and "curiosity" as two separate strengths. However, in Inuit culture, we have *sanatunirmiik tukisiniarniq,* which literally means "thinking in all directions" and "seeking to understand". Do you think this notion is the same as "love of learning" and "curiosity"? Or does it suggest something else?

8. After giving some time for group discussions, the teacher can bring students back to the whole class for discussion:

   - *Are there strengths that can be compared or cannot be directly compared?*
   - *Could you share one or two examples that you find particularly striking?*

9. In a final step, the teacher invites students to add to the target filled with their strengths from lesson two Figure 9.2 any *Inuit Qaujimajatuqangit* strengths they feel are meaningful and invites some to share. An example is shown below in Figure 9.3:

10. The teacher takes a screenshot for future reference.

11. Final task: Bridging two languages and two souls, with two learning activity options:

    a. Students revisit the draft they prepared in Lesson 3 and revise and add *Inuit Qaujimajatuqangit* strengths to their letter to their future self when they see fit.

    b. Students can write a completely new letter to their future self with advice about how they can put the best possible use *Inuit Qaujimajatuqangit* strengths. An example is shown below:

Letter—new version:
   Dear Self
   Your love of learning is your greatest asset. However, you have found an additional strength from traditional Inuit knowledge: *Uukturarniq*. The word *Uukturarniq* means "experimentation": Combine your signature strength of *Love of Learning* and *Uukturarniq*, experiment without fear and without judgment! There's no limit to the innovation and ingenious devices that you can create! And no doubt, whatever you do in life, you will find your joy and meaning. What an amazing prospect for the future!
   Yours truly
   Self.

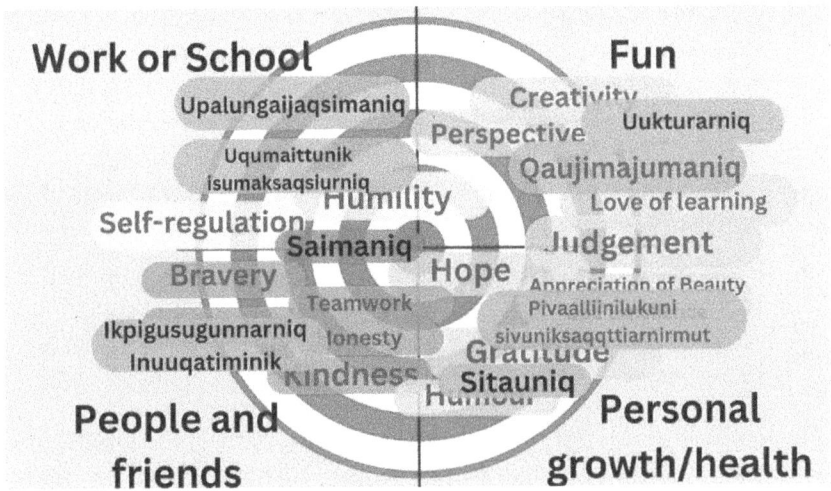

FIGURE 9.3 *An example of a target with both English and* Inuit Qaujimajatuqangit *strengths.*

Alternatives or Extensions

a. For students who are beginning learners, they could do a *strength portrait* (based on the idea of Language Portrait, Prasad, 2014) in which they draw an outline of themselves and color in the parts of themselves where they intuitively "feel" their particular strengths lie. Students can then write a short paragraph or sentences to describe their portrait.

Concluding Thoughts

Learning is a complex, nerve-racking business that involves showing vulnerability, taking a leap of faith, and sometimes being taken somewhere you were not ready to go. In Indigenous educational contexts, the challenges are enormous, as the curriculum and pedagogies are often based on benchmarks and frameworks that assume acceptance of a colonial understanding of the world as universal. Here are some key guiding principles:

1. Teachers have a duty to support their students, particularly linguistically and culturally minoritized students, in offering every possible opportunity to build and strengthen their sense of self, because self-efficacy is the rock on which learning with joy and meaningful outcomes is founded.

2. Students must be allowed to be present with all of themselves when tackling the challenges of learning, which includes not just mobilizing all their linguistic repertoires (i.e., translanguaging) but also acknowledging Indigenous knowledge systems as equally valuable worldviews (i.e., transknowledging). This supports decolonizing English language teaching and allows Indigenous students to celebrate the fullness of their identity and enables them to straddle the two worlds.

3. Engaging students, whether Indigenous or non-Indigenous, in reflecting on the similarities and differences between cultural frames or references supports their metalinguistic and metacultural awareness, promoting their sense of self as they navigate their intercultural worlds.

The purpose of this chapter is to show a practical offering that boosts language learning and self-efficacy through allowing students to be present with all of the language and knowledge repertoires they possess. What is more, engaging students with other languages and cultures through translanguaging and transknowledging will likewise broaden and enrich their critical meta-conversations and reflections about the connections between language and self. For ESL teachers, it might be daunting to include other languages and cultures in their classrooms. However, this willingness to put themselves in a position of vulnerability will enable them to become co-learners with their students, gaining insights from their cultural wisdom traditions and re-imagining their relationships with the world (Donald, 2021). This also allows them to provide more authentic learning situations that are pertinent to their multicultural students' lived realities. This critical approach supports self-determination and invites an honoring of meaning in learners' own lives, without imposing values on them. When students explore these important issues of self and identity and make links between the target language and other languages they use, they take ownership of all the words available to them. The unit plan described in this chapter can be easily modified for high school students with different language and cultural backgrounds. The key principle is not to teach the English language and its associated worldviews as if they are universal truths; rather, it is to teach the language and culture in relation to students' own languages and cultures, validating these alternative knowledges and values and making ESL learning more relevant to their multilingual lives.

References

Abe, A. (2017). Indigenization in the ESL classroom. *TESL Ontario Contact Magazine* (pp. 30–36).

Antia, B. E., & Makoni, S. (2023). *Southernizing sociolinguistics: Colonialism, racism, and patriarchy in language in the Global South*. Routledge, Taylor & Francis Group.

Ball, J., & McIvor, O. (2013). "Canada's big chill." In C. Benson & K. Kosonen (Eds.), *Language issues in comparative education: Inclusive teaching and learning in non-dominant languages and cultures* (pp. 19–38). SensePublishers.

Battiste, M. A. (2013). *Decolonizing education: Nourishing the learning spirit*. Purich Publishing Limited.

Bérubé, D., & Marinova-Todd, S. H. (2012). The development of language and reading skills in the second and third languages of multilingual children in French Immersion. *International Journal of Multilingualism, 9*(3), 272–293. https://doi.org/10.1080/14790718.2011.631708

Canagarajah, S. (2023). Decolonization as pedagogy: A praxis of 'becoming' in ELT. *ELT Journal, 77*(3), 283–293. https://doi.org/10.1093/elt/ccad017

Cummins, J. (2017). Rethinking monolingual instructional strategies in multilingual classrooms. *Canadian Journal of Applied Linguistics, 2*, 221–240.

Cummins, J. (2021). *Rethinking the education of multilingual learners: A critical analysis of theoretical concepts*. Channel View Publications.

de los Rios, C. V., & Seltzer, K. (2017). Translanguaging, coloniality, and English classrooms: An exploration of two bicoastal urban classrooms. *Research in the Teaching of English, 52*, 55–76.

Derakhshan, A., & Karimi, E. (2015). The Interference of first language and second language acquisition. *Theory and Practice in Language Studies, 5*, 2112–2117.

Dmitrenko, V. (2017). Language learning strategies of multilingual adults learning additional languages. *International Journal of Multilingualism, 14*(1), 6–22. https://doi.org/10.1080/14790718.2017.1258978

Donald, D. (2021). We need a new story: Walking and the wâhkôhtowin imagination. *Journal of the Canadian Association for Curriculum Studies, 18*(2), 53–63. https://doi.org/10.25071/1916-4467.40492

Duckworth, A. (2016). *Grit: The power of passion and perseverance*. Ebury.

García, O., & Kleifgen, J. A. (2020). Translanguaging and literacies. *Reading Research Quarterly, 55*(4), 553–571.

García, O., & Wei, L. (2014). *Translanguaging: Language, bilingualism and education*. Palgrave Macmillan.

Heugh, K. (2017). Re-placing and re-centring Southern multilingualisms. A de-colonial project. In C. Kerfoot & K. Hyltenstam (Eds.), *Entangled discourses: South-north orders of visibility* (pp. 209–229). Routledge.

Heugh, K. (2021). Southern multilingualisms, translanguaging and transknowledging in inclusive and sustainable education. In P. Harding-Esch & H. Coleman (Eds.), *Language and the sustainable development goals: Selected proceedings of the 12th Language and Development Conference* (pp. 37–47). British Council.

Kanu, Y. (2011). *Integrating aboriginal perspectives into the school curriculum: Purposes, possibilities, and challenges*. University of Toronto Press.

Lin, A. M. Y. (2015). Conceptualising the potential role of L1 in CLIL. *Language, Culture and Curriculum, 28*(1), 74–89. https://doi.org/10.1080/07908318.2014.1000926

Makoni, S., Kaiper-Marquez, A., & Mokwena, L. (2023). *The Routledge handbook of language and the global South-s*. Routledge.

Makoni, S., & Pennycook, A. (2007). *Disinventing and reconstituting languages, bilingual education and bilingualism*. Multilingual Matters.

Maturana, H. R., & Varela, F. J. (1992). *The tree of knowledge: The biological roots of human understanding*. Shambhala Publications.

Niemiec, R. M. (2014). *Mindfulness and character strengths: A practical guide to flourishing, mindfulness and character strengths: A practical guide to flourishing*. Hogrefe Publishing.

Nunavut Department of Education, Curriculum and School Services Division. (2007). *Education Framework Inuit Qaujimajatuqangit for Nunavut Curriculum*. https://www.gov.nu.ca/sites/default/files/publications/2024-01/Inuit%20Qaujimajatuqangit%20ENG.pdf

Peterson, C., & Seligman, M. E. P. (2004). *Character strengths and virtues: A handbook and classification*. Oxford University Press.

Prasad, G. (2014). Portraits of plurilingualism in a French international school in Toronto: Exploring the role of visual methods to access students' representations of their linguistically diverse identities. *Canadian Journal of Applied Linguistics, 17*(1), 51–77.

Seligman, M. E. P. (2011). *Flourish: A visionary new understanding of happiness and well-being*. Free Press.

Sterzuk, A. (2020). Building language teacher awareness of colonial histories and imperialistic oppression through the linguistic landscape. In D. Malinowski, H. H. Maxim, & S. Dubreil (Eds.), *Language teaching in the linguistic landscape* (pp. 145–162). Springer.

Truth and Reconciliation Commission of Canada. (2015). Truth and reconciliation commission of Canada: Calls to action. https://ehprnh2mwo3.exactdn.com/wp-content/uploads/2021/01/Calls_to_Action_English2.pdf

Turcotte, Y. (2019). James Bay and Northern Quebec Agreement. *The Canadian Encyclopedia*. (https://thecanadianencyclopedia.ca/en/article/james-bay-and-northern-quebec-agreement)

Turner, A., Chakrabarti, S., Rowe, J., & Somaru, N. (2019). *Applied vedanta philosophy from the Routledge companion to management and workplace spirituality*. Routledge.

Yasmin, N., & Khan, W. (2017). *Character strengths and subjective well-being: An exploratory study of Indian youth, 2017*. Positive Psychology, Character Strength, Happiness, Youth Development, Subjective Well-Being.

How Can I Keep from Translanguaging? An Afterword for Difficult Times

Ofelia García

Afterwording in Difficult Times

I find myself writing this Afterword at a difficult time. On January 20, 2025, Donald Trump was elected the forty-fifth president of the United States while wildfires raged in California. Two days later, I had a knee replacement surgery. It has been the coldest January and February in New York City in fourteen years. This all has meant that I have spent much time indoors reading, but not writing, reflecting on daily stories about the effects of a sea of Executive Orders and policies that have further silenced bilingual racialized Americans and attacked our mere existence. The noise is deafening—from news and podcasts, from friends and neighbors, students, family, children. As the United States turns inwardly and is declared to be exceptionally made up of one race (white), one language (English), and two sexes (male and female), we are experiencing greater tumult and strife throughout the world. Traditionally, Afterwords project understandings toward a future. But as I write these words, I do not clearly see a just future for my American bilingual Latine grandchildren or for the teachers for whom this book is written. Thus, this Afterword is written in the spirit of the hymn popularized by Pete Seeger in his protest music of the 1960s, which I played on the guitar as a young adolescent. The translanguaging within these pages obliterates the tumult and strife of an uncertain future with echoes of resistance and hope for freedom so that minoritized multilingual speakers all over the world can keep on living, imagining, learning, growing, and singing.

Translanguaging as Hammer of Justice and Bell of Freedom

The translanguaging of the teachers and learners in this book acts, to keep on drawing from another of Pete Seeger's activist songs, as a "hammer of justice." Translanguaging in this book also acts, as Seeger says, as "a bell of freedom." And so, the case studies in this book do much more than simply provide me with ideas for a translanguaging pedagogy. With a hammer, these case studies remind us that education must move us toward social justice, encouraging English-medium (EM) classroom teachers to resist and crack policies that limit their actions of respect toward their emergent bilingual students. But acting on the translanguaging hammer also simultaneously brings about the ringing of a bell of freedom from English-medium classrooms that restrict, rather than enable emergent bilingual learners to become themselves.

Seeger's hammer and bell reveal at the end of that song what is important—"it's the love between, my brothers and my sisters, all over this land." And so, translanguaging in these case studies acts not only to resist the separation of English from other language practices and to liberate emergent bilinguals from having to do so. Translanguaging in this book reminds us that it can only be enacted through what García & Nuonsy (2024) have called "actionable love," through promoting love between people and their language and cultural practices, their epistemologies, and their transknowledge (Heugh, 2021). And this actionable love is precisely what moves the many resources with which this book provides teachers.

In this book, Tian and Lau reveal the complexities and challenges of yielding a hammer to crack the English-only classroom, while ringing a bell to announce the freedom from the colonial logic of English and moving the classroom to a translanguaging space of actionable love. Many times, as the cases show, the resources exist, but the policies work against using them. So, where do we start?

How Do We Start to Crack Policies and Ring Freedom? Putting The Translanguaging Cart before the English Language Horse to Bring in Love

To open up cracks in educational policies and practices, it would be important for teachers to develop a *translanguaging stance* (García et al., 2017). Ringing attention to a translanguaging stance becomes Part I of this book. But what makes this book unlike any other is that the focus of the chapters is not simply a theoretical exposition of the importance of stance. The case studies act on translanguaging's actionable love by proposing and describing important resources for teachers to develop their translanguaging stance. Such is the case, for example, of the *Dominant Language Constellations (DLCs)* described in the first chapter by Nayr Correia Ibrahim.

A well-known resource to enable teachers of emergent bilinguals to become conscious of their multilingualism is Brigitta Busch's language portraits (2012), used especially in Europe (Lau, 2016). But despite warnings from Busch herself, the use of different color felt-tip pens to represent languages in the body-shaped silhouettes has meant that languages are portrayed in different body parts and usually displayed as separate. In contrast, the DLC artifacts described and shown in Ibrahim's chapter move from awareness of distinct languages to that of language interdependence and translanguaging. Images such as dream catchers, trees with overlapping leaves and fruits, and wheel mechanisms are given as examples, along with actions taken in the classroom, which include not only the multimodal creation of artifacts, but also discussion, reflections, and writing. In entering these activities from a different starting point—a starting point that begins by acknowledging the dynamic ways in which multilingual people language in their lives—the students' awareness of translanguaging is given an intellectual and actual space in the classroom. Translanguaging is thus acknowledged as important to make sense of multilingual lives and to become liberated from a monoglossic ideology of bilingualism. In many ways, this reflects what Muchira in her chapter refers to as "putting the cart before the horse." Most English language teachers start with language, the horse, which then might pull a multilingual cart with translanguaging practices. The case studies in this book attempt to invert this practice, ensuring that teachers of English first develop their own and their students' translanguaging stance, putting first the ways in which multilingual people language with a dynamic, fluid, and unitary linguistic/semiotic repertoire that includes all multimodalities. That is, the case studies in this book recognize the standard English language taught in English-medium classrooms but differentiate this understanding of language from the one that centers actual human beings engaging in communicative/semiotic practices. It is the latter, rather than the former, that then informs instruction in these classrooms. A translanguaging stance, as Seltzer (2022) says, is not only personal and individual; it is also political.

When emergent bilinguals and their teachers in English-Medium classrooms are framed as experts, no matter how their languaging differs from the English language of instruction, classroom translanguaging spaces are not only safe; they become spaces of "shared trust and responsibility," as Child and his co-authors say in their chapter. It is this shared trust and responsibility that nurtures love.

Building Translanguaging Spaces of Shared Trust and Collaboration: Incompletion and Interconnectedness

The chapters in Part II (Elementary classrooms) and Part III (Secondary classrooms) in this book become a sharing feast—sharing linguistic practices, multimodalities, bodies, knowledge, expertise, responsibility, identities and experiences, resources, curricula and lesson plans, selves. In other words, enacting translanguaging in classrooms requires sharing love, plain and simple. When rigid language standards and fixed identities said to be "complete" are the absolute goal of English-Medium classrooms, love is hardly present. Translanguaging spaces are instead based on a philosophy of incompletion and interconnectedness that Leketi Makalela (2016) has referred to as *Ubuntu translanguaging*, based on South African philosophy. The goal of English language teaching cannot simply be to have students use English as monolingual and native (considered finished) English speakers. Instead, it must be based on a conviction that language learning is always *incomplete* because it depends on the shifting contexts, experiences, interlocutors, spaces, and modes in which language users *do* language. Furthermore, the only way to engage fully in languaging is always through *interconnections* with others and other things. Languaging is never an isolated event or experience; it always relies on external interconnections.

The *incompletion* of translanguaging is experienced in these pages time and time again. The multilingual Kenyan learners in Muchira's chapter express this clearly. These students are multilingual but often not regarded as "complete" in the sense given to us by language textbooks. They certainly can "hear" their Indigenous languages, but they often "do not know how to speak." This is an important statement, for it reminds us that language is always political and is included or not in education depending on its sociopolitical status. Speakers are never incomplete, whether deemed to be bi/multilingual or not; it is language education policies that exclude that are incomplete, silencing many. To ensure that teachers view their students as complete, the chapter by Rowe and Lau describes how to apply a model of well-being that builds students' positive emotions, engagement, relationships, meanings, and accomplishments. Working with Inuit communities in North Québec, the authors adapted the model through an Indigenous framework. English-medium teachers must foremost commit to the well-being of their students according to their own desires and epistemologies.

Interconnections, through collaboration, in the sense of co-labor, are what good English-medium classrooms look like. The interconnections that are built in translanguaging spaces are also felt in these pages—interconnections among peers, and between teachers and students. Following the Common European Framework of Reference for Language (CEFR), teaching and learning focus not just on developing receptive and productive modes of communication. Communication also depends on two collaborative aspects—interaction, or the social use of language, and mediation, or facilitating meaning-making beyond possible linguistic or cultural barriers.

In this book, teachers are not positioned as experts but as co-learners who have much to learn about the multilingual lives of their students and who embrace vulnerability and risk-taking. This interconnection of co-teaching and co-learning is described fully in the elementary classrooms in the chapter by Li and colleagues. At the secondary level, the chapter by Oliveira and Lau also gives evidence of this interconnection between teachers and students in classrooms in Brazil. This collaboration between teachers and students results in teachers who are not simply English teachers but who are seen, as named by Li and colleagues, as "incipient bilinguals." It is not just the students who are emergent bilinguals; the teachers, in taking this more co-learner goal, start learning from their students as they shift from monolingual English-only identities to those that recognize their emergent bilingualism. In so doing, teachers transposition from their role as experts to that of also learners.

Grouping peers purposefully also emerges from these pages as an important collaborative interconnected aspect of the translanguaging space. Students are positioned as working together in English-medium classrooms in Brazil, Canada, Norway, South Korea, and the United States. The purpose of these groupings also cracks the English monoglossic ideology of the English-medium classroom, for in working together students start appreciating their linguistic diversity. These English-medium classrooms are much more than simply English-medium. They are, as the chapter by Muchira makes clear, "a launchpad for exploration of linguistic resources" in a process she calls "multilingual augmentation."

Student grouping is purposeful. The difference between spontaneous translanguaging and pedagogical translanguaging that Cenoz and Gorter (2022) make disappears in these translanguaging spaces. A translanguaging pedagogy rests on opening up translanguaging spaces where students can use language freely, using all their full unitary repertoire of linguistic/semiotic and other multimodal resources. A translanguaging pedagogy must start with the "spontaneous" translanguaging with which bilinguals language and communicate and that liberates them from the sociopolitical constraints of solely using features and ways of languaging that are considered "standard" and dominant. Learning is never individual but social, and peer-teaching/learning collaboration is an important part of establishing translanguaging as a valued resource for multilingual learners.

Nowhere is this point more important than in the design of just assessments. In their chapter, Ascenzi-Moreno and Conte describe how having students retell stories using their full linguistic/semiotic repertoire is the best way to gauge students' understandings of reading. Portfolio assessments, documenting student practices and voices as they act on different circumstances, are preferred to a standardized assessment that measures students against native-speaking norms that are unattainable for multilingual speakers.

Without what has been called "spontaneous translanguaging," a translanguaging pedagogy cannot stand. Translanguaging is not simply about using pedagogical strategies that develop learners' metalinguistic awareness. First, students must develop an awareness of translanguaging in their lives, in society, in the media, and then reflect on the reasons why it is seldom admitted in schools. Why is this so? Who is being left out? How can we create English-medium classrooms where students' translanguaging is leveraged as an important resource to teach the standard English of school? A translanguaging pedagogy puts the cart before the horse.

To do so, educators must adopt a decolonial logic (Mignolo, 2000), delinking language and knowledge from the colonial/imperial matrix of power. Oliveira and Lau's chapter shows how to act on these decolonial efforts, as teachers search for cracks in the textbooks of instruction.

This collaboration/interconnection extends not only to the people in the classrooms—teachers and students—but also to the many things that populate language classrooms—plants, animals, word walls, vocabulary charts, graphic organizers, worksheets, books, dictionaries, digital tools such as translation apps, assessment instruments, portfolios, curricular guides, and policy documents. It also extends to the ways in which learning takes place. In classrooms for refugee students in Canada, there are adolescent youths who have not previously gone to school. Van Viegen describes the efforts of an Arabic-speaking student who is learning English but, given his prior experience, cannot read or write Arabic. For the translanguaging space to include him, the focus of communication in this English-medium classroom has to go beyond developing receptive or productive skills, or even the collaborative interactive skills of the teacher and his peers. It also must address the mediation aspect of the communication between his peers, teacher, and him, ensuring that they all facilitate this student's meaning-making. People, their language, and the space and world in which they live are never incomplete; they exist only in relationships, in interconnections with each other.

Beyond Bridging to Working with/in the Translanguaging Corriente

The collaboration of people, artifacts, language, and semiotic systems in translanguaging classrooms cannot simply be a bridge to get to the "other side" of English dominance. Translanguaging cannot lean students toward English language completion and those people who consider themselves dominant in the world. The translanguaging space also must not lean students toward the separation of English from the students' own language practices. Instead, a translanguaging space must embrace incompletion and interconnectedness, and the idea that as speakers we are always drawn by a communicative corriente that is fluid and relational.

García, Johnson, and Seltzer (2017) have used the metaphor of the seashore with its shifting limits of sea and shore to express the impossibility of exactly delineating one language from another in the discourse of bilinguals and their translanguaging. Just as the materiality of the seashore depends on tides, the reality of language depends on the gravitational pull of why, what, and who is producing the communicative act. There is no structure that can be built to clearly separate water from sand/land at a seashore. Likewise, the dynamic communicative act of bilingual people cannot be delineated by government and educational policy, no matter how hard it tries.

We think of bridges as structures that connect two masses of land often over water and that help people and goods cross over obstacles to get to the other side. But there is no other side to get to within the translanguaging space. The translanguaging space is a dynamic corriente that enables us to be ourselves as bilinguals, "above the tumult and the strife." We don't perceive our linguistic and cultural practices, our transknowledge, as obstacles; we recognize our strength. We situate ourselves as educators with our bilingual students in the river's corriente—not in land that seems safe and steady and yet creates differences and separation, nor in bridges that can collapse at any time. Translanguaging is for the brave and the loving. It is for those teachers who hold a hammer of justice and a bell of freedom. And it is for those who sing the love between people and languages that have been constructed to separate us and dominate some of us, when our souls as human beings have always been interconnected. This book guides us to step into the translanguaging corriente, giving us the resources to be with our emergent bilinguals. It reminds us that translanguaging in action starts with all the practices of emergent bilinguals, rather than with English as simply a language devoid of life and unable to hammer justice or ring the bell of freedom. Holding on to the words of Pete Seeger's songs and the love that they project enables us to keep translanguaging, even as some attempt to silence us. With a hammer and a bell, teachers in translanguaging English-Medium classrooms will continue to sing about the love between people, objects, language practices, and knowledges that keep us above the tumult and the strife that we are experiencing this late February 2025 as I write this.

References

Busch, B. (2012). The linguistic repertoire revisited. *Applied Linguistics, 33*(5), 503–523. https://doi.org/10.1093/applin/ams056

Cenoz, J., & Gorter, D. (2022). *Pedagogical translanguaging.* Cambridge University Press.

García, O., & Nuonsy, S. (2024). Actionable translanguaging love in education and research. *Critical Inquiry in Language Studies, 21*(4), 414–428. https://doi.org/10.1080/15427587.2024.2336449

García, O., Johnson, S. & Seltzer, K. (2017). *The translanguaging classroom: Leveraging student bilingualism for learning.* Caslon.

Heugh, K. (2021). Southern multilingualisms, translanguaging and transknowledging in inclusive and sustainable education. In P. Harding-Esch & H. Coleman (Eds.), *Language and the sustainable development goals: Selected proceedings of the 12th Language and Development Conference* (pp. 37–47). British Council.

Lau, S. M. C. (2016). Language, identity, and emotionality: Exploring the potential of language portraits in preparing teachers for diverse learners. *The New Educator, 12*(2), 147–170. https://doi.org/10.1080/1547688X.2015.1062583

Makalela, L. (2016). Ubuntu translanguaging: An alternative framework for complex multilingual encounters. *Southern African Linguistics and Applied Language Studies, 34*(3), 187–196. https://doi.org/10.2989/16073614.2016.1250350

Mignolo, W. (2000). *Local histories/global designs: Essays on the coloniality of power, subaltern knowledges and border thinking.* Princeton University Press.

Seltzer, K. (2022). Enacting a critical translingual approach in teacher preparation: Disrupting oppressive language ideologies and fostering the personal, political, and pedagogical stances of preservice teachers of English. *TESOL Journal, 13*(2), 1–11. https://doi.org/10.1002/tesj.649

Index

action research 139, 141, 145, 156, 159
actionable love 202–3
artificial intelligence (AI) 120
arts-based 33, 161
assessment
 accommodations 122
 accuracy 120, 123–4, 131
 adaptations 123–4, 134
 alternative 155
 bias 120
 classroom-based 123, 124
 cultural knowledge 121
 monolingual 120–1, 123, 133
 multilingual approaches 123
 multilingual language learners (MLLs) 120, 133
 portfolio 152, 206
 reading 124, 125, 131
 scoring 121, 131
 script 128, 130, 131
 self-assessment 152
Aulajaaqtut Principles 186
Aware-Explore-Apply Strengths Model 179, 183, 187, 194
awareness viii, 20, 28, 34, 86, 91, 203, 206
 linguistic 94
 multilingual language learning 94
 critical xi, 33
 decolonial x
 language 6
 metacognitive 186
 metalinguistic 7–8, 65–66, 186, 198, 206
 metacutlural 198
 multilingual viii
 phonological 92

Beeman, K. 65–7; *see also* teaching for biliteracy
Bhasin, A. 113
bilingual education 3, 5, 40, 62–66, 78–79
Brazil 151
 Brazilian Democratic Movement 140
 co-teaching in 63–4, 66–7
 two-way dual language bilingual education (DLBE) 63–4, 77–8
 English-side teachers 77–9
 Indiana context 63–4
bridging 66–7, 71–3, 78–9
 definition and purpose 66–7
 habitat lesson example 67–71
 planning and co-reflection 71–3
Busch, B. 203

capitalism 143, 151
case study research 161
Cenoz, J. 17, 19, 103, 105, 109, 174, 205
Chesnut, C. 63
co-labor 205
co-learner 74, 76, 205
co-learning 61–6, 74, 76–78, 205
 definition and teacher role 74–6
 process 77
 student empowerment 76–7
 translanguaging connection 76–7
co-teaching 71–4, 78–9, 205
 collaborative instructional cycle 72
 models 73
code-switching 5, 174

INDEX

collaboration
    explore mindsets through 39
    team 44, 45
    translanguaging spaces 39
colonialism 142, 180–2
    colonial narratives 154
    coloniality 143–4
    modernity/coloniality 143–4
colonial 197
    histories 142
    logic 202
    matrix of power 144
corriente 207
    dynamic *corriente* 207
comprehension 124, 131, 132
context-sensitive 4
Covid-19 pandemic 144
Creese, A. 1, 103
critical literacy 139, 140, 153
    critical repertoire 147
Cummins, J. 84, 103, 181
cultural homogenization 149, 151
curricular
    constraints 140
    openings or cracks 140, 144–5, 147–8, 152–5

decolonial/decoloniality 143–4, 154
    logic 206
    option 140, 144, 155
    teaching and learning 141
decolonize/decolonizing/
    decolonization 19, 140, 141, 143, 146, 150, 151, 181, 182
    modernity/coloniality project 143
decorations
    multilingual word wall 43, 45
    question words color-coded by language 43, 50
    student-centered 48
demonolingualize/
    demonolingualizing 18–19
Deroo, M. R. 102–3
developing ideologies
    enact new understanding 40
    locally manifested 40
    teacher beliefs 41
documentation of reading 129, 130

dominant language constellations (DLC)
    artifacts 17, 18, 20–31, 33, 34
dynamic 1–6, 8–9, 12

emergent bilinguals 202–3, 205, 207
    learners 202
    students 202
emerging multilingual learners (EMLs) 100–1, 107, 114
English as a foreign language (EFL) 99–101, 139
English-medium classrooms 202–6, 208
English second language (ESL) 140
English-only
    Medium 84, 92
    space 85
equitable 2, 6, 9, 11, 12
equity 2–3, 5–7, 12
    education 54
    more equitable environments 40
    promoted through translanguaging 42
Escola Sem Partido 141
ethnolinguistic 85–8, 90, 93
expressive writing task 193

financial literacy learning 170, 172
fluid 1, 3, 9, 12
fluidity
    linguistic 83, 84, 87
    multilingual 95
    nuances of 91
forced migration, refugees 159
framework 28, 33
    four-stage 33
    teaching 34

García, O. 17, 19, 39–42, 62, 64–5, 101–3, 107–8, 111, 113–114, 122, 132, 142, 154, 158, 174–5, 180–1, 201–2, 207
Global North 181
Global South 140, 149, 182
globalization 144–51
grit 183
grouping
    purposeful 49, 53
    student choice 45

INDEX

heteroglossic spaces 2
home language 124
   flexibility 42, 43
   greetings 43, 45, 47
   seeking opportunities to use 44, 51, 53
   student ownership 47
   support 40, 42
   teacher expertise not required 42, 48, 51

identity(ies) 18, 19, 21–3, 25, 27–9, 31, 33, 34
   development 107, 110, 114
   identity-affirming practice 162
   language 19, 23, 25
   linguistic 29
   multilingual 18, 20
   texts 33
ideologies 17–19, 41, 61–63, 100, 103, 123, 140, 160, 174
incipient bilingual teachers 61, 64, 77–9
   definition 64
   role in translanguaging 74–8
Indigenous 182
   languages/ILs 85, 86, 89–92, 94, 95, 204
   non-Indigenous 198
instructional
   planning 104–6
   steps 132
interconnectedness 204, 207
interconnections 204–6
interdependence 22, 25
   language 22, 23, 25, 33, 34
Inuit communities 204
Inuit Qaujimajatuqangit Education Framework 186
Inuktitut 180

justice 34, 66, 161, 175, 184, 202, 207
   -oriented 1, 7

Kachru, B. B. 99
Kenyan
   English 85
   linguistic practices 84, 85
   and other African languages 92
   school 83, 90
   space 92
Kiswahili 84, 86, 88–94
knowledge systems 2, 6
Korea, South 99–101, 103–4, 108–9, 111–13
Kuujjuaq 180

Lachance, J. 65, 72–3
   collaborative instructional cycle 72
   co-teaching models 73
   and Honigsfeld, A. 65, 72–3
language
   approximation 128–30, 132
   awareness 167
   of the catchment area 83, 84
   development 132
   portraits 203
Latin-America 141
learning collaboration 206
LGBTQ 141
linguistic
   justice 139, 145–7, 154–5
   repertoires 1, 4, 7–10, 12, 121, 122, 134
   resources 205
love 202–4, 207–8

Makalela, L. 204
mathematics education 169, 170
mediation 205–6
metalinguistic and metacultural 198
metaphor 23, 25
metaphorical 21, 29
   affordances 17, 18, 31, 32
   space 33
Mignolo, W. D. 206
monoglossic ideology 203, 205
monolingual
   approaches 6
   biases 11
   ideology/ideologies 3, 12, 102–3
   native speakers 10
   norms 1, 3, 7
   policies 5
   teachers 64, 66, 77–8 (*see also* incipient bilingual teachers)

Morita-Mullaney, T. 5, 61–3
mother tongue 22, 84–5, 87, 89, 92, 152
multilingual 187
    learners 1, 4–6, 10–12
    learning strategies 165
    students 2, 6, 10
multilingual language learner (MLL) demographics
    fast-growing 39, 40
    teacher misalignment 39–42
multimodalities 203–4
multimodal resources 205
multilingualism 18, 19, 21–3, 25, 29, 31–4

neoliberal 139
Niemiec, R. 183
non-Englishes 85, 89
North Quebec and James Bay Agreement 180
Novo Ensino Médio 141
NPD Grant Project
    enhance capacity 39
    taught and positioned as experts 43
Nunavik 180, 187, 194–5
Nunavusiutit Principles 186

pedagogical 19, 22
    affordances 17
    approach 34
    design 34
    implications 32, 33
    knowledge 19
    opportunities 18, 27
    practice 18
    shift 34
    tool 20
    translanguaging 9, 19, 103, 106–7, 114, 205
peer-teaching 206
PERMA model of well-being 7, 183, 185–7, 194–5
portfolio assessments 206
power
    did not impose upon students 44
    examine dominant structures 41
practitioner-oriented 2

Quijano, A. 140, 143

reading 124
reflective/reflection 18, 19, 21, 27–9, 31–4
refugees
    students 206
    Syrian 160, 161
    youth 159–61
relationships 204, 206
repertoire(s)
    learners' linguistic 83, 84, 86, 88–91
    multilingual 94, 95
    speaker's complex 85
research-informed 1–2, 12
residential schools 180
responsive adaptations 119, 123, 124, 130, 134
retelling 131, 132
running record 130

Santos, M. 146–7, 151–2
schooling history 126
self-efficacy 180, 183, 185
Seligman, M. 183
semiotic 205, 207
    repertoire 203, 206
Sheng 85, 91–3
Spanish–English classrooms 67–71
spontaneous translanguaging 205–6
standard English
    code 84
    Kiswahili 88, 91
    varieties 96
student background 126, 127
    culturally responsive 48
    present in classroom artifacts 46–7
students with limited or interrupted formal education (SLIFE) 159
superdiverse ethnolinguistic heterogeneity 86–7

teacher/s
    agency 120, 125
    Andrea 51
    feedback 130, 131

INDEX

as learner 48, 52
Madison 45
Michelle 43
reflection 107, 110
resist dominant ideologies 41
willingness 42, 54
teaching English in English (TEE) 100–1
policy backlash 100
teaching for biliteracy 65–7
transformative
learning 2
lens 1
potential 2
practices 7
teaching practices 4
transknowledge/transknowledging 7, 179, 180–2, 194, 198, 202, 207
translanguaging 17–22, 25, 27, 28, 33, 34, 61–2, 64–7, 77–9, 122, 123, 139–44, 146–7, 154–6
approach to assessment 122, 127
choice 41, 47, 50
classroom 115
and co-teaching 66–7, 71–4
and co-learning 74–7
everyday practice 42, 44
knowledge 123
linguistic repertoire 45
MLs as linguistic experts 41
as pedagogy/pedagogical 40, 41, 61–2, 64–5, 103–7, 114, 158, 173, 174
perspective 28
practices 19–21, 27
purposeful action 41, 45, 48
spontaneous 108–10
impact on participation 109–10
stance 17–22, 24, 25, 27, 32–4, 102–3, 107, 110–11, 202–3
development 77–9
theory 41, 122
turn 17
translanguaging-in-action 103–6
classroom excerpts 104–6
translanguaging spaces 202–7
co-constructed 41, 42
freely make meaning 41
leverage assets 41, 42, 45, 54
require effort 40, 48
shared 42
stance 77–9
translation 122, 131, 174
translingual turn 141
trauma-informed pedagogy 159, 160, 174
Truth and Reconciliation
Calls to Action 182
Truth and Reconciliation
Commission of Canada 180

Ubuntu translanguaging 8, 84–6, 88, 91, 95, 204
ultraconservative 139
unitary repertoire 205
Uqausiliriniq 186
transpositioning 66, 76
Urow, C. 65–7; *see also* teaching for biliteracy

Valdez, V. 63
visual/visualize 18, 20–3, 32, 33

Wei, Li 17–9, 33, 41, 66, 76, 122, 142, 180
well-being 204–5
wrap-around approach 162
Wright, W. 62–5